SOLDIERS OF THE CASTLE
Dover Castle Garrisoned

G M Atherton

Cover: Parade ground at Dover Castle, 1844 (Burgess)
The painting upon which this print was based dates from 1844. It depicts the Well tower and part of the barbican adjacent to Palace Green. This tower was demolished to make way for the Victorian barracks later constructed on the site.

Published by: Triangle Publications, 5 East Cliff, Dover, Kent CT16 1LX

ISBN 0-9539478-3-1

Printed by: Geo J Harris, The Press On The Lake, Sandwich

To Maurice for his forebearance
With love and gratitude

CONTENTS

FOREWORD

One of the hazards of being, in that awful phrase, a television historian is that I am often asked to write forewords to books. Sometimes it is a real pleasure to agree; the book sits squarely in the middle of my research interests, and is an original contribution to the literature. But sometimes the reverse is true; perhaps it is not really in my area, or perhaps it is, but I have profound reservations about the authors' abilities or approach. At times like that I mutter darkly (and not wholly dishonestly) about my work–load or the dangers of over–exposure.

When Wendi Atherton ambushed me with her book at a regimental gathering in Canterbury I confess to fearing the worst, and wondered how I might extract myself. How wrong I was. For her book is not simply a beautifully researched piece of local history, but an invaluable source of reference for historians interested in Dover Castle, for so long one of the most important of the 'keys of the kingdom' and often one of the first and last man–made sights seen by those entering or leaving Britain. She does not simply catalogue the changes in the castle's garrison with an almost quartermaster–like care for detail and a praiseworthy regard for primary sources, but she expands to throw light on the men who garrisoned the castle and the fortunes of their commanders.

In about 1337 the Deputy Constable received a royal summons to 'immediately deliver the money you received from us for the men lacking from the number that you should have brought…for the guarding of our aforesaid castle.' Two hundred years later the Governor was entitled to claim fourpence a week for 'every woman of light character following the camp.' William Eldred, the author of *The Gunner's Glasse*, was Master Gunner of the castle 1619–26, and recommended that gunners should be 'sober, honest and of good conversation.' James Wolfe, the future victor of Quebec, commanded the regiment in garrison in 1753–54, and complained that 'there is not in the King's dominions a more melancholy dreadful winter station…the winds rattle pretty bad, and the air is sharp, but I suppose it is healthy because it causes great keenness of appetite.' When the 14th Foot returned from Waterloo in 1815 they found that their countrymen had already expended their limited stock of enthusiasm for Wellington's army; they remembered 'being kept under arms for hours in the cold' while customs officials submitted them to a rigid search. At the very end of the Castle's time as a garrison, the Cameron Highlanders, fresh back from Aden, admitted that: 'it is not the barracks one would choose: the Quartermaster's Stores are dank, dismal dungeons, suitable for growing mushrooms.'

This is a little gem of a book: would that all authors made it so easy for me.

Richard Holmes
Professor Richard Holmes, CBE, TD, JP
Colonel of The Princess of Wales's Royal Regiment

PREFACE

About twenty–five years ago I was asked by the architect then in charge of Dover Castle to compile a list of the regiments stationed in the castle. It was originally intended to be just that – a list of units and dates, but I kept finding additional snippets of information and anecdotes that I found interesting, and which also perhaps give a picture of life in the Castle ... and so the document grew! The lay–out is maybe rather unconventional, but is a personal preference, in that I dislike having to keep looking up references at the back; and some of the content may seem very obvious to those who know their subject, but include explanations that I personally did not know when I started. I make no claim that my list is totally accurate nor fully comprehensive – perhaps a framework for others to build on and correct. In fact, I would be grateful to receive any comments, corrections or amendments. I am very aware that there are traps for the novice, not knowing which sources are considered reliable and to be trusted, and that I may on occasion have misinterpreted a record.

Many of the units named in the earlier centuries will have been billeted on the Town, or in other quarters, especially during periods of disrepair or rebuilding of the Castle; but most will have been doing duty in the Castle, usually guarding prisoners, and so have been included for interest. The early records mainly just state 'Dover'; Archcliffe Fort and Moate's* Bulwark were built by 1540, and the town wall towers were used as guard houses, the soldiers often being billeted in 'inns, livery stables, ale-houses and victualling houses.' There are some periods when no units were actually in the Castle, except perhaps a small maintenance party, though there seem always to have been a few gunners – sometimes very elderly and infirm! Apart from its defence, Dover was an embarkation port for small units, drafts, etc, with a steady stream of such units passing through.

[* variously spelt Moat's, Moate's or Mote's]

Where a regiment was known by a Colonel's name, I have added in brackets (where applicable) the number or title by which that regiment later became known – but I have not followed right through to modern titles, as this would make the list impossibly long. Most of those interested in their regimental history will already know the numbers of their parent regiments [*see* Appendix D]. From 1751, numbers for regiments started to be used instead of the Colonel's name, though I have continued the entries as they appear in the record. The month quoted may be disputed; it was not possible to include the actual dates of occupation, and where, for instance, a Marching Order may be dated 27th April, the entry will be May - i.e. to the nearest full month. Occupancy may not even have been until the following month – a long route march could take 4–6 weeks from the date of the Order (and was sometimes even changed en route!). A shorthand form often used in these Marching Orders was: 'It is HMP that you cause (*name of regt)* under y^{r}C to march from their PQ by the S and MCR'.. *[It is His Majesty's Pleasure that you cause the (name of regt) under your Command to march from their Present Quarters by the Shortest and Most Convenient Route]*. Today we might think the long route marches a trial, but to some they were a positive attraction. George Calladine recounts in his diary one reason given for joining up in the 19th Ft with some friends, when serving as militiamen in Dover in 1812, was that the Depôt coys were in Hull, 'and we wished to have a long march through the country'. They were 'to rest the Sunday and every 3rd or 4th day on their March as the Officer in Chief shall see Cause...'. Also, although the main body of a regiment may have moved out some time before the next unit arrived, advance and rear parties were normally there to effect the handover.

ACKNOWLEDGEMENTS

As an amateur with very little prior knowledge of military history, I have had much help and encouragement from many people I would like to thank. Mr R H Forey (Army Historical Branch, Ministry of Defence (MOD)) gave me my first rough framework from 1800, and Gregory Blaxland stands out as the first to show me how to start unravelling the mysteries of the Public Records Office, from whose staff I have also had unfailing courtesy in response to my endless naïve questions. Brigadier Lewenden produced a list from Royal Artillery records in Woolwich for me, and I have also had encouragement, advice and assistance from Brigadier Tommy Collins, David Chandler, Douglas Welby, Lord Ballantrae, General Sir Willow Turner, General Sir Peter Hunt, Major General Rowley Mans, Colonel Geoffrey Powell, Colonel Bunny Arnold, Major Bill Fox, Colonel Les Wilson, Jonathan Coad, the many regimental secretaries to whom I have written, as well as countless other individuals who have furnished me with odd details. Dr Alan Guy of the National Army Museum gave me some very helpful pointers on sources to try, and has looked over the list for glaring historical errors (though any that remain are entirely my own). Jon Iveson has also checked for errors, and has kindly helped with many of the illustrations from the Dover Museum collection. Cecil Humphery-Smith valiantly deciphered some of the ancient documents for me. Ivan Green (who has generously allowed me to use some of his photographs) and Terry Sutton's local knowledge has also been a great help. I have worked in the Public Records Office (now National Archives), the MOD Library in Whitehall, the British Library, the National Army Museum Reading Room, Dover Library and Museum, Canterbury Cathedral Library, the East Kent Archives at Whitfield, and the County Archives in Maidstone, to all the staff of which I also extend my warmest thanks, and I apologise if I have left anyone out. Some of the reference sources used are listed at the back.

I would also like to record my thanks to English Heritage for a grant towards the cost of publication.

GMA

With regard to the necessarily frequent use of certain words and phrases, the following abbreviations have sometimes been used:

DC	Dover Castle
CDC	Constable of Dover Castle
LW	Lord Warden (of the Cinque Ports)
LtDC	Lieutenant of Dover Castle (or Governor or Lieutenant-Governor –nowadays Deputy Constable)
W/H	Western Heights
RE	Royal Engineers
AA	Anti-Aircraft
CA	Coast Artillery
RA	Royal Artillery
RGA	Royal Garrison Artillery
GA	Garrison Artillery
RN	Royal Navy
RNVR	Royal Naval Volunteer Reserve
Inf	Infantry
Arty	Artillery
Bde	Brigade
Regt	Regiment
Bn	Battalion
Bty	Battery
Coy	Company
Det	Detachment/detail
disb	disbanded
OR	Other Rank
CO	Commanding Officer
pdr	pounder (guns)
HQ	Headquarters
RHQ	Regimental HQ
DYRMS	Duke of York's Royal Military School
QEPP	Queen Elizabeth's Pocket Pistol
S/L	Searchlight
HAA/LAA	Heavy/Light Anti-Aircraft
TA	Territorial Army
RAMC	Royal Army Medical Corps

*<u>Layout</u>: RA indented; units positively named as in the Castle in **bold**; units not in bold are believed to have been in the Castle, but were not specified, or were either working on building or guarding prisoners in the Castle but quartered elsewhere. Those in Dover, but more likely in the Town, are shown in brackets [ ]; Dragoons and Cavalry in Italics, as mostly in Town. In World War II, the different indentations are intended to show: HQs, Infantry, RA, then smaller units.*

The reference abbreviations in small italics on the right of the text are expanded in the Bibliography.

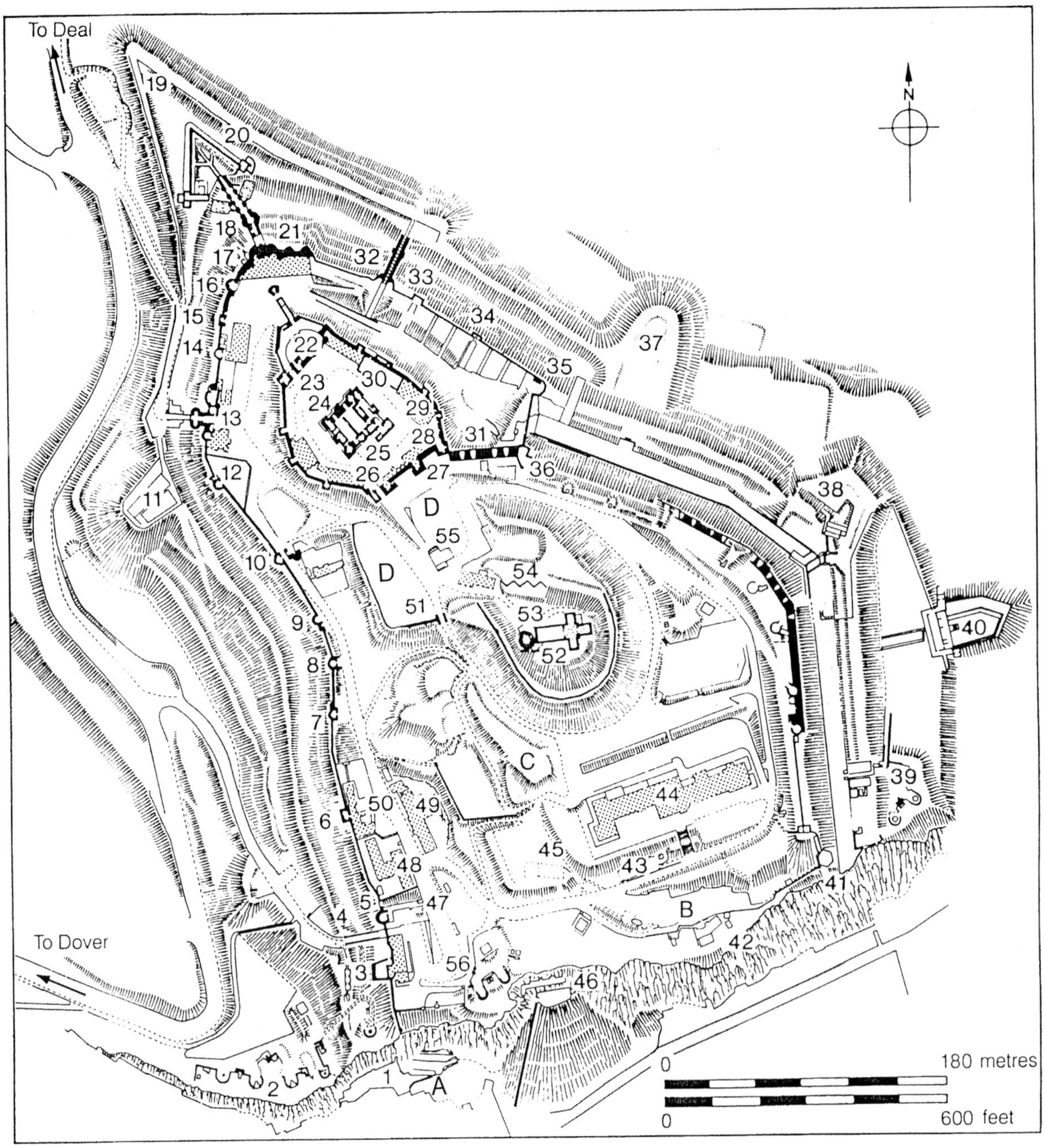

KEY

1 Moat's Bulwark
2 Shoulder of Mutton Battery
3 Tudor Bulwark
4 Canon's Gateway
5 Rokesley's Tower
6 Fulbert of Dover's Tower
7 Hurst's Tower
8 Say's Tower
9 Gatton's Tower
10 Peverell's Tower
11 Constable's Bastion
12 Queen Mary's Tower
13 Constable's Gateway/Tower
14 Treasurer's Tower
15 Godsfoe's Tower
16 Crevecoeur's Tower
17 Norfolk Towers
18 St John's Tower
19 Spur
20 Redan
21 Underground Works
22 King's Gate Barbican
23 King's Gateway
24 Keep
25 Inner Bailey
26 Palace Gateway
27 Arthur's Gateway *(site of)*
28 Keep Yard Barracks
29 Arthur's Hall
30 Keep Yard Barracks (regimental museum)
31 Bell Battery
32 Fitzwilliam Gateway
33 Mural Towers
34 Mural Towers
35 Averanches Tower
36 Pencester's Tower
37 Horseshoe Bastion
38 Hudson's Bastion
39 East Demi-Bastion
40 East Arrow Bastion
41 *(site of)* Radar
42 Port War Signal Station/ Admiralty Lookout
43 Stairs to Cliff Casemates
44 Officers' Mess
45 Long Gun Magazine
46 Cliff Casemate Barracks
47 Powder Magazine
48 Royal Garrison Artillery Barracks
49 Regimental Institute
50 Cinque Ports'/Debtors' Prison
51 Colton's Gateway
52 Roman Pharos (lighthouse)
53 St Mary-en-Castro Church
54 Four-gun Battery
55 Well
56 Shot Yard Battery
A Guilford Battery *(site of)*
B Cliff Block Hospital *(site of)*
C Saluting Battery *(site of)* and Beacon
D Palace Green Barracks & Married Quarters *(site of)*
E Well Tower *(site of)*

from a drawing by Kate Morton (courtesy of English Heritage)

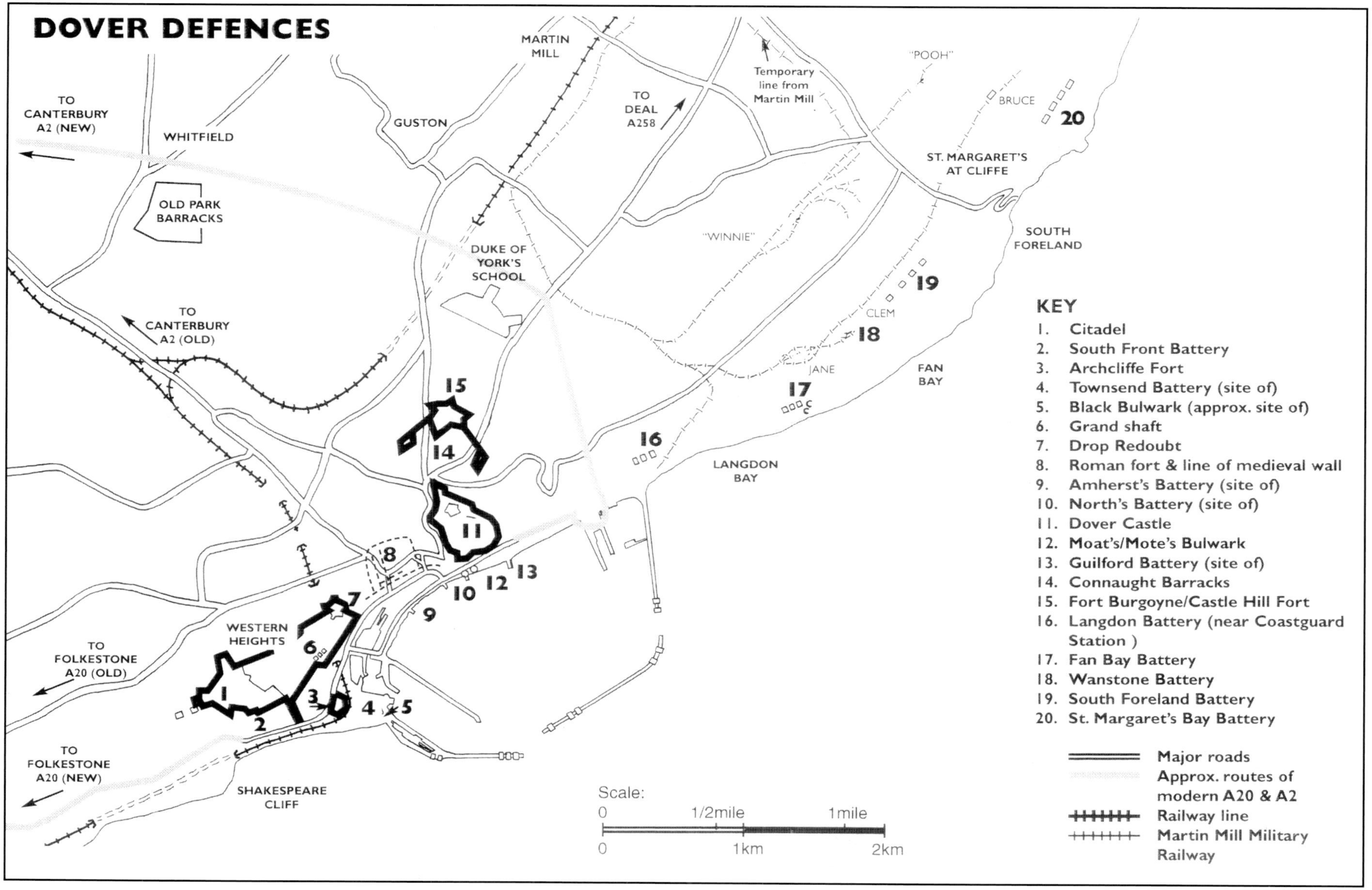

Map of Dover defences. Not all the defences are included: during World War II there were many more gun batteries, both inland and along the piers and breakwaters. *By Clare Limbrey*

ILLUSTRATIONS

(with grateful thanks to those mentioned for their courtesy in allowing me to use them)

Page No

I have tried to trace the original artists, but in some cases this has not so far proved possible; notably the Knotting Class cartoon, drawn by sailors in PWSS.

The 1st century Pharos
The tallest surviving Roman building in Britain

Soldiers manning a burgh
as depicted in an early 11th century manuscript

INTRODUCTION

One of the oldest and most important castles in the kingdom, Dover Castle is also one of the few to have been almost continuously garrisoned right up to the 20th century. Built on a site of considerable natural strength, and overlooking the narrowest part of the Strait of Dover, it protected a harbour of growing importance in the Middle Ages, which itself became known as the Gateway to England. Matthew Paris, writing in the 13th century, called it 'The Key and Bar (or Bolt) of the whole Realm' *(clavis et repagulum totius Regni)*; I have also heard: 'If Dover is the Gateway to England, then its Castle is the Lock and Key'. It is one of the finest examples of medieval fortification in Western Europe, and has been constantly adapted and modernized up to the standards of the time, to suit changing methods of warfare – a castle that has moved with the times, mainly because of Dover's unique and strategically important position as Britain's port nearest to the Continent. It has long stood for defence against invasion, the protection of essential communications, and as a base for launching continental expeditions. Caesar was deterred from landing at Dover, as he originally intended, by the defence capabilities of the heights, and Sir Walter Raleigh's book 'A Discourse of Sea Ports' declared that: 'No promontory, town or haven in Christendom is so well-suited for annoying the enemy, protecting commerce, or sending and receiving dispatches from the Continent.' (written for him by Thomas Digges, the Elizabethan engineer responsible for building Dover harbour).

The clifftop site is generally believed to have been an Iron Age hillfort, and would no doubt then have been well defended, as it would in Roman times with the existing evidence of the 1st-century Pharos (lighthouse) within its walls. Some old histories claim the Roman garrison of Dover to have consisted of a body of Tungrians (auxiliaries recruited from what is now part of Belgium) in the time of Constantine the Great (306-337AD), being strengthened later in the 4th century by Theodosius the Younger (378-395AD), with the 1st cohort of the 2nd Augustan Legion (a cohort was normally 480 strong, but the 1st cohort probably nearer 800); from this force there would most likely have been a detachment up on the hill. After Roman rule ended early in the 5th century, little is known of the next few centuries, but it is believed the site became an Anglo-Saxon burgh, or defended township. The church is believed to be late Saxon (10th/11th century) and, together with the Pharos, stands within the 'Saxon Oval'. The Pharos was later used as a soldiers' guardroom, then as a bell tower up to 1690.

There is no early record of how many troops would have defended the Castle hill – even at the time of the Conquest, when some traditions have it that the small garrison, under the command of Bertram de Ashburnham, briefly offered somewhat feeble resistance against William I's army *(Lyon, Akers, B-J)*. Others claim that the castle surrendered peacefully! Dover was poorly manned at this time, as many of the townsmen were away on ship service with King Harold in the north–east (battle of Stamford Bridge), as also were part of the Castle garrison. The chronicler, William of Poitiers, relates that the ill–disciplined French army caused a lot of damage by fire to the castle and almost totally destroyed the town, just as the defenders were about to surrender, and that William, not wishing to further alienate the defenders who had begun to treat with him, spent eight days rebuilding or strengthening the castle; this may not have been much more than a motte–and–bailey at the time. Many of his soldiers are said to have died in Dover from dysentery, after eating fresh meat, and drinking the local water. William left a sufficient garrison (*Darrell* suggests 500), plus his sick and wounded, before proceeding to London, and appointed his half-brother, Odo, Bishop of Bayeux, as Constable of the Castle and Earl of Kent.

According to William of Poitiers, Odo was a man of outstanding ability, quoting his goodness and sagacity, his liberality and eloquence – 'Normans and Britons alike followed him gladly as one whom they would rather have as lord than any other'. A different picture of him soon emerges as rapacious and overbearing, and he made himself so unpopular with the leading men of Kent that in 1067, during William I's absence in Normandy, they invited Count Eustace of Boulogne over to seize Dover and the castle. The English inhabitants of Dover, however, who had been protected since 1048, first by Godwin, then by Odo, from previous assaults by Eustace, supported Odo. Together with the Norman force at the castle, also loyal to Odo, they succeeded in repulsing Eustace and the rebellious barons and men of Kent. *Statham, Blaxland*

'The spectacle of English forces contending against one another was a common one in the five years following Hastings; some fought doggedly against the new monarchy, but others supported it in steadily increasing numbers. There were widespread English revolts in 1069, but after 1071 the English were remarkably loyal to the Norman kings.' *C Warren Hollister*

In 1137 the custody of the castle changed hands several times during the conflict between King Stephen and the Empress Maud (Matilda), and again during the Civil War between Henry III and the Barons led by Simon de Montfort, (1263-5), when Dover took the side of the Barons. Prince Edward (later Edward I) was kept prisoner and hostage in the castle for a few months, after the Battle of Lewes in May 1264.

A siege tower and scaling ladders - as might have been used during the siege
courtesy of Ivan Green

Model of a Trebuchet or 'Malvoisin' at Dover Castle

Hagioscope or squint at west door, St Mary-en-Castro

After Henry II's massive rebuilding programme in the 12th century, from 1160, but mainly between 1180-1188, a system called Castleguard came into use. *Camden* says there should be 'as many knights as foot-soldiers'. The garrison, 'in time of war, was to consist of 1000 men and 100 horse, in addition to the constable, his knights, and their military tenants' *(Akers)*. Over 1000 men are again mentioned as being the required garrison in the time of Edward III (c 1350), counting three men to every two battlements: ('que chascun ij kerneaux eyent troys hommes pur defense'). *Colvin's History of the King's Works*

The Castle withstood a long siege in 1216 (from 24th June to shortly after the death of King John, on 19th October) under the command of Hubert de Burgh, the Justiciar of England. He had a garrison of 140 knights with their men-at-arms, 'and a number of retainers'. Some accounts say 170 men, which could include those retainers. When the Dauphin landed in Kent, on 21st May 1216, to join the rebel Barons against King John, he captured all of Kent, except Dover, and advanced to London, where he was received with open arms. ('All Kent hath yielded; nothing there holds out but Dover Castle' - *Shakespeare: King John*). The King of France, recognizing the importance of the Castle, and upon hearing that his son was at Stamford, is reputed to have said: 'Hast my son not gott Dover Castle? Then, by the arm of St James, (allegedly his accustomed oath*)* my son hath not one foote in England'. *Lambarde, Camden, Montagu Burrows*
And so, in June 1216, the Dauphin returned to besiege the Castle, bringing up many and varied siege machines, including a giant 'petraria' (stone-thrower), called a 'Malvoisin' ('Bad Neighbour'), and succeeded in undermining one of the towers of the northern entrance. The defenders managed to repel those that gained entry, and eventually a truce was arranged. King John died during the siege, and a French chronicler of the time is reputed to have written: 'The truce between Hubert de Burgh and Louis (the Dauphin) so upset King John that he died'! After the King died, the Dauphin tried to persuade Hubert de Burgh to surrender – unsuccessfully – so he abandoned the siege. He made another attempt in May 1217, having returned to France for reinforcements, but left soon after the French were defeated at the battle of Lincoln three days later. The next attempted attack came from a strong French force under Eustace the Monk (English, and a renegade priest), which embarked on 24th August, 1217, but was defeated by Hubert de Burgh at sea – with an inferior fleet, but by the clever tactic of positioning themselves with the wind behind them and throwing quicklime to blind the French troops, before boarding their ships and cutting the rigging. Hubert de Burgh realised there was a weakness at the northern entrance of the castle, vulnerable to attack from the high ground to the north-east, and set about building the fine new gateway now known as Constable's Tower, (1217-1227), and then repairing the damaged northern tower, completely sealing that entrance. He also built a tunnel underneath this blocked entrance, the round St John's Tower with sally ports into the ditch, and the Spur outwork, among other alterations and modifications. At about this period alterations were made to the church of St Mary–en–Castro – an unusual feature of which is the soldiers' altar and double piscina in the SE corner of the nave. There was once a screen across the chancel steps, beyond which the soldiers could not go, and they had their own chaplains. There is a curious little window near the west door, called a hagioscope or squint, through which the military guard on his rounds could look to ensure the light on the soldiers' altar was always lit – the priests refused to look after any lights not *within* the chancel! [*see* Statute IX, Appendix A]. It is still kept lit today.

However, the Castle's military importance had declined by the end of the Middle Ages, and general maintenance was rather neglected. Dover Castle was a royal residence as well as a fortress, and many of the alterations, to the Keep during the 15th century for instance, were designed to achieve greater comfort in the royal apartments for the occasional visits by the monarch, rather than towards better defence. By 1573 these apartments were apparently not in very good order for the visit of Queen Elizabeth I, from 25-31 August. William Brooke, Lord Cobham, who was Lord Warden at the time, reported on the state of the royal apartments for her Progress: '...the state of Dover Castell. The Lodgings whereof I have seen and do ffynde them (by reason they have nott been of Longe tyme Lyen in) to be both dampysse *(sic)* and mustey and therefore verey necessarey that some *(be)* sent downe to make ffyres in the sayed Lodgings a good while beffore her Ma^{ty} come thether and to see the same well eyerd and sweted ffor otherwyse they wilbe noysome unto her highnesse. And thus I committ yor good Lordship to the t'ntie *(?)* of Almighty God ffrom my howse att Cobham the 13 Julii 1573'. *Arch Cant XI*

In 1625, despite much refurbishment for her arrival prior to her marriage to Charles I, Henrietta Maria was said not to be greatly impressed by the state of the Castle nor by her reception. From the mid-17th century the castle ceased to be used as a royal lodging, and became solely a garrison, further alterations being then for military needs. Despite the adaptations, there were periods when the castle was allowed to fall into a state of serious disrepair, and by the 18th century it was in very sorry condition – little more than 'a delapidated billet for passing regiments of foot'. The church was so ruinous that it was abandoned in 1690, and St James's Church at the foot of Castle Hill became the garrison church.

Gun Salute for the death of H M Queen Elizabeth the Queen Mother, 2002

courtesy of 100 (Yeomanry) Regt RA (Volunteers)

25-pdr gun at Dover Castle

That was until 1745, when fears of invasion from France prompted the start of major modernization by the Duke of Cumberland, with more major building works in 1756 and during the period 1794-1799, for the same reason. The most drastic alterations were the cutting down of the old towers in 1756 to create gun platforms and clear the field of fire, giving the present-day castle its somewhat 'modern' look. Since then, the castle has been continuously modernized and maintained in good repair – latterly as an Ancient Monument rather than a garrison. The church was restored in 1860 by Sir Gilbert Scott.

The pattern of occupancy has changed frequently, and the numbers too, ranging from only a few invalid gunners to, on occasion, several battalions. In the 17th century, the resident garrison (normally a company) was often assisted by constantly changing Marching Companies, usually from Rochester or Chatham. At the time of the American War of Independence, the militia alternated every six months with the regular army, when the latter were at summer camp and used the Castle as winter quarters. A regiment would often be scattered across the county, with only one or two coys here and there – at, for instance, Dover, Deal, Hythe, Folkestone, Chatham, Maidstone, Upnor, etc. It is amazing how frequently they moved around. During the Napoleonic wars, 1793-1815, the militia seems to have been almost permanently in occupation, except during brief periods of peace. From 1820-1850 there was always one company of gunners in the Castle, two companies from 1850-1860, and from 1860-1925 the Castle became exclusively a Royal Artillery station, with only small detachments of infantry to 'guard the gates and approaches', the main body of which was then stationed at the Western Heights, or in 'Castle Hill Fort' (Fort Burgoyne). In 1925 the Castle reverted to an infantry station.

During World War I, Dover Castle was used mainly for mobilizing reservists, with Territorial gunners manning the coast defences, but was kept relatively empty as an ultimate retreat for outlying troops (reserve rations for 5500 men for 7 days were held). It was again very much in the front line during World War II, a main HQ for the Navy, Coast Artillery and Anti-aircraft defences, housed chiefly in the bombproof underground tunnels. 'Once again the plan was drawn up so that in the event of Dover being cut off on the landward side, and the withdrawal of the infantry to within the Castle, the whole unit would become completely self-contained, able to operate seawards, and remain a strong point behind the enemy's lines of communication'. *(Col B E Arnold, TD, Fire Commander in the Castle during the war).*

The last troops actually stationed in the Castle moved out in 1958, when the barrack accommodation was deemed no longer suitable. The church of St Mary-en-Castro is still the military chapel for the use of the battalion stationed in nearby Connaught Barracks.

The only military presence now in the Castle is the Deputy Constable of Dover Castle (the modern successor to the Lieutenant of Dover Castle perhaps) who resides in The Constable's Tower, and is the senior military officer in the district. Also, the museum of the Princess of Wales's Royal Regiment and the Queen's Regiment, most of whose forebear regiments have been stationed in the Castle, is housed in the Keep yard; it was founded in 1978 and moved to Dover Castle in 1987.

Gun salutes are still fired occasionally from the Castle – it is an official saluting site, though not so often used now, as there are very few artillery units in the South East. For many years they used to be fired by HQ Bty, Depot Regt, RA, at Woolwich. 100th (Yeomanry) Regt, RA (Volunteers) from Luton fired one of the more recent salutes on 1st April, 2002, to mark the death of HM Queen Elizabeth The Queen Mother, Lord Warden of the Cinque Ports – a 41–gun salute. On other occasions, one of the custodians at the Castle, a retired gunner, fires a single English Heritage 25–pdr gun: in 2002, for instance, on HM the Queen's Accession day in February to mark the Golden Jubilee; for the lighting of the beacon for the Jubilee week-end in June; and for the two–minute silence on 11th November, Armistice Day.

An Inspector of Ancient Monuments commented in 1961:-

'One of the few Roman lighthouses in the world, one of the noblest Norman Keeps in the kingdom; visible evidence of a famous siege as far back in time as 1216, together with what are probably some of the mines and countermines employed. Add to these Tudor coastal defence work, extensive artillery works of the Napoleonic period and the mid–19th century, and the war room from which Admiral Ramsay controlled the evacuation of Dunkirk, and it is clear that no other ancient monument in the country can equal, let alone challenge, the breadth and scale of the historical compendium that is compressed within the 75 acres at Dover. It is of the first importance that it shall be preserved inviolate as one of the richest and most vivid survivals in the national heritage.'

Sketch of the Great Siege of 1216
by Peter Dunn, courtesy of English Heritage

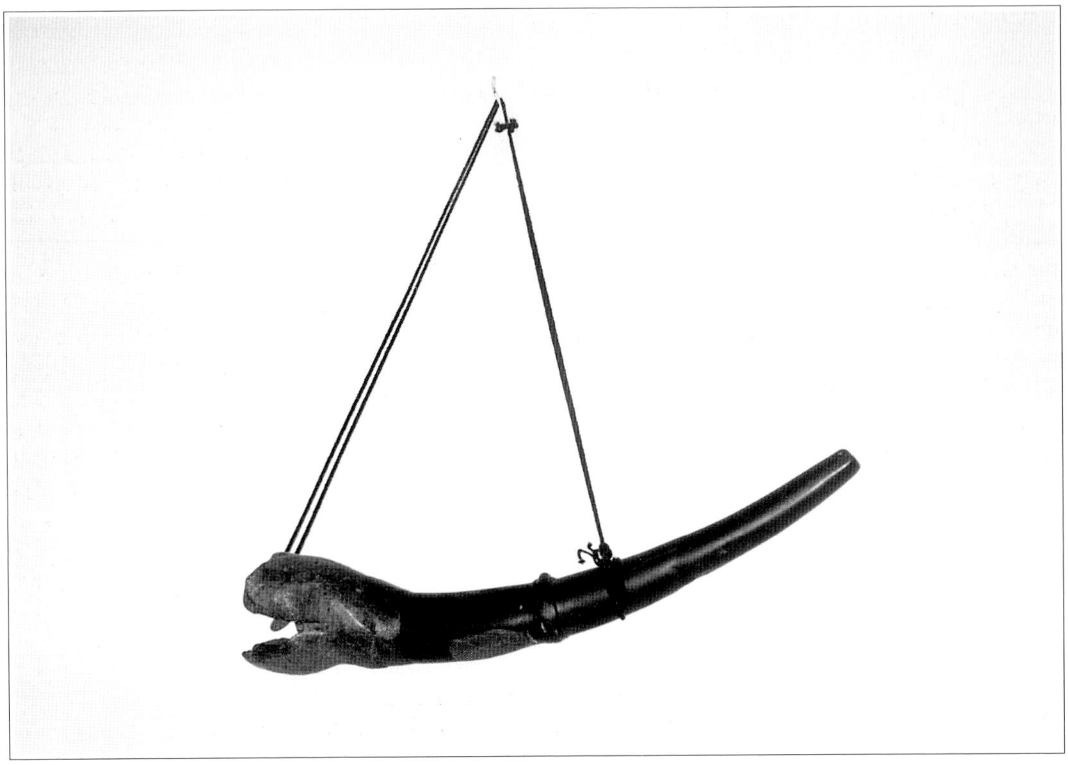

Ancient Horn at Dover Castle
(not on view)

UNITS STATIONED AT DOVER CASTLE

from 1166– **Castle Guard** *ArchCant XLIX*

Castleguard operated from Henry II's reign up to 1541, during the reign of Henry VIII. It was a system devised by Henry II in 1166, at first for the defence of the kingdom in general and its fortresses, but gradually seems to have centred just on Dover by 1211/12. Certain knights held lands ('knights' fees') and baronies from the Crown (many from Bishop Odo's estates, which were forfeit in 1084), in return for manning and maintaining the various towers of the Castle – the responsibility for guards constantly changing each month. Apart from the Constable, the eight knights first mentioned, (c.1166-1211/2), some of whose names are reflected in the names of the towers today, were:

William d'Albrune/de Albrinces/Albrunce/Albrance Albrincis/d'Averanches/Averenches	Averanches Tower	21 soldiers	28 weeks
Fulbert Lucy/Fulbert or Fobert de Dover	Fulbert de Dover Tower	15 "	20 "
William Arsic/Arsick/d'Arsich/Arsicke	(now called Say Tower)	18 "	24 "
Galfride Peverel/Geoffrey/ Jeffrey de Peverell	Peverell's Tower	14 "	20 "
William Maynemouth(e)/Mamignot/ Maminoth/Magminot	(now Norfolk Towers)	23 "	32 "
Robert Port/de Porth/Porthe	(now Queen Mary's Tower)	12 "	24 "
Hugh/Hugo (de) Crêvequer/Crêvecoeur/ de Crepito Corde/Crackte Harte	Crêvecoeur Tower	5 "	24 "
Adam Fitzwilliam	Fitzwilliam Gate	6 "	24 "

'112 soldiers, so divided that 25 were continuously to keep watch and ward' *(Kilburne, also Leland); Lyon* says 115. *Kilburne* and *Harris* both say the garrison consisted of 1000 men at this time, and *Lyon* and *Akers* 1000 foot and 100 horse in time of war, as well as the Constable, his knights and their retainers. For a garrison of one thousand men, the provisions for forty days (in case of siege) were: 'Meal for 1000 loaves a day; 600 gallons wine (2½ quarts per man); beef, pork, or mutton on 18 days – 100 casks of beef, 270 hogs, 162 casks of mutton; Fish on 22 days – 44,000 herrings (5 herrings a day per man), 1,320 cods, 6,000 stock fish or middle cod; cheese and oatmeal, salt; almonds, rice, vinegar, pepper and spice, kidney beans. Wax, cotton and beef suet for candles, sea coal. For 100 horses: 100 cartloads of hay (40 bundles per cart); oats ($^1/_3$ bushel per horse per day); 50 cartloads of litter; 600 horse shoes; 6000 nails; mutton suet and tow – for wounded horses'. *Lyon*

The number of soldiers required for the Constable himself is not mentioned, nor for other parts of the Castle – possibly there was accommodation for up to 1000 in times of trouble, with a smaller peacetime garrison being maintained. (The Constable's 'knight's fees' correspond to the de Montfort (later, Henry de Essex) estates, including 'the great honour of Haughley', escheated to the Crown in 1163).

1216 (siege) **140 knights and their men-at-arms and the Constable's retainers** *Roger of Wendover,Akers*

This would have been c1000 men. Some accounts say 170 knights, which may have included the Constable's retainers. Many local histories refer to a relief force of 400 brought in by a de Penchester during the siege, but this is not mentioned in earlier contemporary records. The siege was raised shortly after the King's death in October, and not resumed until the following April, during which time Hubert de Burgh had time to replenish both men and provisions.

After the siege of 1216, Hubert be Burgh reformed the system of Castleguard, as it was found to be unsatisfactory with such constant changing of guards; instead, the knights due for ward had to pay a rent of 10s per month (scutage) in lieu of actually providing the men, known as 'Castleward rent', payable to the Constable or his deputy at Dover Castle, who then found and paid his own men as a standing garrison out of these rents, in line with the increasing professionalism of armies started by Richard I. (*Arch Cant XLIX*). 'This garrison was not so considerable for the number, as for the intrepidity, fidelity, experience and alertness of those who composed it. There was a continual watch kept during the night (sometimes under the inspection of the marshal and sometimes of the judge); and every hour a horn or trumpet sounded to keep them all awake at their respective posts'. *(Darrell) [There is an ancient horn kept at Constable's Tower, acquired from the Tower of London Armouries c 1978, with a label that it belonged to Dover Castle – could this be it?].*

1258–1265 – A time of great unrest, and eventually civil war, Dover Castle several times changing hands between the King and the rebel barons led by Simon de Montfort. The Castle surrendered to de Montfort in July 1263, and remained in his hands until 1265, his son Henry being Constable of Dover Castle (CDC) at the time. After the battle of Lewes in May 1264, Prince Edward *(later Edward I)* was for a short time a prisoner in the Castle, later being sent to Wallingford Castle and then Kenilworth, before escaping the following May.

June 1265 – Simon de Montfort, the younger, escorted his mother, Eleanor de Montfort (Countess of Leicester, Simon's wife and sister of Henry III) when she sought refuge in Dover Castle, with a strong band of supporters. She held a dinner there on 12th July, trying to ensure that the leading townspeople of the Cinque Ports should remain favourable to the Baronial cause. Many of the supplies came from Brabourne, one of the Countess' Kentish manors: a tun of wine (252 galls.) might last a household 2-3 weeks, but during her stay at Dover Castle ('worried days'), with many soldiers there, a tun was used almost every 2nd day; grain 1½ qtr; wine 2 sextaries, 3 galls of red 'from the

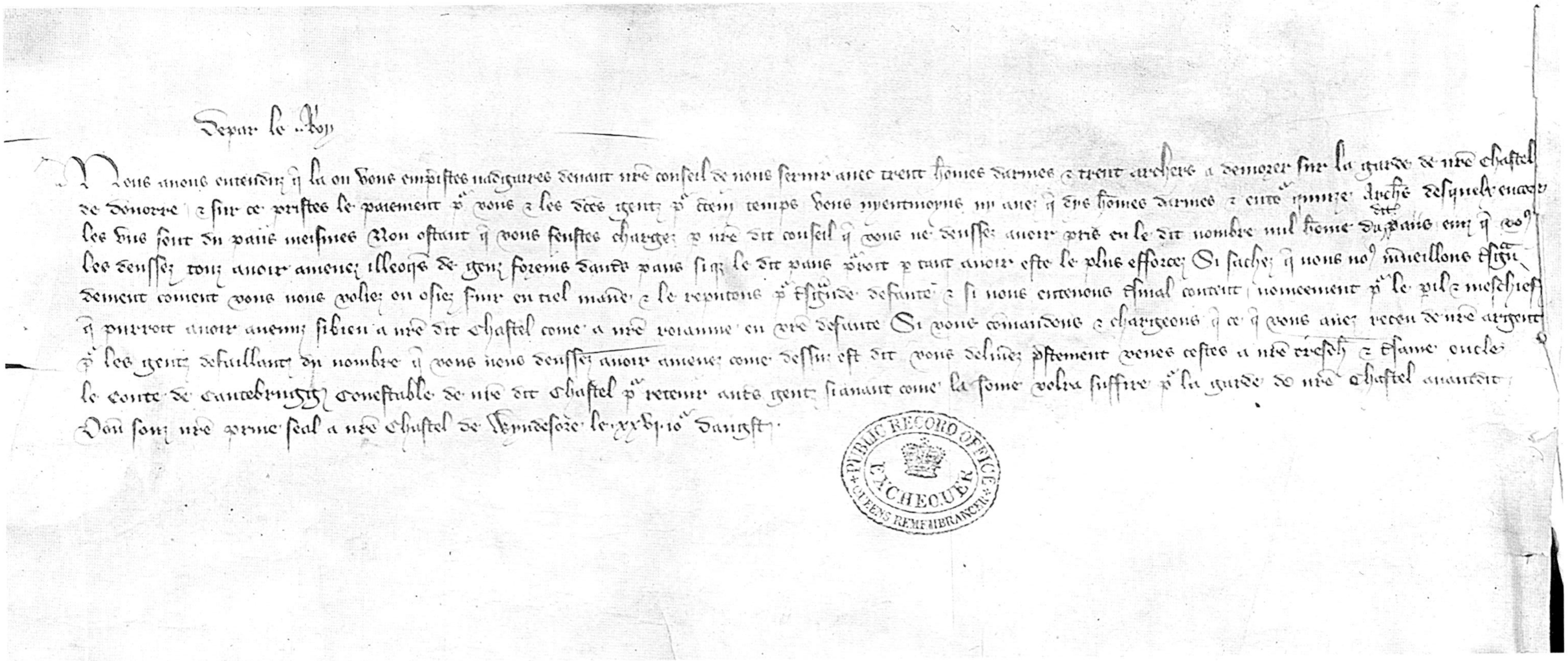

Depar le Roy

Nous avons entenduz que la ou vous empristes nagaires devant nostre conseil de nous servire avec trente homes d'armes et trente archers a demorer sur la garde de nostre chastel /2/ de douerre et sur ce prist le paiement pour vous et les dites gentz pour vous, nyentmoyns ny avez que dys homes d'armes et entour quinze archers, desquels encores /3/ les uns sont du paiis meismes, Non obstant que vous fustes chargez par nostre dit conseil que vous ne deussez avoir pris en le dit nombre nul homme du dict paiis, einz que vous /4/ les deussez tous avoir amener illeoques de gens foreins dautres pais, sique le dit pais pourvoit par tant avoir este le plus efforcez. Si sachez que nous nous merveillons tres gran- /5/ dement comment vous nous voliez ou osiez servir en tiel maniere et le reputons pour tres grand defaute et si nous entendons tres malcontent nommeement pour le peril et meschief /6/ que purroit avoir avenuz sibien a nostre dit chastel come a nostre roiaume en vostre defaute. Si vous commandons et chargeons que ce que vous avez receu de nostre argent /7/ pour les genz defaillantz du nombre que vous nous deussez avoir amenz come dessuz est dit, vous deliverez presentement veues cestes a nostre trescher et tresame oncle /8/ le conte de cantebrugge, conestable de nostre dit chastel, pour retenir autres gentz, si avant, come la somme volra suffire pour la garde de notre chastel avantdit.
/9/ Donne souz nostre prive seal a nostre Chastel de Wyndesore, le xxvj. jour d'augst

[Nos /-/ relate to lines on original document]

courtesy of National Archives (PRO/E101/37/11)

Castle stores'; 1 sextary *(about 1 pint?)*, 1 gall of white; beer, for 45 galls, 22½d. For the kitchen: half an ox from Brabourne and two sheep, 1 pig; poultry 2s.8d., peas in pod 2d, eggs 16d, milk 3½d. Spices were valuable – ginger, pepper, almonds, saffron, cinnamon, galingale (a mild form of ginger), cloves. Rice, sugar, grapes. For stables: grass for 27 horses, oats 1 qtr, 6½ bushels – sum 6s.2d. *EK D/91 Misc*

(Simon was killed at the Battle of Evesham, 4th August 1265).

29 archers under John de Warre, were paid by the Countess to reinforce the defences of the Castle during August and Sepember, 1265. She was allowed to leave for France in October. *Maddicott*

1267 – Discipline must have suffered during this period, as Stephen de Penchester, when appointed Constable of Dover Castle (CDC) in 1267, produced his Statutes of Dover Castle, laying down the conduct required of the garrison. No reference to the numerical strength of the garrison - only that the guard should consist of twenty warders on the Castle walls [*see* Statute I, Appendix A]. De Penchester also pleaded for arrears of pay for the garrison (a recurrent theme through the ages!), neglected under the previous CDC, Matthew de Bezille – for 25 foot sergeants, also knights, sergeants and watchmen.

1274 – The garrison of Dover Castle was sent to quell a riot in the Town. *Chanc.Misc.14/6,19, Murray,p92*

1278 – Stephen de Penchester was to have 100 chestnut stumps for the works at Dover Castle; also 6 oak stumps in the woods of 'Chastaynere' (chestnuts) for his fuel – 'of the King's gift'. 27 tuns of wine laid up in Dover Castle before the late disturbances in the realm to be examined, and if rotten *(it was)* to be disposed of. *Close Rolls*

1339/40 **100 men – 60 men-at-arms and 40 archers** *E101/22/15*

From the accounts of William de Clynton, Earl of Huntingdon, CDC. The wages were 20 men-at-arms @ 12d per day; 40 @ 6d, and 40 archers at 3d per day.

1346 – A garrison of 1000 men (t. of Ed III, 1327-1377). The supposed number of 1000 is based on the number of battlements in the Castle, at three men to every two battlements. 'en le foreine mur du chastel sont Dlv kerneaux ... et pur ceo qe comme appar est en chascune garnesture du chastel, ou ville enclose de mur kernellé qe chascun ij kerneaux eyent troys hommes pur defense, qe amounte a viijcxxxij hommes' (832 men), with a note that the Keep and inner bailey required 168 men more. This must have been for times of trouble *(see under* Castleguard*)*. A letter from the Royal Surveyor to Ed III, dated 1346, translates this as: '...the sub-Constable and I went to count the loopholes in the Castle, and found that in the outer wall there were 555 loopholes, and in the same wall are 19 towers with a grand tower outside the gate, and another grand tower on the north side (of which grand towers the loop holes are included in the aforesaid number, viz 555). And because the rule in every castle or town enclosed by a wall is that there should be three men to every two loopholes, 832 men will be required for this outer wall. And in the tower round the Keep and in the inner bailey there are 378 loopholes to guard which 168 men would be sufficient making 1000 in all'. *Hist of K/W II*

1355 – An account of Roger de Mortimer, CDC, for wages, names one knight @ 2/- per day, 6 men-at-arms @ 12d. & 6 archers @ 3d; this must be for manning one tower only under Castleguard. *E101/27/2*

c1377 **10 men-at-arms and 15 archers**

t. of Richard II – between 1377 & 1380, when Edmund Langley, Earl of Cambridge was CDC. Account of Richard de Grene for paying these men for the guard of Dover Castle, addressed presumably to his deputy.

(Translation of illustration opposite) 'By the King

'We have heard that there where, not long ago, you undertook before our Council to serve us with thirty men-at-arms and thirty archers, to remain as guards of our castle of Dover, and for this you took the payment for yourself and the said men for you, nevertheless you have only ten men-at-arms and about fifteen archers, of whom furthermore some are from the district itself, despite the fact that you were charged by our said Council not to take any of them from the district, but that you were to bring them all from other lands, so that the district would in this way be more enriched. Know then that we are greatly amazed how you were willing and dared to serve us in this manner, and regard it as a very great fault, and are very unhappy because of the peril and mischief that might have come to our said castle as to our kingdom through your fault. We therefore command and charge you immediately to deliver the money you received from us for the men lacking from the number that you should have brought, as was said above, to our very dear and very beloved uncle the Count (or Earl) of Cambridge, constable of our said castle, to retain as many other men, as before, for the guarding of our aforesaid castle, as the sum will support.

Given under our privy seal at our Castle of Windsor, the 26th day of August'. *E101/37/11*

(This was probably written for Richard II by his uncle, John of Gaunt, as he was only 10 at the time – his uncles, Edmund Langley and John of Gaunt were part of his council of regency).

1520 – Henry VIII stayed a night at DC with Emperor Charles V of France. He also stayed before embarking on his ship, the 'Great Harry', on his way to the Field of the Cloth of Gold – sometimes described as 'that glorious picnic'.

1540 **25 gunners, 8 soldiers, a trumpeter, a drummer** *L & P HVIII*

Henry VIII made radical changes, since he found the revenues and privileges of the estates provided for Castleguard were being abused and the duties not performed. By 1541, the King had appropriated many of the Castleguard estates to the Crown, and ordered all the revenues therefrom to be paid direct to the Exchequer (and not to the Governor or Constable), and from then on the Castle was manned only by the King's troops - 'a great number of all

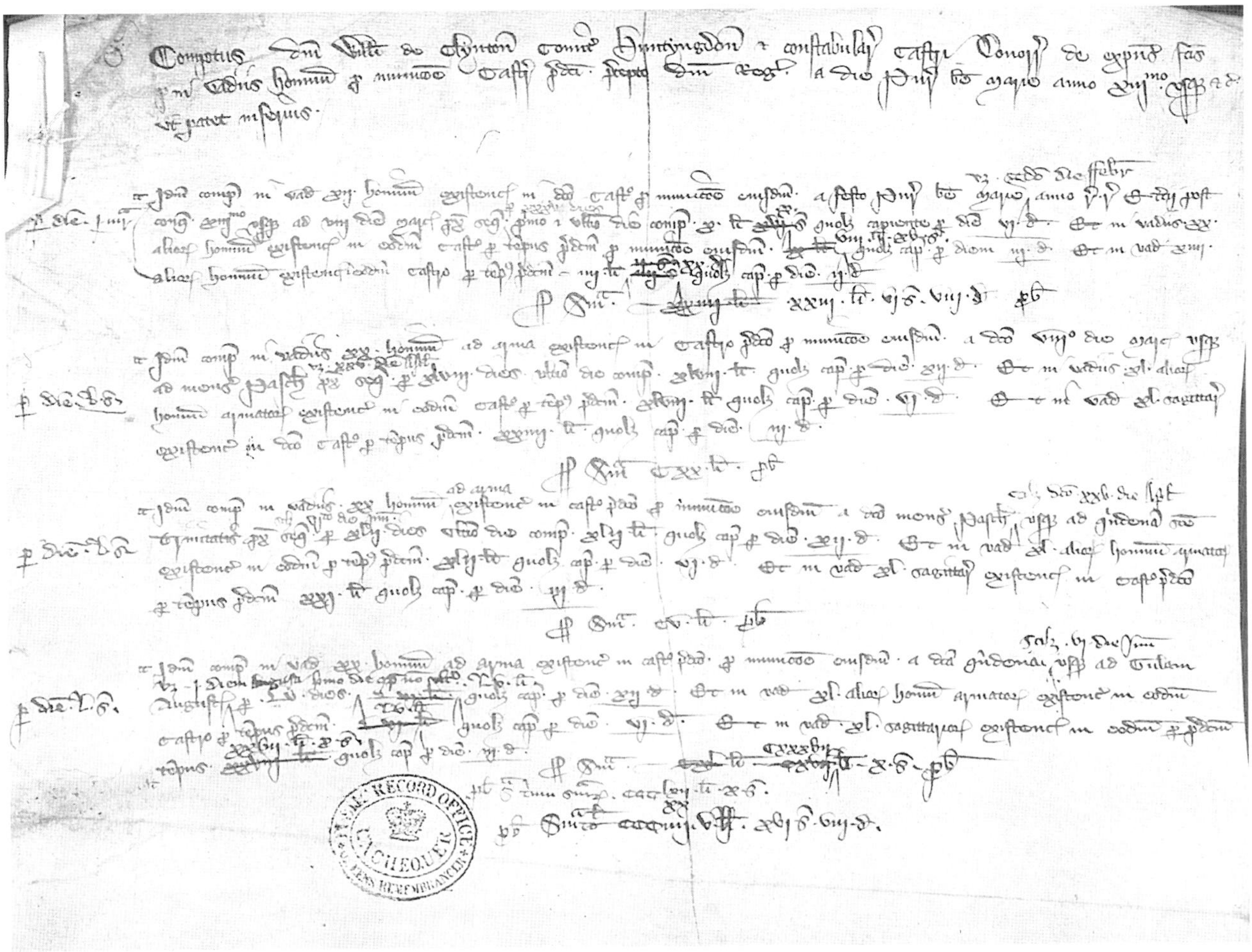

William de Clynton's wages bill, c 1339 *(see page 3)*
courtesy of National Archives (PRO/E101/22/15)

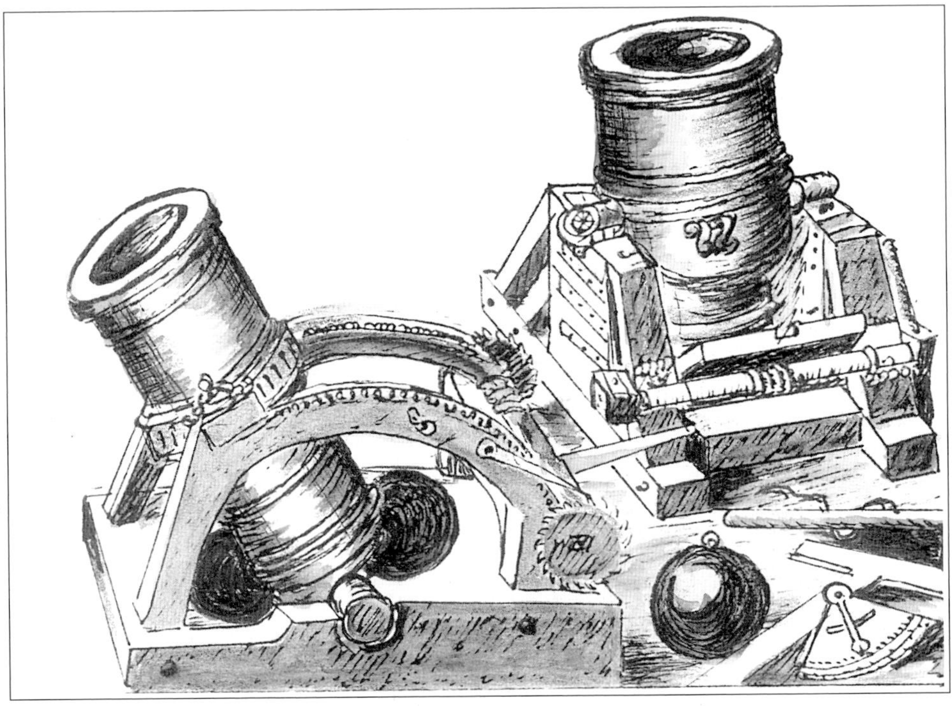

Mortars, c.1575

soldiers there always keeping watch and ward, furnished sufficiently with Harnesse Artillerie and other Municions of Warre, for Safeguard of this Realm' *[see* Appendix B – *transference of payment from Castle to King].* *EK/CPW/R01*
Captain Thos Wingfelde (or Wynkfelde, of Sandwich, also Wingfield) is mentioned as in command. In 1536, Thos Wingfield was comptroller to John Whalley, paymaster to the King's Works at Dover, who was not often present.
1539 – Dover Castle was in bad repair, and 'there is but one gunner belonging to the said Castle'. In 1540, the wages of the garrison were, per day: Captain, 12d or 16d; deputy, 8d; porters, 6d or 8d; and gunners 6d. The Constable was entitled, among other emoluments, to two pence for every pound paid by the King to stipendiaries and men-at-arms within his jurisdiction; to fourpence a week of every dealer selling goods to his men; the same of every woman of light character following the camp; and one penny for every barrel of ale or beer sold to his men Also 'for every great beast brought into the castle at night, 1d for the poll, and for every four sheep, 1d. £4 pa for the pasture of the Castle above the tithe paid to the church of the same'. *Lyon, CSP(D)*
The Castle was regarded as being of little military importance at this time, but was used as an administrative HQ during the building of Henry VIII's coastal forts: Sandown, Deal, Walmer and Sandgate. 'The coming of artillery doomed the high-walled medieval castle and town; military engineers developed a new kind of fortification – low in silhouette, to resist bombardment and with rounded towers, which deflected gunfire better than straight walls,' although this latter principle was already in evidence in the 13th century, when D-ended towers were built in lieu of square ones in the curtain wall of Dover Castle. *Hist of K/W, Corelli Barnett*
However, after the death of Henry VIII in 1547, the garrison was neglected, the Castle in poor repair, and the troops mainly billeted on the town. Even so, the Castle had a small permanent artillery garrison (or 'District Establishment') for the maintenance of guns and stores, and to train detachments of Infantry, Militia, seamen or Trained Bands as 'extraordinary or additional gunners'. [Appendix C– *H VIII's orders for Castles under LW's care*]
1548 – 6 brass sakers, 2 brass culverins (1 damaged) and 1 brass demi–culverin [QEPP] – 'quite insufficient for defence of so large a castle *[a saker is an old form of cannon smaller than a demi–culverin].* *Hist of K/W*

1553– **7 gunners, 7 soldiers and a janitor** *CSP(D)*

1554 – Feb 1, Sir Thomas Cheyne fought against Wyatt in Kent, going to the aid of Lord Abergavenny.
Oct 1556 – Cheyne was instructed by Queen Mary to guard the Castle well for fear of an attack from disaffected factions then in France – Earl of Devon, Captain Thos. Ormesby and others. Sir Thomas Cheyne (Cheney) was Constable of Dover Castle, May 1536-1558, a Privy Counsellor from 1540, Lord Lieutenant of Kent, and in 1558 Treasurer to the Household.

Jan 1558 **100 men under Sir Thomas Cheyne** *CSP(D)*

In Jan 1558, about 5000 soldiers mustered in Dover and were sent over for the relief of Calais, of which number Sir Thomas had to raise 1000 men in the Cinque Ports area. After the fall of Calais, on 10th January, and their return, he was to choose 1000 of the ablest men for the defence of the Castle. However, by the end of January he had only been able to raise 100, and they were poorly armed. He furnished his own household servants with all the armour and weapons he had. ('in the last wars was a hole *(sic)* hundred.'). Later in the year, ailing and ageing, he asked permission of the Queen to retire to his estate on the Isle of Sheppey and defend Queenborough Castle (of which he had also been Constable, since 1512), leaving the defence of Dover Castle to his Lieutenant, William Crispe, with the 100 men. He died 16th Dec 1558. William Crispe complained in 1559 of the difficulties of clothing the forces, and that the wages were always in arrears – a frequently recurring complaint.

1559–1572– **15 Gunners** *CSP(D)*

William Cecil (Secretary of State to Elizabeth I), re: Dover Castle – 'the repayringe of the lodgings if anye should lye in them – the reparations of all the ordenances for stocks and wheels to be done presently – powder demi last to be sent thither for that there is but 15 gonners *(sic)* belonging unto it and no sowldiours'.
1573 – Queen Elizabeth I visited Dover on her annual progress, and stayed in Dover Castle as the guest of Lord Cobham (CDC). *E351/3208*
1584 – Moate's Bulwark had 2 officers, 1 Master Gunner, 2 soldiers, 8 gunners and a porter.

1586– **18 Gunners and Lord Warden's retinue** *CSP(D)*

Again mention of 100 soldiers in time of war. In the late 16th century and early 17th century, it was the Constable/Lord Warden's job to provide the garrisons for all the Cinque Ports Castles, and he had a retinue of officers under him to carry out the everyday affairs: His deputy, or Lieutenant of the Castle, (who in turn had a deputy), the Marshall, the Sergeant-at-arms and Boder (later on, in the 18th century, these three posts were combined in one man), the Registrar, Clerk, Gentleman Porter and four Yeoman Porters, Warriners *(also spelt* Warreners*)*, Master Gunner, Chaplain, etc. Quite often neither the Lord Warden nor the Lieutenant of the Castle would be present, and the day-to-day business more usually fell to a deputy lieutenant or governor. In Henry VIII's reign the title was 'Captain of the Fort', but became 'Governor' in Charles I's time, and it is not always clear when and whether there is a difference between the 'Governor' and the 'Lieutenant'. The Lieutenant's military control of the Castle ceased in the mid-17th century, when the garrison was composed of regular troops under their own officers.
With mounting danger of invasion from Spain, the need was for a better trained defence force, and training became an accepted if unpopular part of life. In 1586–7 Dover was transformed into a great citadel. In the 16th century, the worst elements (poachers, thieves, drunkards) were sent abroad as expeditionary forces (more expendable!), the best endowed men being reserved for home defence – the Government considered it safer and cheaper to rely on prosperous citizens (householders, farmers, yeomen) for the militia and trained bands, who were more able to buy

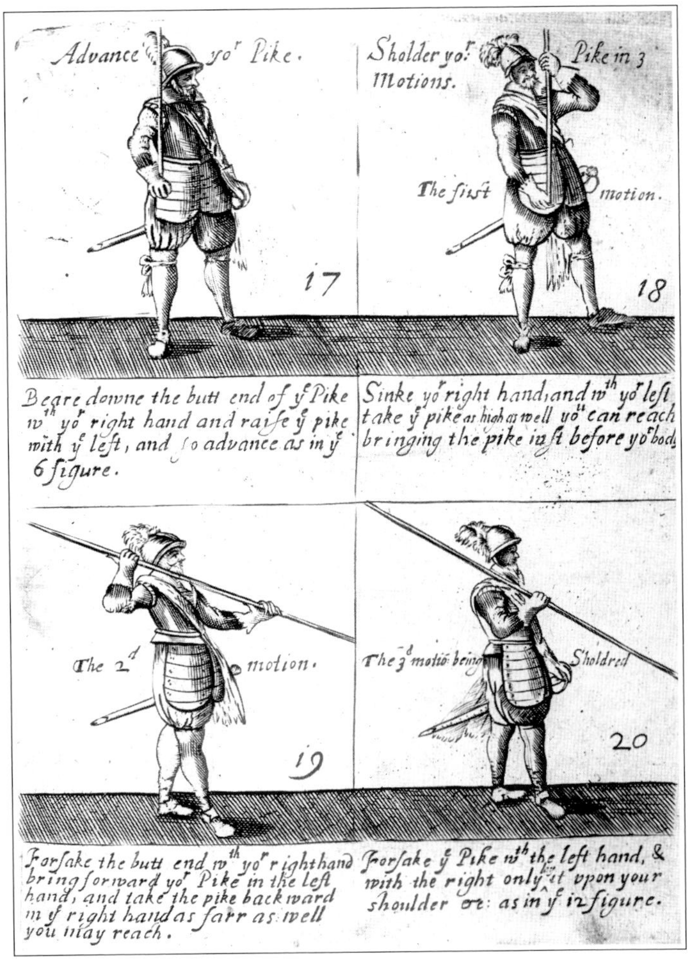

Pike Drill
courtesy of The National Army Museum (NAM 13385)

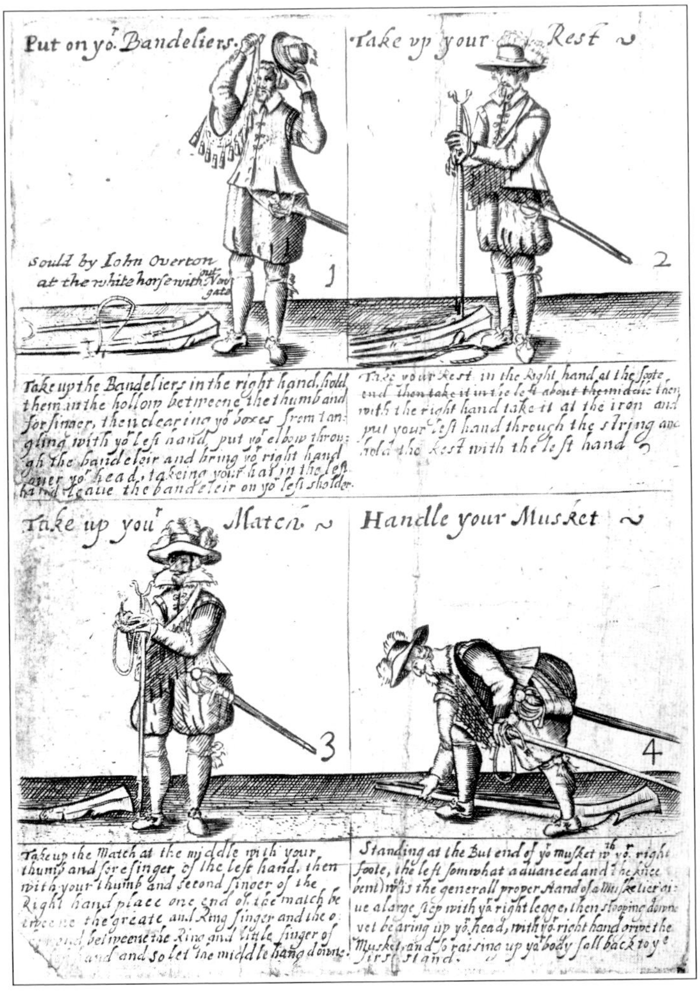

Musket Drill
courtesy of The National Army Museum (NAM 13369)

their own arms and pay for their training; they also feared to arm and train the lower orders! 'The propriety of the time expected gentlemen to fight with pikes; the nimblest men with firearms; the clumsiest with bills, and the blockheads with pick and shovel, as pioneers'. The pike was considered a more honourable weapon than the musket. *Boynton*

1588 **1 Master Gunner, 47 Gunners** *[Armada]* *M-J*

1604 **4 officers, 4 under-officers and 12 watchmen;**

The LtDC: £8.8s.8d pa; watchmen: 30/- pa, paid by the Lord Warden. *Records of Dover, B-J*

1611 **A Captain and 4 soldiers, Porter, 9 gunners, 7 assistant gunners** *SP 14/66*

1613–1642 **Manned by 16-17 Gunners** *CSP(D),SP14/110*

and Lord Warden's retinue, including Assistant (LtDC), Marshall, Gentleman Porter, soldiers and watchmen – 32 in all. 9 gunners @ 8d per day, 7 assistant gunners @ 6d per day. *EK/CPW/R01*

During the first half of the 17th century, gunners, watchmen and soldiers of the ordinary garrison were appointed by the Lord Warden and sworn in individually to the King's allegiance; the jobs were much sought after – they were: 'Privileged Exempted and Freed from being Returned Impanelled or put in any Juryes Assizes or Inquests by the Sheriffe ... or do any other Service of Personal Attendance in any place other than the said Castle'. Soldiers (mainly gunners) due for service at Dover Castle, either regularly, or as an 'out-guard', made plea to be exempt from the county musters and other local duties, and were excused these. Some gunners lived in, but some lived quite far away, and did not always answer the Castle musters. Oct 1615, 'only 7 out of 16 gunners are to be seen'. The Marshall, Nicholas Knott, 'recommends certain inhabitants to supply the places of those gunners who live at a distance…complains that some of the gunners neglect their duty, only ten of them residing in or near Dover, and those refusing to obey authority. He knows persons who are fit substitutes for those who do no duty'. 16 gunners are named and 14 substitutes, who were paid pro rata out of the original gunners' pay. They appear to have had to be on guard duty in pairs every 8th day, and often would find regular substitutes. W Eldred, whose name appears on the roster, later became Master Gunner at the Castle in 1619. It may be noted that he performed his own guard duties ('by himselfe'). *(see page 8)*

Musters – mustering the militia for inspection was an old-established custom, but training as a regular adjunct to peacetime musters was virtually unknown before 1573. The larger musters would be a formal public inspection of all the county forces, but 'special' musters were often private reviews of a company or even smaller units, such as the Castle ones would have been, followed by training.

Form of Oath – for Soldiers and Gunners (extracts) *EK/CPW/RO1*

> 'You shall sweare to the uttermost of your powers witt will and cunning you shall be true and faithfull to the Kings Maj[tie] our most dread and being Sovereign Lord King James of Great Britain France and Ireland King Defender of the ffaith and in earth Supreme Head immediately under God of the Church of England to his Highnesse Heirs and Successors Kings of England.
>
> 'You shall not knowe or heare any thing that may in anywise be prejudiciall to his Maj[tie] or to his Heirs and Successors or to the Comonweale peace and quiett of this his Maj[ties] Realme and Dominions or to the surety strength or defence of this (fortresse) but you shall with all diligence reasonable discover and upon the same onto one of his Maj[ties] Privie Counsell or to such other person as you shall think may and will convey and bring it soonest to his Maj[ties] knowledge….
>
> 'And all such statutes Ordinances and Rules as now bee or hereafter shall be made or devised for the surety good Order or Stablishment of this said Fortresse, you shall not only for your own part well and truly observe fullfill and keepe to the uttermost of your power, but alsoe in case you shall knowe any person or persons of the said Fortresse that shall at any time infringe violate or breake the same or any of them, you shall reveal and disclose itt att the next Musters to the Lord Warden….
>
> 'You shall bee not Quarrel-picker nor Maintainer of Quarrells, affrays, discord or variances'….

A petition of Dec 1618 is made by the Lord Warden's retinue and gunners of Dover Castle to be exempt from watch and ward in town. *CSP(D)*

Aug 1615– [Captain Thomas Andrews & a Select Band of soldiers] *CSP(D)*

Almost certainly in the Town and Port, and probably earlier – Captain Andrews was *re*-appointed by Lord Zouch (LW). There were forces of different types: Trained Bands, Selected Bands (c 117 men), Serviceable Inhabitants, Militia, General (c 255 men) and Untrained Bands. Men were *selected* from the general musters as being the most able to be *trained* in the use of pikes and firearms. The Trained Bands were a military body controlled by the Lord–Lieutenant of each county, but in the Cinque Ports by the Lord Warden, (at times in Kent one and the same man). Trained men were sometimes unwilling to attend for training, and would send a substitute (permitted if from their own household); some were too flabby and unfit, and would send their sons! (Press gangs were for those 'of no fixed abode' and other misfits). *Boynton*

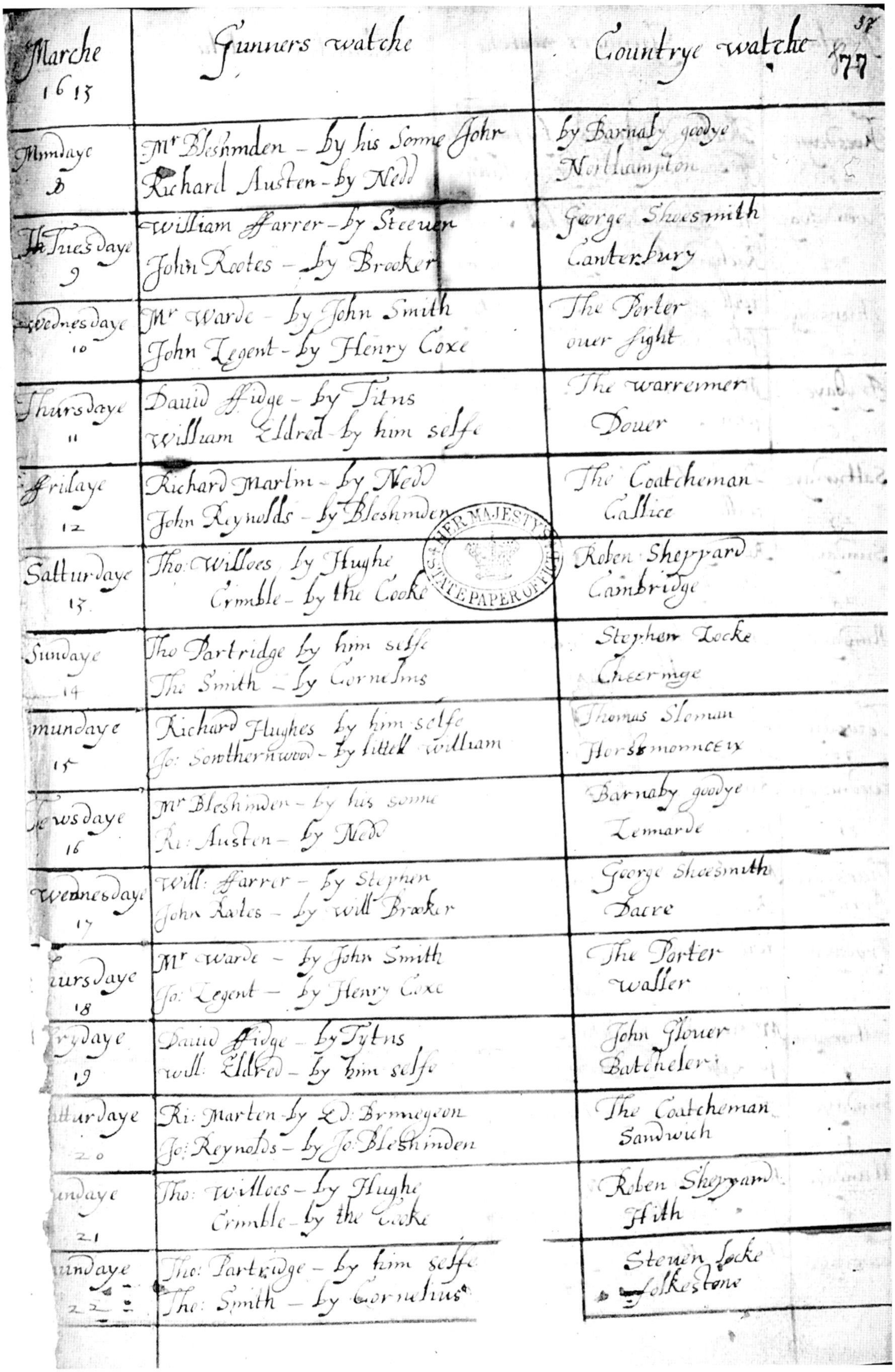

Marche 1613	Gunners watche	Countrye watche 57 / 77
Mundaye 8	Mr Bleshmden – by his Sonne John Richard Austen – by Nedd	by Barnaby goodye Northampton
Tuesdaye 9	William ffarrer – by Steeuen John Rootes – by Brooker	George Shoesmith Canterbury
Wednesdaye 10	Mr Warde – by John Smith John Legent – by Henry Coxe	The Porter ouer fight
Thursdaye 11	Dauid ffidge – by Titus William Eldred by him selfe	The warrenner Douer
ffridaye 12	Richard Martin – by Nedd John Reynolds – by Bleshmden	The Coatcheman Gallice
Satturdaye 13	Tho: Willoes by Hughe Crimble – by the Cooke	Roben Sheppard Cambridge
Sundaye 14	Tho Partridge by him selfe The Smith – by Cornelius	Stephen Locke Cheeringe
mundaye 15	Richard Hughes by him selfe Jo: Southernwood – by littell william	Thomas Sloman Horsmonncex
Tewsdaye 16	Mr Bleshmden – by his sonne Ri: Austen – by Nedd	Barnaby goodye Lemarde
Wednesdaye 17	Will: ffarrer – by Stephen John Rotes – by will Brooker	George Shoesmith Dacre
Thursdaye 18	Mr Warde – by John Smith Jo: Legent – by Henry Coxe	The Porter waller
ffrydaye 19	Dauid ffidge – by Tytus will: Eldred – by him selfe	John Glouer Batcheler
Satturdaye 20	Ri: Marten by Ed: Brmegeon Jo: Reynolds – by Jo: Bleshmden	The Coatcheman Sandwich
Sundaye 21	Tho: Willoes – by Hughe Crimble – by the Cooke	Roben Sheppard Hith
Mundaye 22	Tho: Partridge – by him selfe Tho: Smith – by Cornelius	Steuen Locke ffolkestone

Roster for Gunners' Watch at Dover Castle, 1613 *(see page 7)*
courtesy of National Archives (PRO/SP14/74)

1619 – The 16 gunners and Yeoman Porter were permitted to share tips of under 10/-; over 10/- the Gentleman Porter, Marshall and Master Gunner got a look in at double the rate, but only those in attendance the day the tip was given! The Yeoman Porter could keep for himself anything given directly to him. *EK/CPW/RO1*

W Eldred, Master Gunner at Dover Castle from 1619–1626, writing about gunners: 'Touching the quality and condition of a man that will be a gunner, in my judgment he ought to be first and principally a man fearing God, with upright heart, not given to much talking or many words, no quarreller, or drunkard, or idle gamester; but sober, honest, and of good conversation ... I do verily think that a fort that is pestered and cloyed with unskilful and obstinate gunners were as good be furnished with so many traitors, for there is no good to be expected from them in time of need'. Eldred produced a plan of Dover. He also described test–firing the 'Basilisco', later to become known as 'Queen Elizabeth's Pocket Pistol', on three occasions – 1613, 1617 and 1622, finding 'by reason of her length will shoot very right, and do not reverse much above a foot by reason of her great weight, and therefore shoot very true'*(see* p 23*)*. *'A Gunner's Glasse', Eldred.*

1616–1620 [Captain Mainwaring's Coy] *CSP(D)*

1620 – Captain Sir Henry Mainwaring, MP, was LtDC Feb 1620–May 1623, but fell out with Lord Zouch, the Lord Warden, who dismissed him in 1623; he was accused of brawl, going to Canterbury without permission, neglect of duty, and sleeping in the town instead of the Castle – ?a sea captain, referred to as 'the late pirate'! Lord Zouch took over the duties of LtDC himself, until Sir John Hippesley was appointed in October 1624, when **a garrison of 34** was named. No 'units' were posted to the Castle at this time; the permanent garrison was appointed by the Lord Warden, as individual positions.

Jan 1616–1619 [Captain Hill's Coy] *CSP(D)*

'lately serving at sea under Captain Mainwaring' – there were two coys in Dover at the time – ?marines.

Apr 1619– [Captain Francis Wilsford – selected band (160 men)] *SP 14/108*

1619– [Captain William Ward, gent – general band (320 men)]

1616–1623 – there are records of Lord Zouch (CDC, July 1615-July 1624) mustering and provisioning Trained Bands. *EK/CPW/RO1*

In 1619, a Return to the Sheriff names **32 men as forming the garrison of Dover Castle**, so the companies in brackets will have been in the Town, albeit still the responsibility of the Lord Warden to pay, and it would seem command. There was either a problem with discipline or the opportunity for a fiddle – in Mar 1619 the powder in the Castle was discovered to be all ashes and sand, most of the gunpowder barrels being filled with sand! *CSP(D)*

Feb 1620 – there was a petition to the Lord Warden from the gunners that the night watch be kept by only two men instead of the usual four, and the day watch by four instead of two. They claimed their health was being injured by loss of rest – only one of the four needs keep awake, and he rouses the others when anyone comes. *CSP(D)*

Jul 1623 – Castle garrison numbers included a Warrener of the 'Outbounds, Confines & Purlewes onto the Warren belonging to the Castle'. 1620–1624 garrison numbers between **32–34**. *EK/CPW/R01*

Dec 1624–Jan 1625 [up to 12,000 troops in Dover (Count Mansfeldt)] *B-J*

At the end of 1624 Dover was very full of troops over a period of about a month, some for as much as three months, waiting to be shipped to Holland with Count Mansfeldt, for the recovery of the Palatinate; they caused a lot of damage in the area through unrest at not being paid, but were not much to do with the Castle – the Mayor being instructed to call out the Select and General Bands, although the LtDC appears to have had command of these troops in the town as well as in the Castle. Sir John Hippesley (LtDC) complained to the Lord Warden that they 'pulled down and burned houses, ships, masts or boats, and any put to prison are rescued, all the base people of the kingdom being gathered there. The other Commissioners stand aloof.' He says he has little help, **only 17 men in Dover Castle**, and is 'ready to sink under the burden.' The pay does not seem to have altered much since 1539 – Gentleman porter 8d, 9 gunners @ 8d, 7 assistant gunners @ 6d per day!

1623–1642 – Coast Garrisons were neglected under the Stuarts, who were always short of money, and again the troops were mainly billeted on the Town. *CSP(D).*

The permanent garrison was never discharged nor paid, so they just got old, poor, disabled and unfit, and often had to 'moonlight' to make ends meet. *M-J*

9 Oct 1626–23 Mar 1627 – the Duke of Buckingham (LW and CDC) required the LtDC to billet and supervise 1000 soldiers from Devon and Cornwall, throughout the Cinque Ports area, so only some will have been in Dover. The LtDC had to contend with much bad behaviour from these men: 'with compleynte of sundry [?---?] for the many disorders, misdemeanours, wrongs, [?---?] and too often Robberies, Felonies done by soldiers billeted under your command infect this Countie, and of those several notorious murders committed within the Cinque Ports and their members' *(very hard to read).* He had to oversee their 'Trayning and Exercising, and to have an eye to all their other actions and demeanours during this period awaiting drafts overseas.' *EK Do/CPz19*

1627 – again many troops, landed in Dover from La Rochelle, caused problems – 'most unwellcome guests', and often no payment for their billets. Trained bands were mustered and the Castle 'outguard' called up. Sir John Hippesley (LtDC) 'earnestly asks for reinforcements.' *[War with France]*

1635 – Some of the prisoners kept in the Castle included: those caught 'evading the press' (press gangs for the Army); those refusing the Oath of Allegiance on entering the country; for piracy; also some French seamen.

1636–1639 – Requests for supplies for the Castle from both Lord Warden (the Earl of Suffolk) and LtDC (Sir John Manwood) – most guns 'unuseful' for want of carriages; and 'the miserable defects of Dover Castle which is wholly

Daux's surprise of 1642 (Burgess)

courtesy of Dover Museum (d00464)

wanting in all kinds of warlike provision'. The LW recommended selling Camber Castle, and adding the soldiers to the garrison of Dover Castle, where there were only **16 gunners**. 1640 – Mr Increased Collins was Deputy LtDC. Spanish prisoners at Dover Castle. *[War with Spain, James I]* *Akers*

Aug 1642– **Col Rich's Regt** (Det) (Sir Edward Boys) *CSP(D)*

1642 – Dover Castle taken by surprise for Parliament on 20th August, by eleven Dovorians led by a man variously referred to as Richard Daux/Dawkes/Drake, aged 28, and described as 'a wild young fellow' *(B-J)*. 30 men were appointed to assist Dawkes in securing the Castle, but 20 deserted. Sir Edward Boys was at that time the LtDC (1640–1645), a Royalist at first who changed sides, and he is said to have connived at the surprise. There was a **garrison of only 20** at the time, under an elderly deputy governor, Robert Fleming, who was loyal to the King. A detachment of about 50 men of Col Rich's Regt (Earl of Warwick's) was sent from Canterbury to hold the Castle 'after the surprise', plus another 70 men from London. *[1st Civil War, 1642-45].*

1642–1660 – No royal flag flew from Dover Castle.

1645–May 1648 **Major Sir John Boys** – 3 Trained Bands of Kent *CSP(D)*

Major Sir John Boys, (LtDC 1645–May 1648, and MP for Kent, Sep 1645) son of Sir Edward – **32 soldiers and watchmen named 'of the ordinary garrison';** the 3 Trained Bands to be called for the defence of Dover Castle when necessary (there was another plot to surprise DC in 1645). John Boys was a royalist, but 'neutral' between the Civil Wars, when the Castle was in Parliamentary hands. He was replaced as Governor in May 1648 – the start of the 2nd Civil War – by William Bradfield, who was very unpopular, and held the post only briefly, until Col Algernon Sydney was appointed in June 1648. Sir John Boys was wounded and taken prisoner in a skirmish near Deal Castle in Aug 1648. *Everitt*

[Raising of the New Model (Army), officially formed 4 April 1645 – for 25 years never referred to as an 'Army', and for 29 years was held to be constitutionally illegal]. *Ascoli*

May 1648 – Sir Richard Hardresse (Hardres), with Colonels Hatton (300 men) and Hammond (60 horse) *(Lyon)*, besieged Dover Castle with 2000 Royalist soldiers and Kentish Yeomanry and Militia, but had to abandon the siege when Col Rich and Col Gibbon relieved Sir Henry Heyman defending the Castle with a Parliamentary force on 6th June, 1648. Hardresse had to leave behind all his artillery and stores.

Jun 1648 Major Husband's Coy and several hundred horse of Col Rich's Regt *F & D*

The Castle was then held (for Parliament) by Col Algernon Sydney, (Governor of Dover, Jun 1648–May 1651) and 3 coys of Foot (I believe the three companies formed the garrison of Dover – one in Dover Castle, one at Archcliffe, and one at Sandgate). Lt Col Sir John Boys *(see 1645)* was a prisoner of Col Rich in the Castle, 1659-Feb 1660, as were other Royalist supporters, for petitioning for a free Parliament – most 'rebels' were aggrieved petitioners rather than ardent royalists. *[2nd Civil War, Aug 1648].*

Appointment of Sydney by General Fairfax:

'Thomas Lord Fairfax Commander in Chiefe of all the Land Fforces and on the pay of Parliament in the Kingdom of England Dominion of Wales and in the Islands of Guernsey and Jersey in order to the Securety and [? Peace] of the Kingdome

'To Co^ll^ Algernonne Sydney, Governor of Dover Castle

'By the Power and Authority to mee given by both Houses of Parliament, I doe hereby Constitute and appoint you as Governor of Dover Castle and Commander in Chiefe of all the fforces raised and to be raised for the defence of the same. These are therefore to will and require you to make you present repaire to the sayd Castle and taking the same into your charge as Governor with all the fforts, towers and places of strength in and about the same; together with all the Magazine, Ordinance Armes and Amunicion thereunto belonginge - you are to keepe and defend the same for the service of the Parliament and Kingdome and you are likewise to exercise the inferior officers and souldiers of the sayd Garrison commanding them to obey you as their Governor - for the sayd service and you likewise to observe and follow such orders and [....??...] as you shall receive from my selfe according to the discipline of Warre given my hand and seale the 17th June, 1648'.

Fairfax *U1475/010/4*

Sydney *(or Sidney – the name is spelt variously in different documents)* was something of an embarrassment to his Royalist family, and had a notoriously bad temper. At the age of 21 he was disenchanted and converted to the Parliamentary army, and then was wounded at Marston Moor. He was invalided out of the army, a Colonel at the age of 22. He was only 25 when appointed to Dover Castle, and not popular with the garrison, being more interested in Parliament then in military administration. *Brigid Haydon*

Jun 1648–Jul 1650 **Capt Swan's coy of Foot** (Governor's Coy – for Col Sydney) *CSP(D)*

4 coys of foot to be kept up in Kent – 2 for garrisoning Sandwich, 1 for Dover Castle, 1 for Rochester.

Relationships were sometimes very complicated during the Civil War: Captain Swan was the son of Lady Celia Swan, and stepson to Sir Thomas Peyton of Knowlton, a moderate, and brother-in-law to Henry Oxenden. Oxenden was a Parliamentary Captain of a Trained Band, and 'freely corresponded' with Peyton when he was in prison, saw to his estates, and entertained him when released. Thomas Peyton was much involved in the 1648 Royalist uprising. Captain Swan's Coy became notorious for its 'outrages, murders and other foul acts' *(?ill-disciplined soldiers).* *Everitt*

Apr 1649–May 1650 **Col Cox's Regt** (2 coys) *CSP(D)*

May 1650–May 1651 **Major Gibbon's coy** *CSP(D)*

From Rye, to relieve the two coys of Col Cox's regt, who are to march with the army. The Governor's and Major Gibbon's coys to be made up to 130 men.

July 1650–May 1651 **Capt Henry Cannon's coy** (M/Gen Harrison's Regt) *CSP(D)*

Captain Henry Cannon was deputy governor (Jul 1650-May 1651) under Col Algernon Sydney, and was ordered to remain in person at Dover Castle and not leave without order of Parliament.

July 1650 – second plot by royalists to take Dover Castle, which failed. Col Sydney was also to repair to Dover Castle, as 'the enemy have some designs upon it'. Sydney was again absent Mar–Apr 1651, and ordered back as 'the present state of affairs is dangerous'; Captain Cannon was evidently absent too, Feb–Apr 1651, being several times ordered back.

Aug 1650 – 300 muskets, 50 being firelocks, to be delivered to Capt Cannon, and remain in store in Dover Castle. He was replaced after criticising Col Sydney for 'dereliction of duty', and questioning his loyalty.

March 1651 – 'to forbid horse-racing and like meetings, under pretence of recreation, which might give occasion to the beginnings of insurrection and new troubles, yet we hear a horse race is appointed near Dover.' *(Barham Down).*

Aug 1651 – Sir John Clotworthy a prisoner, sent from Arundel Castle 'with 30 horse and a trusty officer', and moved again in Sepember to Windsor Castle (notable prisoners seem to have been moved about a bit, preferably far from their country seat, and possible support). *[3rd Civil War, April 1650-Sep 1651].* *CSP(D)*

May 1651–Dec 1659 **Lt Col Thomas Kelsey's coy** *CSP(D)*

To release Capt Cannon's coy. At first only 100 men strong, but garrison strength later increased to 200 men in 1656 – some were seamen, now to be trained as gunners. Thomas Kelsey replaced Captain Cannon as governor May 1651. He was in Ingoldsby's Regt, later Commissioner of the Admiralty during the Protectorate, major–general of Kent and Sussex (1655), MP for Dover (1656) and virtually ruler of Kent. Kelsey was away in London more and more on State business, so Captain Thos Wilson, his deputy, had charge of the Castle much of the time.

'The major–general of Kent and Sussex was Thomas Kelsey. Like most of the major–generals, a man of humble origin, he was not a native of Kent but already had connections with the county, having held the office of Lieutenant of Dover Castle since 1651 and taken an active part in the direction of local affairs. He had also been a member of parliament for Sandwich in 1654. The system of government through major-generals was a form of military rule, but it is interesting to note in the letter written by Kelsey, printed below, that he firmly states that soldiers must respect the law and that a soldier under his command who had been behaving in an arbitrary way would be punished.' *Kentish Sources II*

Letter from Thomas Kelsey, Major-General for Kent and Surrey, to the Corporation of Tenterden, 1656:

'Gentlemen,

Yours of the 13th instant I have received, touching one Robert Bayly a souldyer in Dover Castle, and for answere I thought good to signify unto yow that it is not my desire that any souldyer under my command showld be soe turbulent in his accions, to which end I have writt to my deputy in Dover Castle (to whose company he belonges) to keep him upon close duty, or otherwise to discharge him; and as to what yow wright of his makeing a forceable entry one a certaine messuage in Tenterden and keeping possession theire, yow may please to take notice that his being a souldyer will not bare him out in any unlawfull accion. And therefore I doe desire that in what he hath offended contrary to law, he may be delt withall accordingly, which is all at present from

Your affectionatt frend

Tho. Kelsey, London 18th October 1656'. *Kentish Sources II*

1652–1654 **1 Master Gunner, 21 Gunners** *M-J*

Aug 1652 – Col Ingoldsby's regt in Dover and Deal. Only **1 coy in the Castle** (Kelsey's). Reductions in forces – regts reduced from 1200 to 800 men each, and arrears of pay made up (between $3^1/_2$–$5^1/_2$ *years'* worth!). *CSP(D)*

Mar 1655 ...'the strangest of months in England. Royalist agents poured into the country; the dungeons of Dover Castle were perpetually full of them, yet they never failed to escape'. *'King Charles II', Arthur Bryant*

Three prisoners, one purportedly Swedish and two Flemings, caught on board a ship from Dunkirk and seeking employment as soldiers in England, were sent to Capt Wilson at Dover Castle. *[1652–4 – 1st Dutch War].*

Sep 1656 **A second coy under M/Gen Kelsey to be augmented from 80 soldiers to 120,** and added to the establishment of Dover Castle, to join the coy already there. The coy at the time consisting of: a captain, lieutenant, ensign, 2 sergeants, 3 corporals, 1 drummer, a gentleman of arms and 80 private soldiers (?Capt Wilson's).

Aug 1657 – Sir Francis Vincent should be secured 'for preservation of the public peace'. Sir William Waller a prisoner in the Castle for a short time.

Oct 1657 – Wm Cullen (Mayor of Dover 1652) to take care of Dover with his Volunteer coy, whilst M/G Kelsey away in London (?Cinque Ports Militia).

Oct 1658–1659 **Col John Dixwell, MP – 2 coys of Foot**

Dixwell was Colonel of the Cinque Ports Militia Regt of Foot (1651–1659), MP for Dover (1646 and 1659); Kelsey was discharged for his part in the Army petition to the restored Long Parliament, 12 Oct 1659. On the triumph of Parliament Kelsey was consequently deprived of the government of Dover and his regt, and ordered to repair to his house in the country farthest from London, under threat of arrest *(DNB)*. Dixwell was appointed Governor of Dover Castle, 13 Oct 1659 in his place, until March 1660.

Capt Wilson was permitted to recall Capt Cullen *(ex-mayor of Dover)* and his volunteer coy 'for the better security of Dover Castle'. *Commons Journals, vii.*

Jan 1660 – The Governor of Dover *(Col John Dixwell)* to remove Capt Wilson; Capt Cullen to 'take care of Dover'. Sir John Boys and three others to be prisoners in Dover Castle; his father, Sir Edward Boys and three others at Deal Castle.

Feb 1660 – Captain Cannon returned as Governor. *CSP(D), Commons Journals, vii*

At the Restoration (11 May, 1660), Kelsey fled to Holland, and Dixwell, as a regicide, fled first to the continent, then to America. *[Oliver Cromwell died Sep 1658]*

Feb 1660– 2 coys Col Eyre's Regt *F & D*

William Eyres/Ayres was a republican, and not trusted by Gen Monk, so was sent to Kent.

May–Dec 1660 **1 coy under comd Heneage Finch, Earl of Winchilsea** *Statham*

The Rt Hon Heneage Finch, Earl of Winchilsea* and Viscount Maidstone, was made Governor of Dover Castle and Dover Town by General Monk. He later became Lord Warden and CDC (1669–1689), (having spent the intervening eight years as ambassador in Constantinople) – known as 'the amorous peer'!

May 1660 – 'Sir Thomas Peyton *(see* Capt Swan, Jun 1648*)* is gone downe it is heare sayde to commande in the Castell of Dover under the Lord of Winchilsey *(sic)* until such time as the Kinge come.' (Landed 29 May 1660). Peyton was a kinsman of the Earl of Winchilsea. *Everitt/Oxinden & Peyton Letters*

[* The town is spelt: Winch**e**lsea; the earldom: Winch**i**lsea].

This coy is likely to have been **Lt Col Thomas Daniells' Garrison Coy**, which moved to Archcliffe Fort Dec 1660–end Jan 1661, and was disbanded 16 Mar 1661. *EK/U2246/12/A1*

Col Daniells (1618–1682) was LtDC and Governor of Archcliffe Fort – a Royalist in the Prince of Wales's Regt, he lost his estates in the Civil War, and was 6 months a prisoner in Chester. After the Restoration several petitions for a position had failed 'though he hazarded his life and ruined his fortunes by his loyalty'. He was granted the office of Capt of Archcliffe Bulwark and the Black Bulwark on the Pier, with powers to elect 4 gunners and 2 soldiers for defence (having asked for 60!) – 16d per day for himself and 8d for each man, plus allowance for fire & candle, arms & ammunition, & requisite repairs. He was knighted 1662, and only repaid by the Exchequer *9 years* later, for the men he had had to pay himself. *CSP(D). EK/U2246/12/A.*

The establishment of the garrison of *Dover* at this time was laid down as manned by: two companies, consisting of two Captains (the Governor to be one, the other as deputy governor and in command at Archcliffe Bulwark), two lieutenants, two ensigns, four sergeants, six corporals, two drummers and 200 soldiers, one gunner, two gunners' mates and four matrosses; Moate's Bulwark to be manned from these by thirty men and an officer, and Archcliffe was to have one lieutenant, one ensign, one sergeant, two corporals and 60 soldiers, one drummer, one gunner and two matrosses (matross = soldier next in rank below a gunner, or gunner's assistant). *CSP(D)*

After the Restoration Sir John Boys requested the position as Customer of Dover, his fortunes being much reduced after imprisonment *(see* 1648*)*.

Oct 1660–Feb 1661 **Sir Francis Vincent - 2 coys of Foot** (100 men each) *E315/351*
1 gunner, 2 gunners' mates and 2 matrosses

One record claims that Sir Francis Vincent (Lt Governor, Jun 1660–Jun 1663) did not pay his troops for a year as he was unwilling to bother himself with so low a matter! Another that his accounts were not finally settled until Nov 1669, (for the pay of the disbanded garrison of Dover Castle – *see* Col Daniells *above*). He was MP for Dover, May 1661 until his death in 1670 *(see also* Aug 1657*)*.

[Sep–Dec 1660 – Charles II disbanded most of Cromwell's Army; the Standing Army was founded January, 1661; this belonged to the King, and was regarded as part of the King's Household, not formally recognized with the law until 1689. The garrison of Dover, Archcliffe and others in Kent came into the King's pay 1 October 1660, which may account for some confusion and arrears of pay. *Ascoli*

Feb 1661 – To halt the total disbandment of the New Model Gen Monk's Coldstream regt laid down its arms, in a symbolic gesture, on Tower Hill, and took them up again as the Lord General's Regt of Foot in the service of the Crown].

Jun 1661– **1 Gentleman and 17 gunners** *CSP(D), R/H*

'The Lord Warden of the Cinque Ports hath command of this place…£159 14s. $2^{37}/_{48}$d. pa. for pay…for the safetie of this place one Gentleman and seaventeene Gunners…the Gentleman and nine whereof to have 8d pd, and eight to have 6d pd; one Lt and one Clerk £8 pa, and Yeoman Porter £2 pa'. A Gentleman of the Ordnance was described as 'something more than an ordinary soldier, hath a little more pay, and doth not stand Centinel' – not an officer, but believed to be senior to a Master Gunner. *JSAHR IX*

From June 1661, 'Our Guards and Garrisons' were manned by independent coys consisting of former Parliamentary soldiers under Royalist officers, excluded from the Disbandment Act, for the security of the Realm, and in the King's service, charged to the King's account. Not until 1689 would Parliament recognise them as an army. Parliament had control of the civilian militia (?Trained Bands), and the King his standing army of regular (professional) soldiers. *Ascoli*

1st Regiment Grenadier Guards Officer, 1660
By permission of Colonel E T Bolitho OBE, Guards Museum

Once the Restoration was firmly established, garrisons of Coast Forts were cut down. Garrisons had been abnormally large during the Commonwealth, and were reduced by Charles II to the 'Ancient Establishment ... in the time of our Royall Father of Blessed and Happy Memory, and severall others of our Royal Progenitors ... for the Lessening of the Greate Charge and Burthen that is uppon our Revenue'. They were reduced virtually to the same size as at first establishment in the time of H VIII. *(CSP(D))*. Dover Castle was manned only by the Lord Warden, one Gentleman (LtDC), one lieutenant, one Clerk of the Castle, 1 Yeoman Porter and 17 Gunners; Moate's Bulwark by a captain, a lieutenant, a master gunner and 12 gunners – all paid by the Lord Warden. It appears there were always a Master Gunner and a few gunners in Dover Castle as well as the infantry – often invalids and veterans, with some positions even considered hereditary. [1677 – 'Richard Woodward, junior, to succeed his father Richard Woodward, senior, as Captain of Moate's Bulwark for life' – 20d a day, and 6d for soldiers under him].

On hearing of the reduction, the people of Dover petitioned for a decent garrison to be kept at Dover Castle, fearing another 'surprise' like that of 1642, when the 'ordinary garrison' had numbered only 20 'and possessed all along by the enemy, who kept the Loyalists in continued slavery'.

A Dutch artist visiting the Castle in July 1661, describes the approach as: '...very steep and arduous. In front of the gate is a wooden bridge over a deep ditch; inside the gate there are sentry boxes on both sides, and all kinds of weaponry lying ready against the wall; two pieces of cannons stand in the inner court in front of the gate to guard the entrance; nobody, of whatever rank, is allowed inside carrying arms, these have to be handed over to the guard. Then one or two of the guard, carrying halberds, show one round and explain all the interesting things. Inside the innermost wall there is a royal palace with a number of large rooms or halls, not very well kept.' He also mentions seeing six Quakers imprisoned in the Castle (for refusing to bear arms). He refers to Queen Elizabeth's Pocket Pistol as 'an uncommonly long serpent'* and to the 'ancient curved copper horn, with which, so they say, the workers at the building of the castle were called together, and many visitors drink from this horn as a curiosity'. (*see* 1216). *Basilisk/basilisco = a mythical serpent. *Journal of William Schellinks' Travels in England, 1661-1663*

1662 – Sir Francis Vincent 'asks direction about two Quaker prisoners who infect many' – wishes they could be removed. The unfortunate Quakers described their prison as 'a nasty stincking hole'. *Arch Cant CXV*

Aug 1662–Mar 1686 **Capt/Lt Col Strode's Coy** *CSP(D),R/H*

The King's Royal Regt of Guards – later Grenadier. *EK/CPW/R01, R/H*

Jun 1663 – Col John Strode (or Stroode/Strowde) first mentioned as Governor of Dover Castle, a post he held until his death in Mar 1686, although *Dalton* mentions him as Lt Governor in 1660. He had joined up as a volunteer in 1658, and was commissioned into the King's Footguards, then stationed at Dunkirk. The first note of Guards stationed at DC is August 1662, on arrival from Dunkirk, and his company formed the permanent garrison until about 1685. Strode is variously referred to as Captain and Colonel; during this period anyone commanding a company held the rank of Captain/Lieut Colonel. Field officers of infantry regiments held double commissions, being also Captains of companies; the Colonel's company, ranking first in the regiment, was commanded by the senior subaltern, styled Captain/Lieutenant, relieving the Colonel of actual charge of the company. *Reg/Sec*

July 1663 – Strode was ordered to detain as close prisoners the Countess of Vlefelt with her husband and entourage; she was charged with conspiracy against the King of Denmark. However, *unofficially* he was required to favour their escape (and yet keep up the pretence!). She escaped through a window and found a shallop (ship), but was seized at sea and taken back to Denmark. *R/H, Gren. Guards*

Mar 1664 – Robert Tichburn kept prisoner at Dover Castle, convicted of high treason for the death of Charles I.

May 1664 – A coy of foot was sent to Sandown Castle by the Governor of Dover (Strode). An observer remarked: 'pitiful, weak fellows, half-starved and eaten up with vermin, whom the Governor ... cheated of half their pay, and the other half they spent in drink'. *Records of Walmer/Memoirs of Col Hutchinson*

Nov 1664 – Strode had an issue of new arms for one company: '30 firelocks, 30 matchlocks, 40 pikes, 100 swords and bandoliers'. *Hamilton, R/H*

Of his tenure as Governor was written: 'there he lived prince-like, keeping open house and a pack of hounds, and has made a brave park within the Castle walls'. *Hist.Parl. III, 1660-90*

[Feb 1665–Aug 1667 – 2nd war with Holland and France]

Apr–Sep 1667 **Capt Robert Tower's Coy of Le Regiment de Douglas** *CSP(D)*

Later 1st Foot/Royal Scots.

Sep 1667–1669–?1672 **One coy The Lord High Admiral's Regt** (Marines – or 'sea souljers') alternating (?) with **The Holland Regt**

The Duke of York & Albany's Maritime Regt of Foot (disb. Feb 1689, and the personnel transferred to the Coldstream Regt of Footguards) - Prince James, Duke of York was Lord High Admiral and CDC, 1660-1669. The Holland Regt was later The Buffs, 3rd Foot, and parties of both regts served as marines. Record not very clear re these two Regts, but in Apr 1671 a new mixed regt was formed, quartered in Rochester – 12 coys drawn from the King's regt of Guards, 3 coys from the Admiral's regt, 3 coys from the Holland regt, and garrison coys. *Knight, Hamilton, R/H*

1668 – The permanent garrison was one company (Strode's) – a Capt, Lt, Ensign, 2 Sgts, 3 Cpls, 1 drummer and 60 soldiers. Strode had an allowance of 2/- a day for 'fire and candle', (cf today's heating allowance!).

Aug 1671 – Capt William Merriwether and **35** others – 'garrison and watchmen'. *EK/CPW/RO1*

Nov 1672–Nov 1673 Col Strode's Coy to London – and again 11–14 Aug 1675 (Weavers' Riots)

Mortars at Dover Castle
One dated 1684 - the Schulemberg Mortar.

[3rd Dutch War, 1672–3]

1673 Cinque Ports Regt of Militia

Warned to report to Dover Castle, but no record found they actually went there; possibly to replace Col Strode's coy during his absence. Col Strode was Colonel of the 1st Bn of Cinque Ports Militia, from 1666 until his death. He was also Judge of Admiralty, and the Courts of Chancery and Lodemenage, and MP for Sandwich 1665 and 1685.

1 Master Gunner & 4 gunners *WO24/3*

Mar 1674–1676 **One coy of the King's or Coldstream Regts of Footguards** *R/H*

One coy relieved every two months from Rochester. Capt/Col John Strode was LtDC for many years, and had his own permanent garrison coy, assisted by the alternating 'marching companies' from Rochester.

'Dover is to be manned by one of the six coys of those two regiments of Guards quartered in and about Rochester', where there were 4 coys of 1st King's and 2 coys of Coldstream Guards. The Coldstream are descended from a force raised by Oliver Cromwell; they marched from Coldstream in the north to assist in the restoration of Charles II. The regt is actually older than the King's (or Grenadier) guards, but were 'second' in confirming their loyalty to the Crown.

Jan 1675– **30 soldiers of Le Regiment de Douglas** (1st)* *R/H*

Mar–Aug 1678 **Det of the Earl of Dumbarton's Regt.** (1st)* *R/H*

Lord George Douglas became Earl of Dumbarton in March 1675. Le Régiment de Douglas (*see* 1667) was first Le Régiment de Hébron, a Scottish regiment raised in 1633 by Sir John Hepburn for service under the French crown (Louis XIV); it then became le Régiment de Douglas, and came back to Charles II on temporary loan in 1661, only to return to France the following year. It returned to permanent establishment in 1673, and claimed precedence as the Royal Regiment of Foot (1st). (*'A few of Douglas' men for 2–3 years past', so these two entries probably represent continuous occupation). *CSP(D)*

Mar–Apr 1678 **Brett's Coy, The Coldstream Regt of Footguards** *R/H*

Aug 1678–Mar 1679 **Capt Wharton's Coy of Lord Morpeth's Regt** (disb Mar 1679) *CSP(D)*

Reference made to the Castle being so ruined there was no place habitable without repair. However, in Aug 1678, there was a request from the Mayor that Lord Morpeth's Regt be quartered in the Castle 'as they used to be', instead of in the town 'as for the past 2–3 years'. (This is confusing as the regt was only in existence for a year, but perhaps refers to troops in the town generally). 1678–1702 – Many references that troops were quartered in the Town doing duty in the Castle over prisoners and deserters. *CSP(D)*

Aug 1678 – Capt Strode's Coy at Hounslow and Windsor attending the Court. (He was promoted to major on 28th Aug).

Mar 1679 **Lord Salisbury's Regt** (disb 1679) (1 coy) *CSP(D)*

1678/9 – Both these regiments (Morpeth's & Salisbury's) were raised Feb 1678 and disbanded in the Castle, Mar 1679 (Salisbury's was Lord O'Brien's).

1679 – regular forces reduced again. The army was considered a 'Grievance and Vexation to the People'. *(Ascoli)*. A company normally comprised: 1 captain, 1 lieutenant, 1 ensign, 3 sergeants, 3 corporals, 2 drummers and 100 men.

1679 **18 gunners** *CSP(D)*

Jan 1679–1685 [2 coys of the 1st (Western) Regt of the Cinque Ports]

Mainly in Dover Town and Pier. Col Strode's and Major Breame's – 150 men each, Trained Bands (Western Regt of the Cinque Ports, of which Col Sir Basil Dixwell was CO – he became LtDC in 1696). Walter Breame was a descendant of a Flemish refugee. He had been imprisoned at the Castle, a youth of 14 years (a case of mistaken identity during the Commonwealth), thus acquiring the honour of being the youngest prisoner for HM's service!

[1681 – Charles II's treasury again empty, the army unpaid and almost mutinous; however, the King formed an alliance with Louis of France (as he had for the secret Treaty of Dover of May 1670) which guaranteed him an income independent of Parliament].

1682 **8 gunners** *Lyon*

Sep 1684 **2 coys of the Scotch Regt**

From Rochester and Chatham (1st Ft, Royal Scots). There were at this time **only 5 gunners** at the Castle.

Col Strode's Coy ordered to Newmarket. He was made Lt Col 1684, and commanded his regt (1st Regt of Foot Guards) on parade at the coronation of James II, 23rd April, 1685, dressed in a coat of Cloth of Gold 'richly Imbroidered with Silver'. He died 25 Mar 1686. *R/H*

Jul 1685–Nov 1688 **Sir Edward Hales's Regt** (14th) (3 coys) *WO5/1*

Raised 1685 at Canterbury. It is not clear whether these companies stayed all the time, or went to summer camp on Hounslow Heath. Sir Edward Hales was LtDC Apr 1686–Dec 1688. He was also Judge of Admiralty and the Courts of Chancery and Lodemenage of the Cinque Ports 'in place of John Strode'. Sir Edward was a Catholic and favourite of James II – he tried to escape to France with the King from Faversham in Dec 1688, but was imprisoned for 1½ years in the Tower of London (of which he had earlier been Lt!), after which he rejoined James II in France, where he died in 1695. 1688 – Col Tooke was Dep Gov DC. 200 prisoners in Dover Castle.

[Monmouth Rebellion, 1685]

Apr 1688– One troop Royal Regt of Dragoons *WO5/3*

Dragoons first mentioned in Dover. Dragoons were originally mounted foot soldiers, able to act as either infantry or cavalry as occasion required. John, Viscount Fitz-Harding, Colonel of one of the King's Regts of Dragoons at Canterbury, also had responsibility for Dover, including the Militia. There was usually one troop or detachment of Dragoons in Dover, more probably at Archcliffe, and mainly employed on patrol duty between Bourne and Dover or on coastal duty (a detachment usually consisted of a subaltern and about 20 men). However, one or two are mentioned as being in Dover Castle on prisoner guard duties, so they are included for interest *(in italics).* *WO5/6*

Apr & Sep 1688 – much raising of extra men in most regiments. *WO26/2*

Dec 1688–Jan 1689 **3 coys of Coldstream** (Col George Wingfield/Wickfield) *WO5/5*

Apart from a few gunners, there was no effective garrison in Dover Castle at the accession of William III and Mary (Dec 1688). Trained Bands of Dover came grudgingly to the defence of the Castle, which was outside the liberties of the Cinque Ports ('in the foreign'), and Portsmen were never called out of their liberties; there had long survived a belief that men of the Cinque Ports were exempt from military service, but this was only true so long as they were required to provide ships and men for the King's Navy – an obligation which ceased earlier in the 17th century. They considered themselves primarily sailors, but 'as the harbours silted up, they thereafter continued their loyal service in the Trained Bands and Militia of the Ports'. However, the townspeople 'took' the Castle for King William in Dec 1688. 'Many of the soldiers who had assisted the principal supporters of William of Orange during the invasion had been irregulars. Dover Castle had been seized by a disorderly collection of 300 sailors, townsmen and yokels under the dubious leadership of two master mariners, a brewer, a soldier and two bakers. The Prince of Orange had to offer this gang financial recompense for their outlays before they agreed to hand over the Castle to some Kent Militia (the 3 coys of Coldstream) under Col Wickfield'. *Fazan,, British Army of Wm III, John Childs*

The Prince of Orange dispersed all the Footguards 'to the country' to isolate them from the King. *R/H.*

[1689–9 War of Grand Alliance – 'Dutch William's War'].

Regularization of the British Army –which was not legally recognized until the passing of the Mutiny Act in 1689.

Jan–Mar 1689 Col John Hales's Regt (disb 1697) (2 coys) *WO5/5*

Raised for French service, and transferred to the English establishment Nov 1688.

May–Aug 1689 Col Cutz's Regt of Dutch Foot (disb 1699) (2 coys) *WO5/5*

[Or Cutt's]. Raised by him 1674, transferred to the English establishment Nov 1688; converted to Seymour's Marines 1698, and disbanded May 1699.

Sep 1689–Jan 1690 Col Babington's Regt (6th) (2 coys) *WO5/5*

The regt helped William of Orange in Holland, and returned to England with him in 1688, transferring to the English service. *CSP (D)*

Dec 1689– **18 gunners**

Feb 1690–Aug 1691 Duke of Bolton's Regt (Lt Col Norton)(disb 1697) (1 coy) *WO5/5,6*

A private regt, only in existence for 8 years, although he had to raise 400 extra men in Oct 1690.

1690–1746 The Castle was allowed to fall into decay, and was used only as a prison - 'neglected in peace, cared for in war'. The Castle Church remained a ruin until 1860, when it was restored by Sir Gilbert Scott; meanwhile St James's Church at the foot of the hill (itself now a ruin since World War II) was used as the garrison church.

Sep 1691–Jan 1692 1st Regt of Footguards (40 men) (later Grenadier Guards) (1 coy) *WO5/6*

Henry, Viscount Sidney, was LW & CDC 1691–1702, and Colonel of the 1st Regt of Footguards.

Jan 1692– Col Brewer's Regt (12th) (2 coys) *WO5/6*

Apr 1693–Oct 1694 Col Beaumont's Regt (8th) (1 coy)

Jan 1694 – Captain Robert Jacob 'to deliver four barrels of gunpowder out of the Castle for the defence of Dover together with their indent for the same.' Jacob was three times mayor of Dover – 1685, 1688 (when he was removed by the King), and again in 1711. *Do/CPz 22*

Oct 1694?–Feb 1695 Col Coote's Regt (disb 1697) (2 coys) *WO5/7*

Coys also in Deal, Canterbury, Faversham, Sandwich & Ashford. Col Coote later raised the 39th Regt of Foot.

Apr 1695– {Col Beaumont's Regt (8th) (1 coy) *became:* *WO5/7*

Jan 1696 {Col John Webb's Regt (8th) (1 coy) *WO5/8*

This is the same Coy – the Colonel's name changed Dec 1695 (Beaumont & Webb). Col John Beaumont was LtDC and Cinque Ports garrison commander (1688-95). 'The usual duty' – coastal patrols and guarding prisoners in Dover Castle.

Nov 1695– Sir Henry Bellassy's Regt (22nd) (1 coy) *WO5/7*

To guard French prisoners. (Name also spelt Belasyse, Belasize; he was later court-martialled and dismissed the service after plunder at Port St Mary, Vigo in 1702).

Jan–Mar 1696 Col Edward Dutton Colt's Regt (1 coy) *WO5/8*

Was John Hales' regt; converted to Marines 1698, and disbanded c1699.

Mar–Oct 1696 Col Tidcomb's Regt (14th) (1 coy) *WO5/8*

Nov–Dec 1696 Col Columbine's Regt (6th) (1 coy) *(or Collenbine)* *WO5/8*

Dec 1696–May 1697 Marquis of Puissar's Regt (24th) *(or de Puizar)* (1 coy) *WO5/8,9*

Examples of graffiti in the Keep

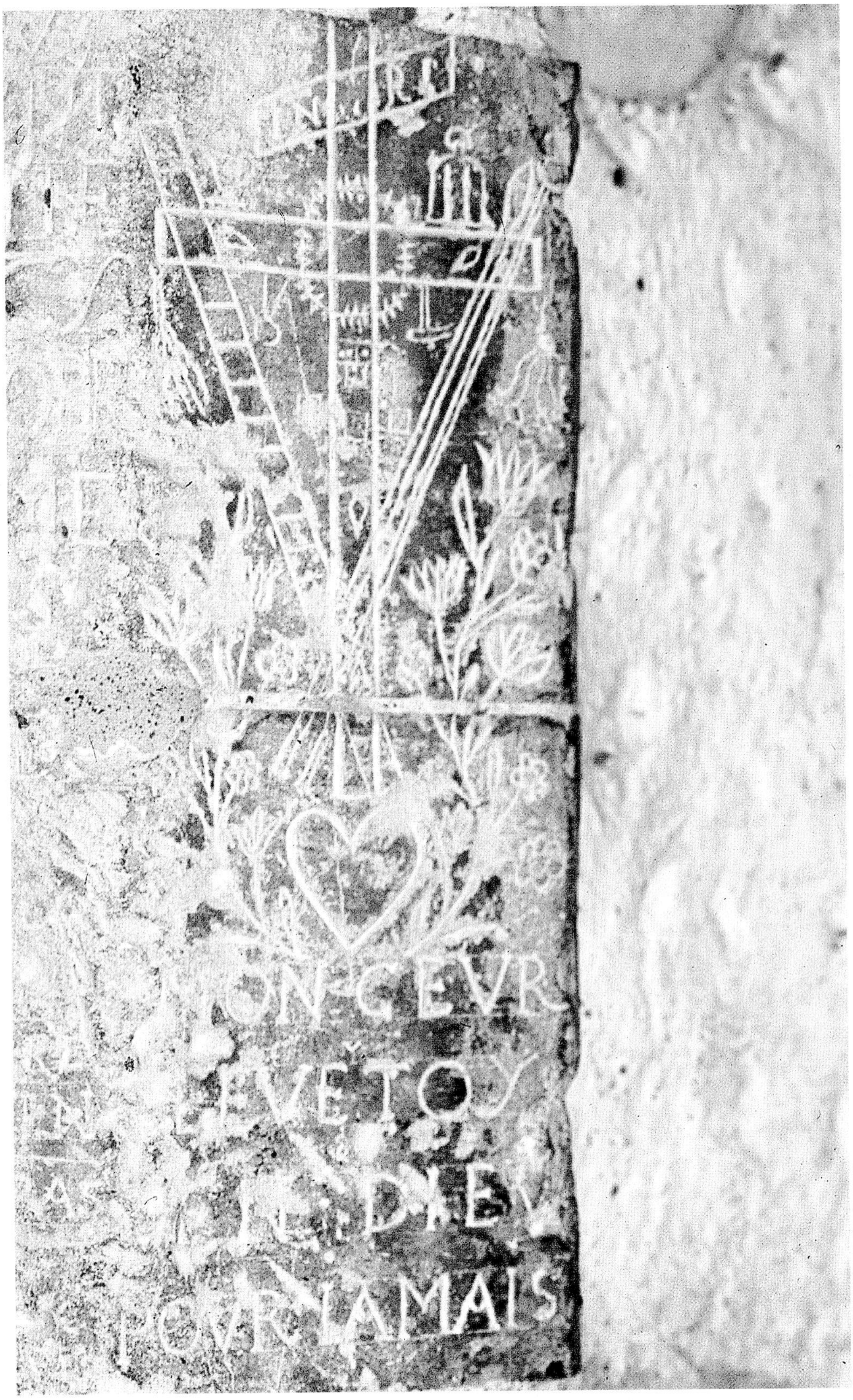

Examples of Graffiti inside the Keep, done by prisoners during the 18th century. Plaintive prayers above and below the one depicting the crucifixion translate roughly as:

'Almighty God deliver/save me please' *(not shown)*

'My heart lift up to God forever'. *(below)*

May–Nov 1697 Dets Col Gibson's (28th) and Col Brudenell's Regts (disb 1698) *WO5/8,9*

Nov 1697 – there is a note about billeting troops returning from Flanders: 'The officers are to take care that the soldiers behave themselves civilly and duly pay their landlords, and all the Magistrates, Justices of the Peace, Constables and other of our Officers whom it may concern, are hereby required to be assisting unto them in providing Quarters and otherwise as there may be occasion'. The word *billet* is from the French word meaning letter or ticket, given to each householder required to lodge soldiers, against which they could claim payment. *WO5/10*

Dec 1697 Col Seymour's Regt (disb 1699) (5 coys) *WO5/10*

Seymour's – was Cutz/Cutt's Regt (see 1689), converted to Marines 1698.

Dec 1697 Brig Fairfax's Regt (5th) (2 coys) *WO5/10*

Came to England with William of Orange and transferred to the English service.

Jan 1698 (2 weeks) Col Webb's Regt (8th) (1 coy) *WO5/10*

'Lately landed at Dover' (from Flanders) – the rest of the regt were in Canterbury and Maidstone until mid–Jan 1698

1697/9 – At the end of the seven-years' Continental war (League of Augsburg), the army was drastically reduced – from 87,000 to 7,000 – to peacetime establishment. The Army 'unloved, unhonoured, underpaid and ill-housed'. *Ascoli*

Dover Castle still in a ruinous state, and gun carriages mostly rotten. No soldiers, only gunners. *CSP(D)*

1698– **18 Gunners** *CSP(D)*

Aug 1698–Aug 1703 Det 3rd Queen Consort's Own Regt of Dragoons (3H) *JSAHR/52*

Troops first sent to the Kent coast to help customs officers against owling and smuggling by Order in Council, June 1698. '... the forces quartered on or near our sea coasts ... to be aiding and assisting to the Civill Magistrates, when desired of them, and the Officers of our Customs, for the Executing Legall Processes and other Matters relating to our Service in hindering the Exportation of Wool, and Illegal Importation of French Silks, Brandy and other Goods, etc ...'. Dets were sent out from HQs in Canterbury and Ashford. There were Dragoons in Kent 1698–1706, and again 1716–1750s, mostly *not* in the Castle, though occasionally they also did duty over guarding prisoners.

Apr 1702 1 coy Lord Shannon's Regt of Marines (raised 1702, disb 1713) *CSP(D)*

1702–1714 (?–1745) Dover Castle used for French and Spanish prisoners – up to 1500 of them! Very full in 1702, and some had to be housed elsewhere in Dover. Prisoners were exchanged, almost as currency, on a rank-for-rank basis, or price per rank. There are many examples of graffiti inside the keep done by prisoners around this time.

[1702–14 War of Spanish Succession & Marlborough campaigns].

May–Oct 1702 **Lord Lucas' Regt of Foot** (34th) (1 coy) *WO5/10,11,R/H*
Oct–Nov 1702 " " " " (2 coys)

Lord Lucas' Regt sent to the Castle 'to do such duty there as the Lord Warden of the Cinque Ports or the Lieutenant of that Place shall direct.' *WO5/10*

The Cinque Ports Garrison at this time comprised: the Lord Warden, Lieutenant, Chaplain, Captain, Officers and Gunners of Archcliffe and Moate's Bulwarks, Dover, Deal, Sandown, Sandgate and 'Walmore' Castles = c. 100 men (so Dover Castle probably only 30-40 men). The pay was: Lord Warden £160 pa; LtDC £50 pa; Captains of Sandown, Walmer and Deal Castles £20 pa; Captain of Sandgate £40 pa; Master Gunner 14d, Sergeant 9d, Gunner, Drummer and Corporal 7d each, and a private soldier 5d – per day (the pay is *less* than in 1539!). *WO55/341*

Nov–Dec 1702 **Lt Gen Churchill's Regt of Foot** (24th) (3 coys) *WO5/11*

Lt Gen Churchill was the 1st Duke of Marlborough.

Dec 1702–Mar 1703 **Lord Shannon's Regt of Marines** (3 coys) *WO5/11*
Mar 1703 **4 coys** " " "

Raised 1702, disb 1713.

Mar–Aug 1703 **Capt Stevenage's Coy of Footguards** (Coldstream)(80 men) *WO5/11,R/H*

Aug–Sep 1703 **Col Roger Elliot's Regt of Foot** (3 coys) *WO5/11,12*
Sep 1703–Jan 1704 **2 coys** " " " " (raised 1703, disb 1713)

Aug 1703–Apr 1706 *Det of Earl of Essex' Regt of Hussars (4QOH)* *JSAHR/52*

Jan–Mar/Apr 1704 Dornell's & Knight's (30th) (2 coys) *WO5/1, R/H*

Col Thos. Sanderson's Marines, raised 1702.

Apr–Sep 1704 Col Elliot's Regt of Foot (disb 1713) (3 coys) *WO5/12*
Sep 1704–Apr 1705 1 coy " " " *WO5/13*

Mar–Apr 1705 Brig Hans Hamilton's Regt of Foot (34th) (2 coys) *WO5/13*

'The late Lord Lucas' Regt'.

Apr 1705 Marines (1 coy) *WO5/13*

'Any coy of our Marine regts', of which there were just six regts at the time. *Ascoli*

Apr–July 1705 Col Heyman Rooke's Regt of Foot (1 coy) *WO5/13*

Raised 1704 on the Irish establishment, disb 1712.

General Thomas Erle, Colonel (19th Foot), 1691-1712

courtesy of The Green Howards Museum

Jul–Dec 1705 Col Edmund Soames' Regt of Foot (2 coys) *WO5/13*

Later Sir Robt Rich's. Raised 1705, disb 1712. …'in ye Guarding and safe-keeping the Prisoners'.

Dec 1705 Marines (1 coy) (*see also* Apr 1705) *WO5/13*

Jan–May 1706 Col Sir Charles Hotham's Regt of Foot (2 coys) *WO5/13*

Raised 1705 in Yorkshire, disb 1713.

May–Nov 1706 Col Livesay's Regt of Foot (12th) (2 coys) *WO5/13,R/H*

'For exchange of Prisoners of Warr and the Guarding and Safekeeping the Prisoners'.

Nov 1706-Apr 1707 – away on election duty & recruiting marches in Yorkshire; no mention of who relieved them - possibly Invalids.

Apr–Aug 1707 Col Livesay's Regt of Foot (12th)(1 coy) *WO5/14,R/H*

Aug–Dec 1707 Lt Gen Erle's Regt of Foot (19th) (1 coy) *WO5/14*

Dec 1707–Jul 1708 Col Livesay's Regt of Foot (12th) (1 coy) *WO5/14,15*

Jul 1708–May 1710 Invalids (?Bruce's) (1 coy) *WO5/15*

One Independent Coy of Invalids became part of the permanent garrison from now on. Invalids included old gunners employed in care and maintenance duties at royal castles and coast fortresses, previously on establishment of 'Guards and Garrisons' in England *(MES Laws)*. Invalid coys had a smaller establishment than a normal 'marching coy' – usually c.60–75 men. 6 coys were formed from the Royal Hospital, Chelsea of 'Out Pensioners' who were fit and able, to do duty on their pension (and were struck off if they refused), each coy comprising: 1 captain, 1 lieutenant, 1 ensign, 3 sergeants, 4 corporals, 2 drummers and 75 private men. Coy numbers were reduced in Jul 1713 to: 2 sergeants, 2 corporals, 1 drummer and 50 private men. *WO26/13*

From 1710–1717 virtually only an Independent Coy of Invalids formed the garrison at Dover Castle.

1713 – For Clothing a Company of Invalids: 'A Coat, Waistcoat and Breeches, a Hatt, 2 Shirts, 2 Neckcloths, one pair of Shoes, one pair of Stockings, a Sword and Belt – once in Two Years'.

Aug 1709 (10 days only) Lord Mark Kerr's Regt of Foot (disb 1712) (1-2 coys) *WO5/16*

Sep–Dec 1709 Invalids only *(see above)*

Jan–May 1710 Col Richard Sutton's Regt of Foot (later Leigh's; disb 1713) (Det) *WO5/16*

May 1710–1714 **Capt Walsh's Coy of Invalids** *WO5/16, N/R Z/17*

June 1712 – a plea, written in French, by 22 French prisoners to the Secretary of State at War for better conditions and food – for two years they have only bread and water, with salt meat three times a week – 'une prison affreuse'. *SP 34/18/76*

Jun 1712 [1 coy 3rd Regt of Footguards (Scots Guards)] *WO5/17*

Embarked for Spain June 1712, returned September 1712 – a few days only.

Aug 1712–May 1713 **Col Kane's Regt** (Det) (disb. 1713) *WO5/18*

1 Lt, 1 Sgt & 20 recruits. Jan 1713 – 9 French prisoners escaped – breaking out at night 'after head count', through a hole in the wall. *SP 34/20/38*

May 1713 { **Maj Gen Wynne's, Col Leigh's & Col Kane's** (disb) *WO5/18}*

Jul 1713 { **Col Newton's, Maj Gen Evans' & Col Pocock's Regts** (disb) *WO5/18}*

All disbanded at Dover Castle. Leigh's was Col Sutton's – *(see* 1710*)*. Pocock's was re–raised Jul 1715 and again disbanded 1718.

1714 – a lot of troops landing at Dover, but passing through. Probably only Invalids at the Castle.

–Jun 1713 *Det Earl of Earl of Strafford's Royal Dragoons (1st)* *WO5/18*

1715–1717 Capt John Cawarden's Coy of Invalids (disb 1717) *WO26/15*

Coast Defences were again cut down in 1716, after the War of Spanish Succession – Dover reduced from 98 guns to 36. *[Royal Regiment of Artillery formed]*. *M-J*

Jan–May 1717 Capt Gwyn Vaughan's Coy of Invalids (disb Jun 1717) *WO5/21,WO26/15*

Jun 1717–Oct 1718 The Prince of Wales' Own Royal Regt of Welch Fusiliers (1 coy)

23rd Foot (Maj/Gen Sabine's). *WO5/21*

1717 –First entry found in Marching Orders about owlers and smugglers (owling = smuggling wool out of England) *(see also* Aug 1698*)*; as early as the time of H VIII, the wool trade with Flanders was described as 'the lifeblood of England's existence'.

1717–1746 – These units were in Dover, mostly 'assisting the revenue officers against Owlers and Smugglers', and billeted on the Town. The Castle was then in poor repair, but housed French and Spanish prisoners some of the time, and these units also did duty in the Castle guarding prisoners, so have been included. The troop of dragoons in Dover was used mainly to assist the revenue officers - riding men being considered more useful than foot soldiers for chasing smugglers – though on occasion they were considered 'more a liability than an asset.' *(see also* 1747*)*. *JSAHR/52, P Muskett*

Oct 1718–Jan 1719 Col Cholm(e)ley's Regt of Foot (1 coy) (16th) *WO5/22*

1719–1721 **Invalids only** *WO5/23*

1719 – Independent Invalid coys were formed into a regt (41st), later the Welch Regt.

Queen Elizabeth's Pocket Pistol

Cast in Utrecht in 1544. A gift to Henry VIII from Maximilien von Egmont, Count of Buren, a distinguished military commander in the service of Emperor Charles V of France. It was at the Black Bulwarke in 1547, and is known to have been kept in the Castle by 1612. It was used during the Civil War in Hull and Sheffield by the Parliamentarians, but surrendered to the Royalists at Lostwithiel in 1644. The old wooden carriage was replaced by the present metal one in 1827, reputedly cast from small cannon brought back as trophies from the field of Waterloo. It was at that time believed to have been given to Queen Elizabeth I by the States of Holland, hence the ER and arms of Holland on the carriage. It is known to have been test-fired by William Eldred, Master Gunner, in 1613,1617 & 1622.

Mr Vernon of Leeds, a one-time drummer boy stationed in the Castle with the KOYLI in 1925, related that one of his duties was to keep the gun regularly polished!

courtesy of English Heritage/Dover Museum (d06242)

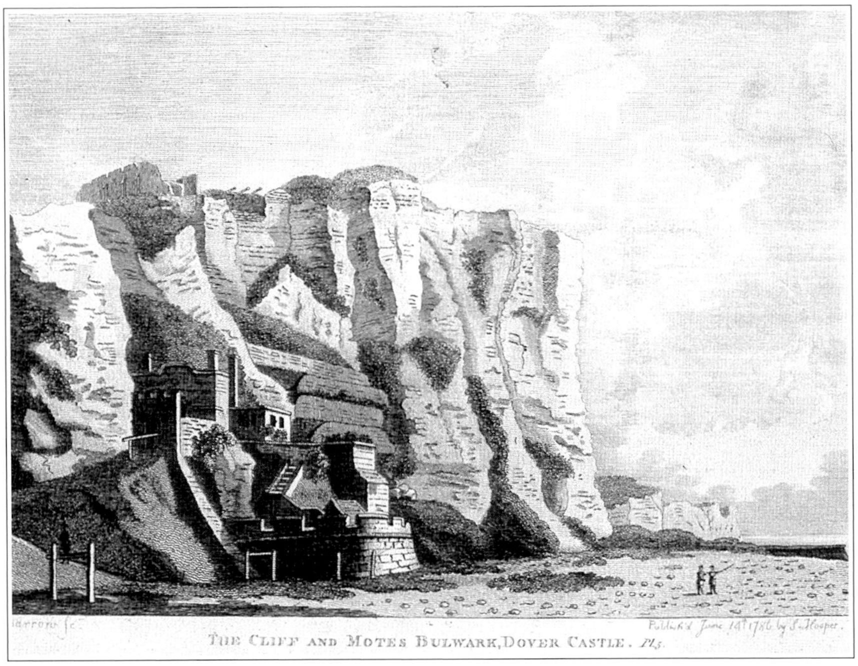

Moat's (or Mote's) Bulwark, built c 1540 by Henry VIII. The site of Guilford Battery was just beyond. *(Darrell)*

c1720 – With war almost continuous, 'marching companies' were not to be spared, so a small permanent detachment of artillery continued for 'keeping and preserving the gunnes, carriages, ammunition and other stores of war' with 'extraordinary or additional gunners' found from seamen landed from the fleet, the infantry garrison, the county militia or even local inhabitants. The number of guns at the Castle was again reduced from 45 ('according to ancient establishment') to 10, but after complaints about the severity of the reduction, this was altered to 15, 'including the long Brass Gun.'

This gun is now known as Queen Elizabeth's Pocket Pistol, but has also been referred to as Queen Anne's Pocket Piece. Earlier referred to as a Basilisco, it is a brass demi–culverin. It has stood in many different positions in the Castle: on the cliff edge near the PWSS; by the present saluting base known as Long Gun Magazine, to the west of the Officers' Mess; on the grass mound above Canon's Gate, etc. It is now housed under cover by the NAAFI block. According to an inventory of royal possessions in 1547 after Henry VIII's death, it was even at one time at the Black Bulwark, near Archcliffe Fort ('one Basillisches of brasse'). Colour Sergeant George Calladine, a militiaman but later of 19th Foot, describes the gun in his diary, in 1812: 'On the Castle hill stands the far–famed Queen Anne's Pocket Piece, being a very long cannon, but of small bore, not being more than a nine–pounder. I believe its length is 24 feet. It once had a gold touch hole, but that metal was too tempting to the eye of a soldier, and was by some sentinel picked out, for which offence I hear the man suffered death. Better for the cannon to have had a common touchhole and the man's life have been spared. The state it was in when I saw it, I conceive would not admit of its being discharged, as it was very much honey–combed or full of small holes'. His translation of the inscription on the gun was: 'Sponge me well, and keep me clean, I'll carry a ball to Calais Green' (a part of Dover!). A more literal translation is: ' Breaker my name of rampart and wall, Over hill and dale I throw my ball'.

May 1720 – On the King's orders: 'No grazing nor plowing nor making gardens' permitted in the 'Outworks, Bastions or Bulwarks', because of damage done to the earthworks. Grass was permitted to be cut twice a year, using ladders where the men could not reach with scythes; grass was to be removed immediately, and made into hay elsewhere.

1722 – there were 1500 French prisoners in the Keep. *M-J, EK/CPW/RO2, EK/D91 Misc*

May 1721–Feb 1722 [?Det Brig Henry Grove's Regt of Foot (10th)] *WO5/24*

Feb–May 1722 [?Det Col Charles Cadogan's Regt of Foot (4th)] *WO5/24*

Both regts 'on coastal duty' – more probably in the Town, 'executing several Legall Processes against Owlers and Smugglers, and all other Matters relating to our Service in the Hindering the Exportation of Wool and illegal Importation of Prohibited and Uncustomed Goods, and to Repel Force with Force in case the Civil Magistrates shall find it necessary'. Other prohibited goods mentioned: French silks, velvets, brandy, tea, tobacco. (Owlers were wool smugglers).

1725– **2 Master Gunners & 8 gunners** *M-J*

The officers & gunners in Dover Castle must have been fairly elderly, as seem to have died and been replaced quite frequently. *EK/CPW/R02*

1725–1739–1762 (?longer) [2 coys The Western Regt of the Cinque Ports (Militia)]

1725 – Militia under Col Sir Basil Dixwell, jun, (LtDC 1714–1739), who resigned 1739, then under Col Thomas Hales (also LtDC 1739–1762) – Trained Band soldiers, and would have been in the Town – Dover Town & Dover Pier coys, but Dixwell also appointed and paid the gunners in the Castle, and would have been able to summon the trained bands to the Castle if need arose. He was 'duly to exercise the officers & soldiers of the same in arms & to use y^r best care & endeavour to keep them in good order & discipline'. Hales' son, Thomas Pym Hales, was also LtDC, Captain of Moate's Bulwark, and of Dover Town Coy of Militia. Moate's Bulwark is regarded as part of Dover Castle. *EK/CPW/RO2*

Mar 1732 – 'The King pays 2d a week part of the salt provision; the soldier receives 1/3d per week for Tobacco, Greens and Necessarys'. The Cinque Ports Garrison received £18 pa for Fire and Candle, and the Garrison pay then was: Lord Warden: £1.7s.4¾d per day (£500 pa); LtDC: 10/- per day (£182.10s pa); Deputy LtDC: 6/- per day, Chaplain to Lord Warden: 2/- per day.

[The regiment survived as 44 Cinque Ports Signal Squadron Volunteers until early 1990s]

Feb–Mar 1727	Col Clayton's Regt of Foot (14th) (1 coy)	*WO5/27*
Mar 1727 (2 weeks)	2 'additional' coys "	
May 1727 (2 weeks)	Col Clayton's Regt of Foot (1 coy)	
Jun 1728–Apr 1729	Queen's Own Royal Regt of Foot (2nd)(Brig Kirke's) (1 coy)	*WO5/27,28*

From review at Blackheath. Coys also at Canterbury (4), Faversham, Ashford and Sandwich.

Jul–Sep 1731	*?1 troop Lt Gen Wade's Regt of Horse (3DG)*	*WO5/30*
Mar 1735–Jun 1736	?Det Col Paget's Regt of Foot (32nd)	*WO5/31*
Aug 1736–May 1737	The late Lt Gen Tatton's Regt of Foot (3rd) (Det)	*WO5/32*
May 1737–Aug 1738	Brig Harrison's Regt of Foot (15th) (Det)	*WO5/32*
Aug 1738–Jun 1739	The King's Own Royal Regt of Welch Fusiliers (23rd) (Det)	*WO5/33*

Sabine's.

Jul 1739–Aug 1740	Gen Whetham's Regt of Foot (12th) (Det)	*WO5/33*

General The Hon. Sir Charles Howard, KB,
Colonel of 19th Foot, 1738-1748 -
courtesy of The Green Howards Museum

Lt General Thomas Howard,
Colonel of 3rd Foot (Buffs), 1737-1749
courtesy of The National Portrait Gallery

Sep 1740-Jun 1741 **Col Campbell's Regt of Foot** (21st) (1 coy) *WO5/34*

Royal Regt of North British Fusiliers – to provide guard upon Spanish prisoners in Dover Castle, the order to continue in force with any relieving company. April 1741 – ordered out of town during elections 'as was usual.' *(see also* 1752*)*

Jun 1741– **Col Houghton's Regt of Foot** (45th) (1 coy) *WO5/34*

Against owlers & smugglers, but also guard duty on prisoners. Regt raised Jan 1741; reviewed at Canterbury, Aug 1741, 'leaving a sufficient guard'.

Jun 1742–Nov 1743 1 troop Lt Gen Sir Philip Honeywood's Regt of Horse *WO5/35,36*

(3KOH? – Honeywood was Colonel of 3KOH until 18/4/1743, then of 1KDG))

[Dettingen 1743; War of Austrian Succession 1740-1748)] – large movements of troops through Dover – 16,000 sent to Flanders in 1742.

Feb–Jul 1743 Col John Cotterell's Marines (6th Regt) (3 coys) *WO5/35, Ascoli*

Disb 1747, and raised again in 1748 as 49th regt of foot.

Jul 1744–Jul 1745 Lt Gen Harrison's Regt of Foot (15th) *R/H*

Also 3 coys at Deal. Aug 1744 – To assist in quelling riots* & against smuggling; prisoners still in Dover Castle. *...'representation having been made to HM that the Smiths at Deptford and Woolwich yards have in a tumultuous manner left their work, and are endeavouring as it is apprehended to induce the Smiths belonging to HM yards at Chatham, Sheerness, Portsmouth and Plymouth to be Rioteur'. *WO5/36*

1745 – Many troops working in Dover Castle, but not necessarily quartered there, during rebuilding of the barracks by the Duke of Cumberland (part of which burnt down again in 1800).

Apr–Sep 1745 **Lord Mark Kerr's Regt of Dragoons** *(11H)* (Det) *WO5/36*

The Dragoons specifically mentioned as doing PoW duty in the Castle, and being relieved by Douglas' Foot.

Sep–Oct 1745 **Brig Gen Douglas' Regt of Foot** (32nd) (4 coys) *WO5/37*

To relieve Lord Mark Kerr's Regt on PoW duty.

–Sep 1745 [Maj Gen Oglethorpe's Regt of Foot (disb 1748)] *WO5/37*

Mentioned as leaving for Hull – ?returning from Flanders, and not resident long.

Oct 1745 Maj Gen Frampton's Regt of Foot (30th) (8 coys) *WO5/37*

Nov 1745 (2 weeks) **Lord John Murray's Regt of Foot** (42nd) (4 coys) *WO5/37*

'to relieve duty over PoWs'.

Nov 1745–Apr 1746 **Lt Gen Harrison's Regt of Foot** (15th) (4/5 coys) *WO5/37*

Apr–Jun 1746 **Maj Gen Charles Howard's Regt of Foot** (19th) (5 coys) *WO5/38 & 379/1*

2 Jun – 'a sufficient detachment' to escort 400 French PoWs from DC to Porchester Castle, and return to Dover.

Jun 1746–Nov 1747 **Lord Beauclerk's Regt of Foot** (31st) (3/5 coys) *WO5/38,39*

Most of these regts in the 1740s would have been billeted in the Town, but with a detachment doing prisoner duty in the Castle.

Nov 1747–Feb 1748 **Lord George Sackville's Regt of Foot** (20th) (5 coys) *WO5/39*

Lord George Sackville was MP for Dover 1741–1760, and son of the Duke of Dorset, who was LW & CDC at the time. The 20th were on PoW duty (plus 3 coys in the Town) – detachments of 1 Sergeant and 12 men were sent to Romney and Hythe 'and Places adjacent', to be 'Aiding and Assisting to the Civill Magistrates and Officers of the Revenue in preventing Owlers and Smugglers from running of goods, and in apprehending the said Owlers and Smugglers and seizing their goods... but not to repel Force with Force unless it shall be found absolutely necessary, or being thereunto required by the Civill Magistrates'.

c1745 there were up to 400 smugglers in Dover; it was said that the military engaged in 'assisting the revenue officers' (militia and regulars) were often suspected of *helping the smugglers...*'What Assistance they gave was chiefly to the Owlers; they left their Stable Doors open, upon compact with ye Exporters, to give them an Opportunity of making use of the Horses in ye Night-Time, for conveying the Wool to the Sea-side where ye Shallops lay ready to receive it'. In an effort to counter the possibility of family ties with them the War Office posted units from counties as far from home as possible! *Douch*

Feb 1748–Jun 1749 **Lt Gen Thomas Howard's Regt of Foot** (3rd Buffs) (7 coys) *WO5/39,40*

Jun–Jul – only 2 coys. Castle and Town – PoW duty.

There were two Colonels Howard at the time – the regts were differentiated by the colour of the facings on their uniforms: this regiment was the Buff Howards, later known as the Buffs (the other became the Green Howards (19th)). Some of their duties were to escort prisoners (PoWs) landed at Seaford back to the Castle; also escorting a shipment of bullion landed at Dover to the Bank of England. *WO5/39*

Jul 1749–Oct 1750 **Col Campbell's Regt of Foot** (21st) (2 coys) *WO5/40*

10 coys in Kent. Royal Regt of North British Fusiliers.

1750 – Some repairs being carried out to the Castle brought forth the comment from the Office of Works: '...the situation of this Castle is so extremely high that he had a remonstrance made unto him that whenever there was any gust of wind the gravel was carried in such whirlwinds as frequently to break many panes of glass; that this is an evil he confessed he knows not how to remedy, for though he believed that in some degree it is true, yet he

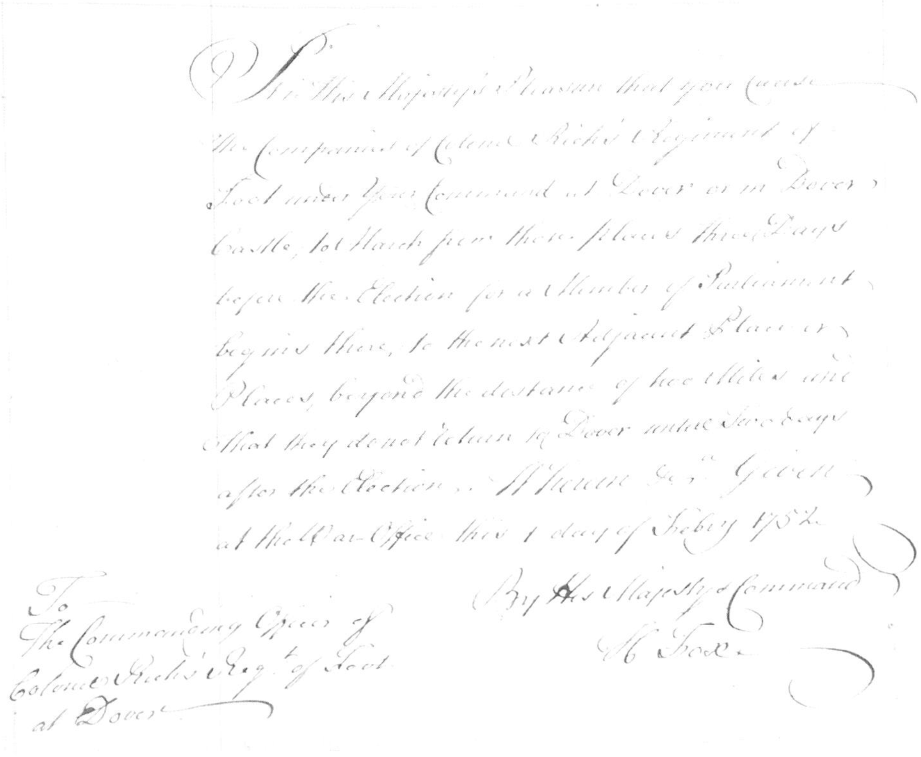

Sir, It is His Majesty's Pleasure that you cause the Companies of Colonel Rich's Regiment of Foot under your Command at Dover or in Dover Castle, to March from those Places three Days before the Election for a Member of Parliament begins there, to the next Adjacent Place or Places, beyond the distance of two Miles and that they do not return to Dover untill two days after the Election. Whereof &c. Given at the War-Office this 1 day of Febry 1752.

By His Majesty's Command
H. Fox.

To The Commanding Officer of Colonel Rich's Regt of Foot at Dover

Col. Rich's Regt ordered out of Dover during an election
courtesy of National Archives (PRO/WO5/41)

Lt Col James Wolfe of 20th Foot (c 1756),
later Maj Gen Wolfe of Quebec
courtesy of The National Trust (Quebec House)

Private and Officer, 20th Foot circa 1760
courtesy of The Fusiliers' Museum Lancashire

apprehends that the effect of every negligence or mischief of the troops quartered therein is attributed to the causes of wind, that he really thinks this deserves some consideration, since the expense of the Office is considerable on this account'. *WO47/36*

10 Mar 1750 – Men of Campbell's were required to escort HM's messengers, bringing from Dover to London 'seven persons concerned in debauching HM's subjects into the French service'.

Oct 1750–Apr 1751 **The Earl of Ancram's Regt of Foot** (24th) (2 coys) *WO5/40*

May–Sep 1751 *Det Col Sir Robert Rich's Regt of Dragoons (4QOH)* *WO5/41*

Sep 1751–Sep 1752 *1 troop Inniskilling Regt of Dragoons (6D)* *WO5/41*

6th Dragoons - Major General Cholmondeley's.

Nov 1751–Apr 1752 **Col Robert Rich's (King' Own) Regt of Foot** (4th) (3 coys) *WO5/41*

1752 – (to the 'keeper of the prison' at DC) – 'It is HMP *(His Majesty's Pleasure)* that you cause the companies of Col Rich's Regt. of Foot under your command at Dover or in Dover Castle to march from those places three days before the Election for a Member of Parliament begins there, to the next Adjacent Place or Places, beyond the distance of two miles, and that they do not return to Dover until two days after the Election.' (This happened during every election). The regiment was also away for a week in March 1752 to be reviewed at Rochester, after which only one coy returned to the Castle.

Oct 1752–Mar 1753 **Lt Gen Huske's Regt of Foot** (23rd) (4 coys) *WO5/41*

King' Own Royal Regt of Welch Fusiliers.

Apr 1753–Mar 1754 *1 troop Lord Tyrawley's Regt of Dragoons (3KOH)* *WO5/42*

Oct 1753–Mar 1754 **Lord Viscount Bury's Regt of Foot** (20th) (6 coys) *WO5/41,2*

The rest of the regiment was in Maidstone. Lt Col James Wolfe was in command, and it may be of interest to quote a little from his letters written home from the Castle. He claimed: 'Lord Bury's Regt is the best in the Army, so far as drill and discipline go'; he lodged 'at the foot of a tower supposed to be built by the Romans', and said 'I am sure there is not in the King's dominions a more melancholy dreadful winter station; the winds rattle pretty bad, and the air is sharp, but I suppose healthy for it causes great keenness of appetite'. He thought Dover socially boring, and was known locally as 'the bookish Colonel'; (other officers were frequently absent from their provincial stations to be at the London scene). He found Dover Castle very uncomfortable, but the advantages were: 'we have no magistrates or inhabitants to quarrel with; the soldiers are under our immediate inspection; and we can prevent them in any evil designs. It would be a prison to a man of pleasure, but an officer may put up with it'. He was only 27 at this time. The climate in Dover did however agree with him, though he complained of 'not being any use in the world' (i.e. not seeing any active service). 'I always encourage our young people to frequent balls and assemblies. It softens their manners, and makes 'em civil, and commonly I go along with 'em to see how they conduct themselves.' He was described as an 'unorthodox and eccentric man', and was a passionately keen professional, bitterly contemptuous of the frivolity and negligence bred by purchase.

Beckles Willson 'Life & Letters of James Wolfe', Correlli Barnett

Wolfe received complaints from the locals against 'some women of loose disorderly conduct, supposed to belong to the garrison'; he considered 'this sort of commerce with the sex as the last and most dangerous degree of brutality, ignominy and vice, and he cannot but entertain an exceeding contemptible opinion of those who have been concerned in it'... who would be 'punished accordingly'. Deserters, considered as cowards and traitors, were sometimes executed as an example to others, and men were put in irons in dungeons for drunken abuse and insolence to NCOs - or 'confined in the black hole'. 'It has been observed that some soldiers go out of these barracks with a full resolution to get drunk, and have even the impudence to declare their intentions, and that such soldiers use insolent and disrespectful language to the sergeants and corporals, pleading drunkenness and stupidity in excuse; these men may therefore be informed, that the first of them who shall take upon him, whether drunken or sober, to insult a non-commissioned officer, either in the barracks or on duty, shall be put into the dungeon in irons, till he be sufficiently convinced that modesty, sobriety and obedience become the character of a soldier'.

Gen Wolfe's Instructions to Young Officers - 1753

Mar–Sep 1754 *1 troop Earl of Ancram's Dragoons (11H)* *WO5/42*

Oct 1754–Apr 1756 *1 troop Lt Gen Hawley's Regt of Dragoons (1RD)* *WO5/42*

Oct 1754–Oct 1755 **Lt Gen Edward Wolfe's Regt of Foot** (8th) (6 coys) *WO5/42*

Castle and Town, against owlers (wool smugglers) and smugglers. Lt Gen Edward Wolfe was James Wolfe's father.

Oct 1755–Mar 1756 **7th or Royal Regt of Fusiliers** (Lord Robert Bertie's) (6 coys) *WO5/43*

4 coys in Town. Dec 1755 – The barracks within the Keep area fitted up for the reception of one battalion. Extra troops were called in to Dover Castle to assist the Engineer with the rebuilding works, 'quartered in the Town, mounting an Officer's Guard in the Castle'. Jan 1756 – bad weather impeded the works: 'so long a continuance of heavy rain and hard gales of wind retarded our making so great a progress in the works at Dover Castle as I could have wished.' *(Capt Desmaretz, RA, architect to the Office of Ordnance)*. A timber building on the eastern wall for the sick and hurt, and the accommodation of French prisoners, was pulled down shortly after erection, to make way for new batteries for the great guns against the opposite commanding hill, and a new hospital and canteen built. The Fusiliers marched for Portsmouth 13 March. A party of sick men was left at the Castle until April. *WO55/2275*

1756–1767 **2 Master Gunners, 4 gunners** *M-J*

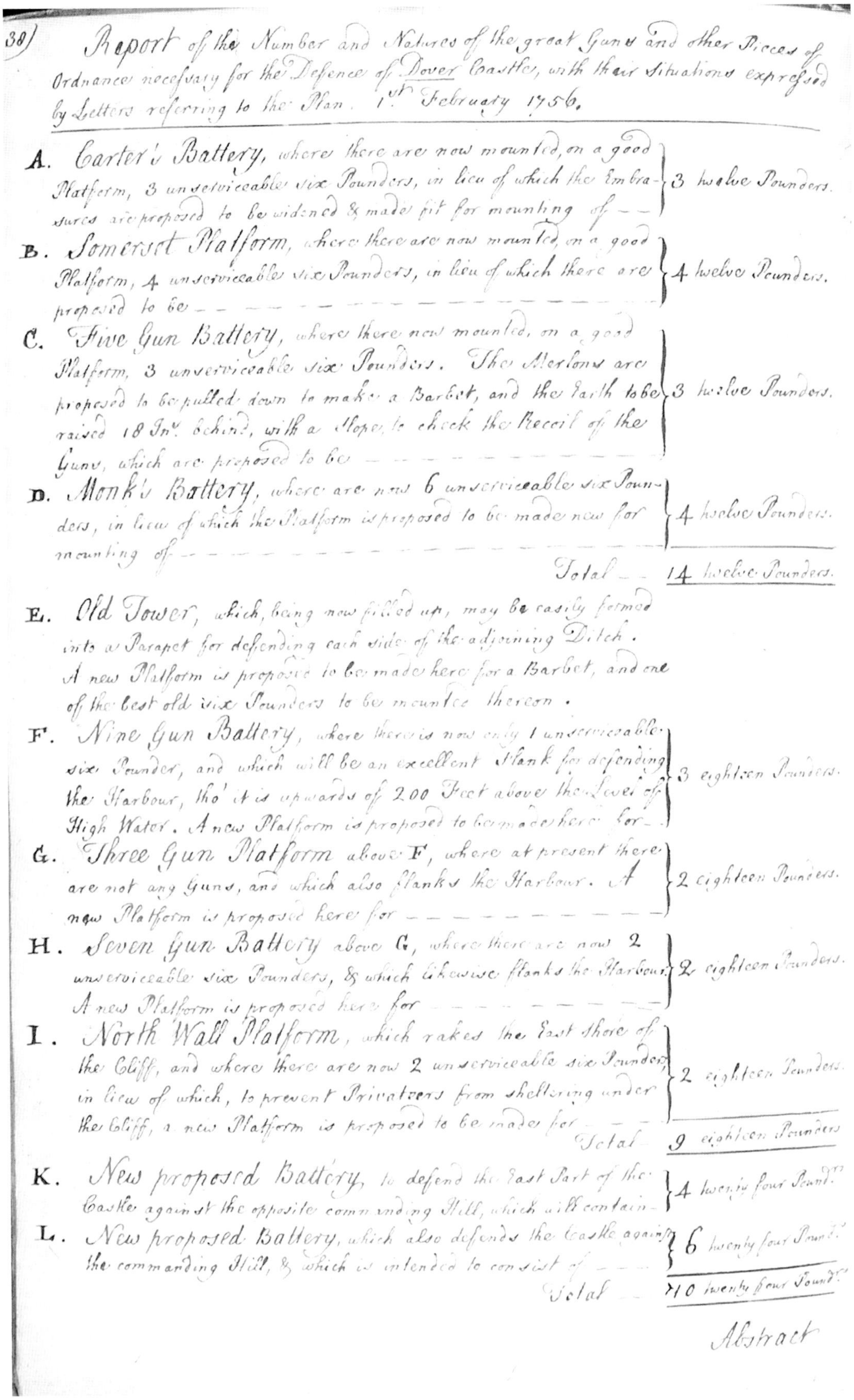

(38) Report of the Number and Natures of the great Guns and other Pieces of Ordnance necessary for the Defence of Dover Castle, with their situations expressed by Letters referring to the Plan. 1st February 1756.

A.	Carter's Battery, where there are now mounted, on a good Platform, 3 unserviceable six Pounders, in lieu of which the Embrasures are proposed to be widened & made fit for mounting of — —	3 twelve Pounders.
B.	Somerset Platform, where there are now mounted, on a good Platform, 4 unserviceable six Pounders, in lieu of which there are proposed to be — —	4 twelve Pounders.
C.	Five Gun Battery, where there now mounted, on a good Platform, 3 unserviceable six Pounders. The Merlons are proposed to be pulled down to make a Barbet, and the Earth to be raised 18 Inc. behind, with a Slope, to check the Recoil of the Guns, which are proposed to be — —	3 twelve Pounders.
D.	Monk's Battery, where are now 6 unserviceable six Pounders, in lieu of which the Platform is proposed to be made new for mounting of — —	4 twelve Pounders.
	Total — —	14 twelve Pounders.
E.	Old Tower, which, being now filled up, may be easily formed into a Parapet for defending each side of the adjoining Ditch. A new Platform is proposed to be made here for a Barbet, and one of the best old six Pounders to be mounted thereon.	
F.	Nine Gun Battery, where there is now only 1 unserviceable six Pounder, and which will be an excellent Flank for defending the Harbour, tho' it is upwards of 200 Feet above the Level of High Water. A new Platform is proposed to be made here for —	3 eighteen Pounders.
G.	Three Gun Platform above F, where at present there are not any Guns, and which also flanks the Harbour. A new Platform is proposed here for — —	2 eighteen Pounders.
H.	Seven Gun Battery above G, where there are now 2 unserviceable six Pounders, & which likewise flanks the Harbour. A new Platform is proposed here for — —	2 eighteen Pounders.
I.	North Wall Platform, which rakes the East Shore of the Cliff, and where there are now 2 unserviceable six Pounders, in lieu of which, to prevent Privateers from sheltering under the Cliff, a new Platform is proposed to be made for — —	2 eighteen Pounders.
	Total —	9 eighteen Pounders
K.	New proposed Battery, to defend the East Part of the Castle against the opposite commanding Hill, which will contain —	4 twenty four Poundrs.
L.	New proposed Battery, which also defends the Castle against the commanding Hill, & which is intended to consist of — —	6 twenty four Poundrs.
	Total — —	10 twenty four Poundrs.

Abstract

List of guns required, 1756

courtesy of National Archives (PRO/WO55/2275)

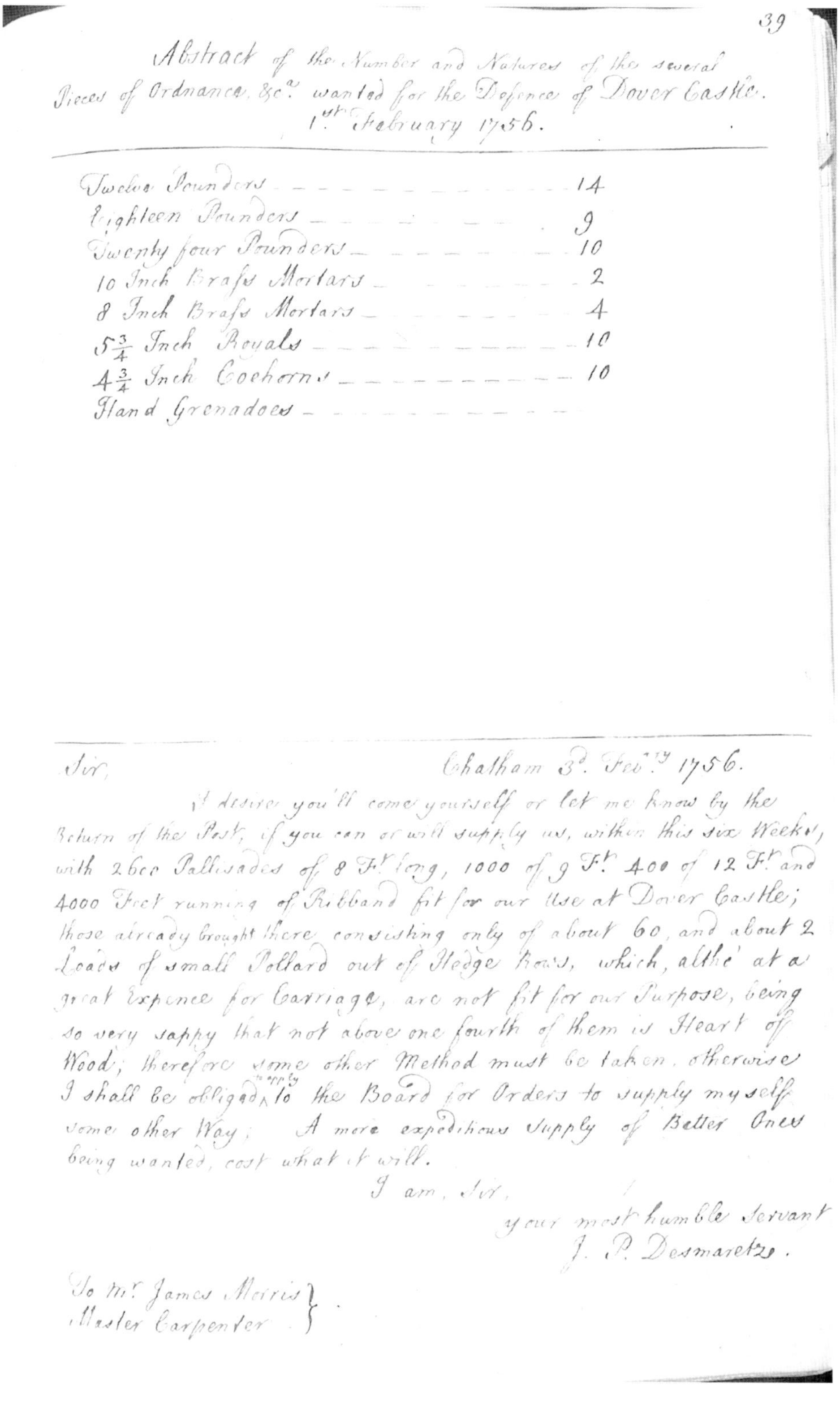

39

Abstract of the Number and Natures of the several Pieces of Ordnance, &c.a wanted for the Defence of Dover Castle.
1st February 1756.

Twelve Pounders	14
Eighteen Pounders	9
Twenty four Pounders	10
10 Inch Brass Mortars	2
8 Inch Brass Mortars	4
5¾ Inch Royals	10
4¾ Inch Coehorns	10
Hand Grenadoes	

Sir, Chatham 3d. Feb.ry 1756.

I desire you'll come yourself or let me know by the Return of the Post, if you can or will supply us, within this six Weeks, with 2600 Pallisades of 8 Ft. long, 1000 of 9 Ft. 400 of 12 Ft. and 4000 Feet running of Ribband fit for our Use at Dover Castle; those already brought there consisting only of about 60, and about 2 Loads of small Pollard out of Hedge Rows, which, altho' at a great Expence for Carriage, are not fit for our Purpose, being so very sappy that not above one fourth of them is Heart of Wood; therefore some other Method must be taken, otherwise I shall be obliged to apply to the Board for Orders to supply myself some other Way; A more expeditious Supply of Better Ones being wanted, cost what it will.

I am, Sir,
your most humble Servant
J. P. Desmaretz.

To Mr. James Morris
Master Carpenter

Complaint about the quality of wood supplied, 1756

courtesy of National Archives (PRO/WO55/2275)

Mar–Aug 1756 *Dets 1st & llth Dragoons* *WO5/43*

On patrol duty between Bourne and Dover 'twice in every day, and once in every night'. Some of the sick and wounded are reported to have been escaping and deserting. A detachment usually consisted of a subaltern and 20 men, or a sergeant and 10–12 men.

Mar 1756 (2 weeks) **King's (8th) and Honeywood's (20th) Regts of Foot** (Dets 100 men each) *WO5/43*

Although this record says the King's Own (4th), this must be the King's (8th) – the 4th were in Minorca, the 8th (Gen Wolfe's) in Canterbury shortly after. Another record says dets of King's and Honeywood's (140 men of the 200 allotted to Mr Bates, the local engineer). They were quartered in the Town, mounting an officer's guard in the Castle, receiving directions from the Engineer carrying on the Works. Troops were employed on the building works as well as civilian labour. 'I have the pleasure to find them much handier, and quite a different set from the others (Fusiliers), being long employed under Mr Skinner in Scotland.' *(Bates)* Tool requirements: 200 wheelbarrows, 400 shovels, 200 ballast baskets, 300 pickaxes with helves (+ 500 spare helves), 6' spikes, 7' spikes, nails, etc).

The total accommodation created for private soldiers was 367 beds for 734 men, as they slept two to a bed; the Keep housed 176 men (88 beds). Subalterns slept two to a room, and the Captain had an 'apartment' - a bedroom 9' x 14', and an ante-room 14' x 14'. *WO55/2275*

[1756–1763 Seven Years War with France – global, including the Carribbean, and the struggle for Canada (Wolfe – Quebec, 1759)]

Mar/Apr 1756 **Det 400 men from the 3 Regts of Footguards** *WO55/2275, R/H*

For four weeks. 'To be made from the four battalions of the three regiments of Guards not under orders to take the field, to be quartered in the Castle', and 'to receive directions from the engineer overseer (Mr Bates) for carrying on the works'. Det eventually comprised: 4 Captains, 4 Lieutenants, 4 Ensigns, 12 Sergeants, 12 Corporals, 8 Drummers, 348 Privates – under Col Hudson, though only 150 men were 'sufficient at present', because the bad weather continued – 'such as no-one local ever remembers as bad'.

Apr–Oct 1756 **Maj Gen James Abercrombie's Regt of Foot** (52nd/50th) *WO5/43*

[Also spelt Abercromby]. 5 coys, and 5 coys to Dover Town, with a det to Deal to guard the hospital, and stop the sick and wounded escaping and deserting! The Colonel at first refused to supply any men for labour, not having received instructions – Bates asked for 150, but had to make do with 30 (scavelmen (?) & labourers), and complained at the frequent change of men. The soldiers were employed until mid-July on the building works – more accommodation, a new hospital and canteen. *WO55/2275*

52nd renumbered 50th, Dec 1756 (*became* Gen Hodgson's, May 1756). The original 50th and 51st were raised in North America, Nov 1754, to recover important stations seized by the French. By August 1756, most had become PoWs, and in Dec 1756 the War Office decreed they 'shall cease to exist'. In Jan 1756, Col James Abercrombie raised one of ten new regts, numbered 52nd, but it became 50th on the demise of the 50th and 51st in America. Regts numbered 52– 62 all moved up two places. *R/H*

?Aug 1756–Apr 1757 *Det 3rd Dragoons (Earl of Albemarle's, 3KOH)* *WO5/44*

Oct 1756–Jun 1757 { **Lord Robert Manners' Regt of Foot** (36th) (7 coys) *WO5/44*
Jun–Oct 1757 { " " " (Det)

14 Oct 1756 – Dover Castle could accommodate only 7 coys, but three weeks later there was room for three more coys, and eventually 14 coys, when most of the building programme was completed. The Keep yard barracks were fitted up for the reception of one battalion. *WO55/2275*

Dec 1756 – There is a comment from the architect Desmaritz to the engineer in the Castle: 'If you can find out the secret to make the soldiers work as assiduously and as well as the country labourers, you may employ them'. *WO47/36*

1756–7 Dover Castle very full. Some of the duties consisted of escorting PoWs to Sissinghurst Castle and Chatham, and also to hospital at Deal. Coys of 36th and 23rd were also stationed in the Town and at Folkestone.

Jan 1757 – 2 of the 7 coys of Manners' regt to be quartered in the Town to make room for recruits for the new 2nd Bn of said regt as they arrive at Dover Castle. Feb 1757 – 2 coys to Folkestone. *WO5/44*

June–Sep 1757–- 2 Bns of Lord Robert Manners (36th) were camped for summer at Barham Down, leaving a det at the Castle.

May–Oct 1757 *Det 10th Dragoons* *WO5/45*

Patrolling duty Dover to New Romney, twice in 24 hours.

Oct 1757–June 1758 *Dets Sir Charles Howard's (3DG) & 1st or Royal Dragoons* *WO5/45*

Oct 1757–Apr 1758 **23rd Regt of Foot** (Royal Regt of Welch Fusiliers) *WO5/45*

Lt/Gen Huske's – 1st & 2nd Bns at Castle, Town & Folkestone

May–Oct 1758 **Col* Hodgson's Regt of Foot** (50th) (7 coys) *WO5/45,R/H*

(*see* Abercrombie's at 1756 – same regt). *He held the rank of Field Marshal eventually, but was *Colonel* of the regt.

2 coys at Deal. Sep – 4 coys of 50th to Sissinghurst to guard French PoWs, and one coy to Chatham.

Also a 'det of sick men of Col Lambton's for recovery' (68th). The 68th had been in Dover and Folkestone until April (as 2nd Bn, 23rd –*see above*), before going to the Isle of Wight for embarkation to Cherbourg in May, leaving behind those sick and unfit for active service. On return in October the regt moved to Rochester, guarding French prisoners, taking their sick with them. A description of camp conditions at this time: 2 blankets between 6 men, sewn together at the ends 'to prevent one man's having a greater share than another', sleeping head to toe. Some sick men of 50th stayed until Jan 1760.

Jun 1758–May 1759 *Det 7th or Queen's Own Dragoons* *WO5/45,46*

Mostly employed on patrols between Dover and Lydd twice in every 24 hours.

Oct 1758–May 1759 **36th Regt of Foot** *WO5/46*

Lord Robert Manners' Regt. Winter quarters. Most regiments went into camp in summer.

May–Aug 1759 *Det 2nd or Royal North British Dragoons* *WO5/46*

May–Aug 1759 **75th Regt of Foot** *WO5/46*

Col Boscawen's Regt. Raised in 1756 as 2nd Bn 37th. Disb 1765.

Aug/Sep 1759 *Det 6th or Inniskilling Regt of Dragoons* *WO5/46,47*

Aug–Nov 1759 **50th Regt of Foot** (9 coys) *WO5/46,47*

The regt had been encamped at Chatham lines. A det of sick men remained until Jan 1760, then rejoined their regt at Hilsea Bks, Portsmouth.

Sep–Nov 1759 *Det 1st or King's Regt of Dragoons* *WO5/47*

Nov 1759–May 1760 **19th Regt of Foot** (9 coys) *WO5/47*

Winter quarters, from Warley Camp; then three weeks at Canterbury when relieved, before going to summer camp at Barham Down.

Nov 1759–Jan 1760 *Det 3rd Dragoons* *WO5/47*

Jan–Mar 1760 *Det 4th Dragoons* *WO5/47*

Mar–May 1760 *Det 10th Dragoons* *WO5/47*

May–Jul 1760 *Det 1st Dragoons* *WO5/47*

Jun–Oct 1760– { **Col Parslow's Regt of Foot** (70th) *WO5/47*

–Jun 1762 " " (Det c. 360 men)

Trapaud's. Gen Trapaud succeeded Gen Parslow as Col, Jul 1760. 'To do the duty on the hospital there', and later (1762) the 31st too *(see also* 14th Ft *below).* *CSP(D)*

Jul–Aug 1760 *Det 3rd Dragoon Guards (Sir Charles Howard's)* *WO5/47*

Aug–Oct 1760 *Det 4th Dragoons (Rich's)* *WO5/47*

Oct–[?Dec] 1760 *Det 7th Dragoons* *WO5/47*

Oct 1760–Oct 1762 **14th Regt of Foot** *R/H*

1760–1763 – dets from 70th and 14th in turn to Pear/Peer (?Pier) Fort 'belonging to Dover Castle'. *WO5/46*

?Jan–Apr1761 *Det 10th Dragoons* *WO5/49*

Apr–Jun 1761 South Bn of Hampshire Militia *WO5/49*

At Dover and Deal, on French PoW duty.

Militia – this was originally a local defence force raised from the civilian population, with some military training - a sort of compulsory 'national service' of the Middle Ages *(see note at* 1615*)*, where men aged between 15-60 had to provide their own weapons, according to their wealth and status, and attend occasional musters. In the late 16th century trained bands started to appear and the militia tended to decline and become more amateur, as the regular army attracted the more efficient men. It had almost disappeared by the early 18th century. However, the Seven Years' War (1756–1763) saw the establishment of a new militia force in 1757, which was the responsibility of the various county Lord–Lieutenants. As not enough volunteers were attracted, a form of conscription by ballot was introduced, involving all eligible males (aged 18-50 at this stage). If those chosen in the ballot were not willing to serve personally, they had to find a suitable substitute. This enforcement was not popular, and led to some rioting; it lasted until 1829, whereafter the militia was raised only from volunteers. In times of war when the regular army was fighting abroad, the militia was embodied and replaced the regulars in certain strategic garrisons, of which Dover was one.

The Militia 'embodied the ancient English principle of the citizens' duty to defend the realm. Its supporters looked on it as 'The Constitutional Force', as against the Standing Army, which 'belonged' to the King's Government, and hence was a threat to liberty and the Constitution'. *Correlli Barnett*

May–Jul 1761 *Det 1st (Royal) Dragoons* *WO5/49*

Jun–Sep 1761 2nd Bn Surrey Militia *WO5/49*

To relieve the Hampshires.

Jul–Sep 1761 *Det 3rd Dragoon Guards* *WO5/49*

Sep–Nov 1761 *Det 3rd (King's Own) Dragoons* *WO5/49*

–Oct 1761– North Bn Lincoln Militia *WO5/49*

Some coys – others at Deal & Sandwich

Nov 1761–Jan 1762 *Det 6th Inniskilling Dragoons* *WO5/49*

Jan–Mar 1762 *Det 10th Dragoons* *WO5/49*

May–May 1762 *Det 1st (King's) Dragoon Guards* *WO5/49*

May–Jul 1762 *Det 3rd Dragoon Guards* *WO5/49,50*

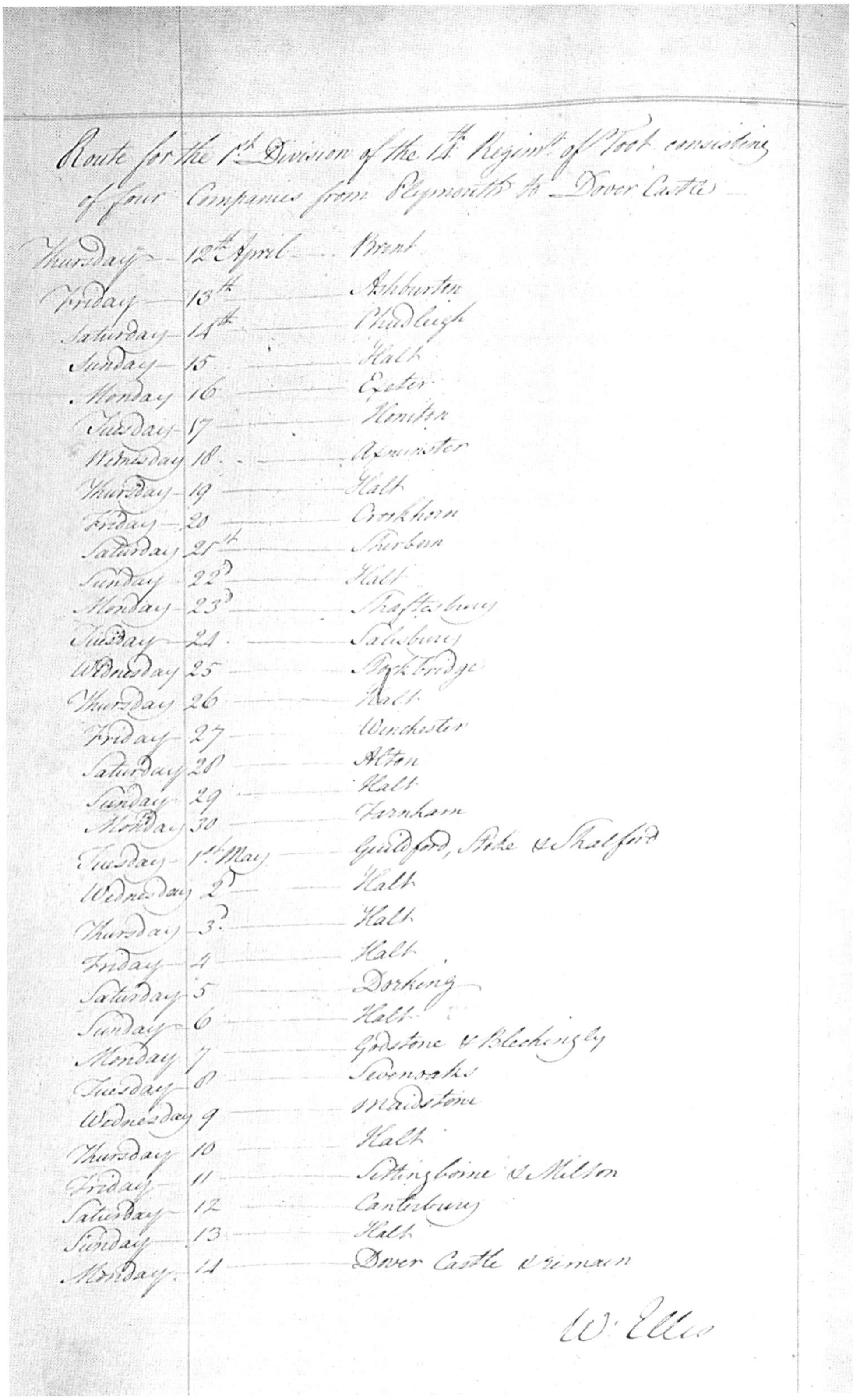

Route for the 1st Division of the 14th Regiment of Foot consisting of four Companies from Plymouth to Dover Castle

Thursday	12th April	Brent
Friday	13th	Ashburton
Saturday	14th	Chudleigh
Sunday	15	Halt
Monday	16	Exeter
Tuesday	17	Honiton
Wednesday	18	Axminster
Thursday	19	Halt
Friday	20	Crookhorn
Saturday	21st	Sherborn
Sunday	22d	Halt
Monday	23d	Shaftesbury
Tuesday	24	Salisbury
Wednesday	25	Stockbridge
Thursday	26	Halt
Friday	27	Winchester
Saturday	28	Alton
Sunday	29	Halt
Monday	30	Farnham
Tuesday	1st May	Guildford, Stoke & Shalford
Wednesday	2d	Halt
Thursday	3d	Halt
Friday	4	Halt
Saturday	5	Dorking
Sunday	6	Halt
Monday	7	Godstone & Blechingly
Tuesday	8	Sevenoaks
Wednesday	9	Maidstone
Thursday	10	Halt
Friday	11	Sittingborne & Milton
Saturday	12	Canterbury
Sunday	13	Halt
Monday	14	Dover Castle & remain

W: Ellis

Marching Order for 14th Foot

courtesy of National Archives (PRO/WO5/52)

Jul–Sep 1762 *Det 3rd (King's Own) Dragoons* *WO5/50*

Sep–Nov 1762 *Det 4th Dragoons* *WO5/50*

Oct 1762–Jul 1763 **31st Foot** (9 coys) *WO5/51,52*

Col Oughton's regt. July – 6 coys to Tiverton & Taunton and 1 coy to Chatham. Dec – 1 coy to 'Pear (Pier) Fort belonging to Dover Castle, to do the duty on the hospital there'.

Jul–Oct 1763 **31st Foot** (2 coys) *WO5/52*

Nov 1762–Jan 1763 *Det 7th or Queen's Dragoons* *WO5/50*

Jan 1763–?Mar 1764 *Det 11th Dragoons* *WO5/51*

Oct 1763–May 1764 **7th Foot** (Royal Fusiliers) (4 coys) *WO5/52*

Mar 1764– *Det 10th Dragoons* *WO5/52*

May 1764–Jul 1765 **14th Foot** (5 coys) *WO5/52*

An instance of orders being changed en route: Original order dated 12th April: (1) 4 coys from Plymouth to Dover Castle (and 5 coys to Chatham); (2) to be reviewed near Guilford on 4th May, and 5 coys to continue to Dover Castle; (3) To be reviewed on 5th May on Wimbledon Common; (4) 3rd review at Hyde Park 7th May, then 5 coys to continue to Dover Castle, arriving 15th May, one month after leaving Plymouth.

24 Aug 1764 – 2 coys of the 14th from Dover Castle to Deal to assist the officers of the Revenue and Commanding Officer of the Cutter, beaten up by smugglers. 'The mob and peoples of the 14 or 15 boats beat and bruised all the men of the Cutter's boat, and carried the Officer to a pond, dragged him through it and very near drowned him, after which they beat him and made him run the Gauntlet from the north to the south end of the Town, when he accidentally fell into a man's house, who sheltered him … the smugglers openly declare they will murder everyone belonging to the Cutter they can get hold of'. *WO5/53*

Jun 1765– *Det 2nd Queen's Dragoon Guards* *WO5/53*

Jul 1765–Jun 1766 **43rd Foot** (2/3 coys) *WO5/54*

And coys at Margate, Ramsgate and Deal; also Chatham, Upnor and Ipswich.

Apr 1766 **22nd & 35th** (Dets) – to assist 43rd.

May 1766– *Det 1st Dragoons* *WO5/54*

Jul 1766–May 1767 **22nd Foot** (Col Gage's) *WO5/55*

Apr 1767– *Det 2nd Royal North British Dragoons* *WO5/55*

Jun 1767–Apr 1768 **8th Foot** (Col Webb's) *WO5/55*

Then to embark for North America.

1768 – first mention of Cinque Ports as an area of command. c1767, the Lord Warden ceased to exercise executive military control, though was still appointing gunners to the Castle. These gunners lived out and followed their own trade (e.g. butcher, boatbuilder, hatter, mariner), rotating their turn for duty. *EK/CPW/R03*

Apr–Jun 1768 **12th** (Apr–May), **& 25th Foot** (Jun) (Dets) *WO5/55*

May 1768– *Det 4th Dragoons [see* Oct 1768 *below]* *WO5/55*

Jun 1768 **13th Foot** (1 coy, from Bromley)

Jul 1768 **13th Foot** (Col Murray's) *WO5/55*

Aug–Oct 1768 " (Det) *WO5/55*

July 1768 – rest of Regt embarked for Ireland. Det remained until mid-Oct.

Aug–Oct 1768 **25th Foot** (2 coys) *WO5/55*

1 coy to join regt at Chatham on 3 Oct, regt then to Guildford and Godalming, where remaining coy to join a week later.

Oct 1768 (2 weeks) **4th Regt of Dragoons** (Det) (dismounted) *WO5/55,56*

To be relieved by 1 coy 17th Foot from Chatham.

Oct 1768–Mar 1769 **17th Foot** (1 coy) *WO5/56*

Then back to Chatham, when relieved by dets of 1st and 17th. 1 coy remained at Chatham and 7 coys at Maidstone.

Mar–Jun 1769 **Royals (2nd Bn, 1st Foot) and 17th Foot** (Dets) *R/H, WO379/1*

May 1769 *Det 1st or King's Regt of Dragoon Guards* *WO5/56*

Jun–Sep 1769 **17th Foot** (Col Monckton's) (9 coys) *WO5/56*

Sep 1769–Mar 1770 " (4 coys)

Mar–May 1770 " (1 coy)

May 1770– *Det 11th Dragoons* *WO5/56*

May–Oct 1770 **15th Foot** (Det) *WO5/57,R/H*

Nov–Dec 1770 " (4 coys) *WO5/57*

Dec 1770–May 1771 " (9 coys) *WO5/57*

May–Jun 1771 **33rd Foot** (Det) *WO5/57*

May–Aug 1771 **7th Foot** (Det) *WO5/57*

Jun–Aug 1771 **23rd Foot** (Det) *WO5/57*

Aug 1771–Mar 1772 **7th Foot** (4 coys) *WO5/57*

Mar–Jun 1772 **7th and 23rd Foot** (Dets) *WO5/58*

Jul–Aug 1772 **67th Foot** (1 coy) *WO5/58*

John Grant, a drummer of 67th Ft, scratched his name on the spiral staircase of the Keep.

Sep–Oct 1772 **3rd Foot (Buffs)** (Det) *WO5/58*

Oct 1772–Mar 1773 **11th Foot** *WO5/58*

Arrived from working on the fortifications at Portsmouth.

Mar–Sep 1773 **11th Foot** (Det) *WO5/58*

1 subaltern, 20 men & NCO – dets changed almost monthly from Chatham.

May 1773–Jan 1774 **14th Foot** (some coys) *WO5/58*

Then to Archcliffe to relieve det 29th.

Oct 1773–Oct 1774 **29th Foot** *WO5/58*

1 coy to Archcliffe Dec 1773–Jan 1774 when relieved by 14th.

Oct 1774–Jun 1775 **36th Foot** *WO5/59*

May 1775–Jun 1779 **Capt James Malcolm's Independent Coy of Invalids** *WO5/59*

c85 men. Dec 1775, quartered in Dover as the Castle too full.

1776/7 – Malcolm's to Sheerness, and occasionally to Archcliffe or the Town, at times when the Castle was too full of regular troops. Invalids – Infantry Invalid coys, formed in 1745, and Artillery coys formed as 4th Bn. RA, in Jan 1771, were raised from the Out-pensioners of Chelsea Hospital. An Invalid coy had a smaller establishment than a normal 'marching coy' (usually about 60–75 men, as opposed to 100), and were supposed to be only for garrison duty in Britain, but seem to have been sent abroad sometimes – for example, to Minorca, Heligoland (1 coy for 14 years), Bermuda (for 13 years), Jersey and Guernsey – where they seem often to have been forgotten. One Invalid Captain died in harness after 69 years' service, having commanded his coy for 33 years! Many were past even sedentary duty in a fortress – one Master Gunner was over ninety; another case reported was of an artillery officer between 70 and 80 years of age, who had been confined to his room for 3 years, mostly bedridden; and yet another described as 'a perfect vegetable, unfit for his duty of the garrison'. There was probably an Independent coy of Invalids in the Castle on and off 1774–1782–1802 (and periodically at Archcliffe); after 1802 they were replaced by Garrison, Reserve and Veteran Bns and coys.

[1775-82 American War of Independence] *JSAHR xxxviii/156*

May 1775–Dec 1779 **Capt Courtenay's Independent Coy of Invalids** *WO5/59*

41st Invalid Regt – a draft from coys in Dover Castle to embark for Minorca, Sep 1775.

Nov 1775–Feb 1776 **Men of the Footguards, with German recruits** *WO5/59*

German recruits arrived end Nov – 'det of Invalids at Dover Castle to bring over the German recruits; men of the Footguards doing duty at Dover Castle to march as soon as recruits are embarked to the respective quarters of their regts'. Foreign units in English pay were used to augment those sent out to North America; troops were hired from Hessian and other German princes. A composite Bn of the three regiments of Footguards was formed for service in the American War – they stayed for six years. It is not clear which Footguards – maybe from the composite Bn.

Hamilton, R/H, Guards Magazine, 1968

Dec 1775–Feb 1776 **27th Foot** (Det) *WO5/59*

May 1776– *Det 10th Regt of Dragoons* *WO5/59*

May 1776 **6th Foot** (Det) *WO5/59*

Oct 1776–May 1778 **18th Foot** (8–10 coys) *WO17/2811*

May 1777– *Det 1st (Royal) Dragoons* *WO5/60*

Jun 1778– *Det 2nd Royal North British Dragoons* *WO5/60*

Jun–Nov 1778 **East Middlesex Militia** (8–9 coys) *WO17/2811,WO5/95*

On arrival at the Castle the Regt reported the 'defenceless state of the Castle', and the 'unskilfulness' of the (Invalid) gunners in the use of guns. Repairs were approved in June 1778.

Nov 1778–Jun 1779 **65th Foot** *WO17/2811,WO5/61*

Winter quarters upon return from the American War of Independence. Summer spent at Coxheath Camp, which was formed in 1778, to provide advanced training and defence against invasion – 17,000 troops spread over 3½ sq. miles.

1778–1782 – the regular infantry moved out of Dover Castle to summer camp (Coxheath, Warley Common, Barham Down, etc), and the militia moved in during the summer months. DC provided winter quarters for regular units.

1779–1789– **A special Cinque Ports Invalid Artillery Coy, RA**

Responsible to the Lord Warden, and not directly part of RA, formed the gun detachments; they were usually elderly and infirm – one mentioned as over 90, another with a wooden leg. *M-J*

Col Tufnell of the East Kent Militia said ' gunners in the Cinque Ports being under the Lord Warden, the (Army) board can give no directions concerning them'. *WO47/91*

Aerial view of Dover Castle

Family fleeing a burning House - *(see page xv)*
from the Bayeaux Tapestry

Norman Horsemen versus Anglo-Saxon foot soldiers *(see page xv)*
from the Bayeaux Tapestry

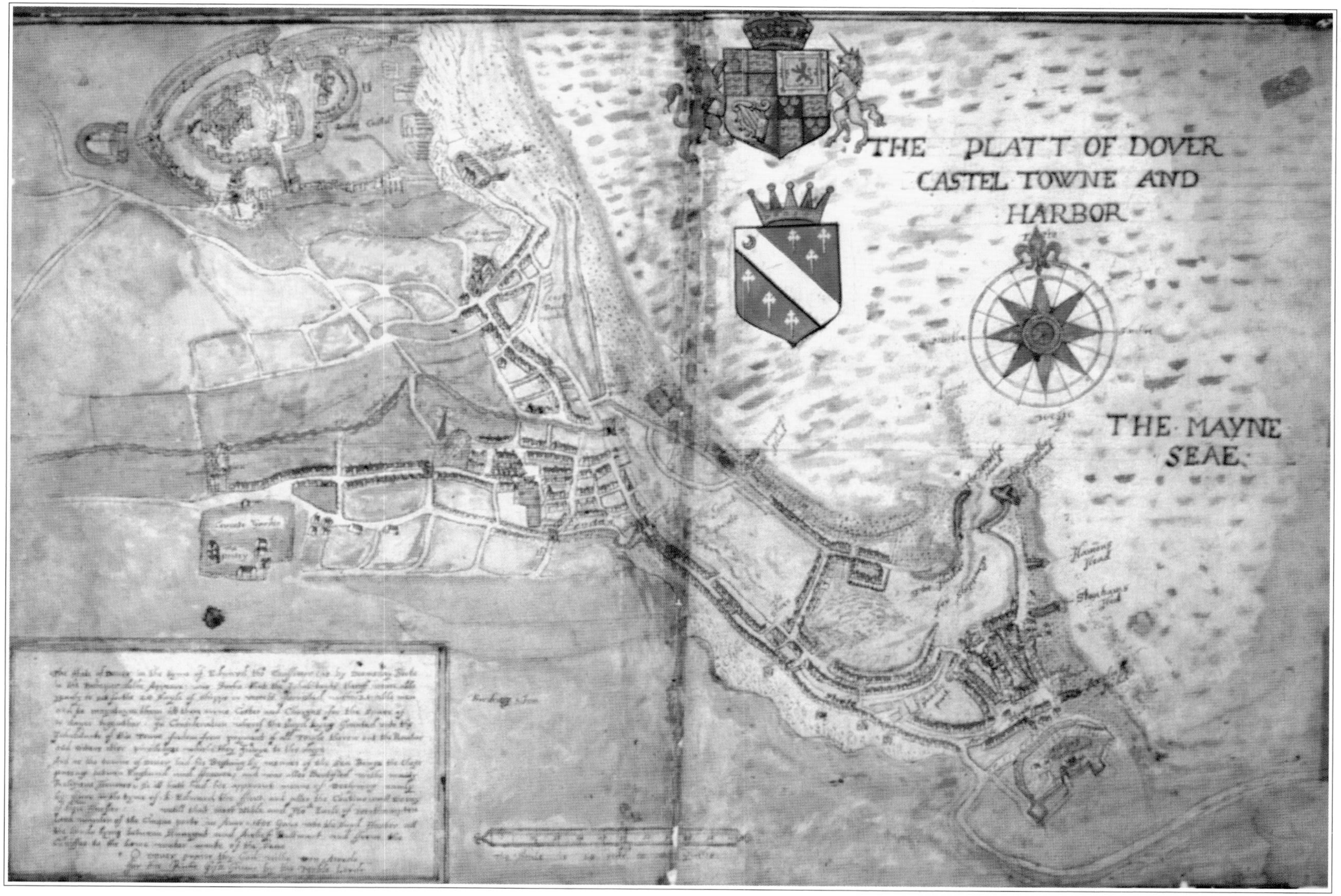

William Eldred's Plan of Dover *(see page 9)*
courtesy of Dover Museum (d02852)

Colonel John Strode - Governor of Dover Castle, 1663-1686 *(see page 15)*
courtesy of St Edmundsbury Musuem

42nd, 79th & 93rd marching past Dover Castle, possbly for review or exercise at Northfall Meadow.
They had all arrived home from the Crimea in July 1856, and left for India, May 1857 *(see page 57)*
courtesy of Dover Museum (d00849)

CAMP OF THE 93RD HIGHLANDERS, WESTERN HEIGHTS, DOVER.

93rd encamped at Western Heights during the building of the new officers' mess and barracks
at Dover Castle, on which they were working *(see page 57)*
courtesy of Dover Museum (d08904)

Troops outside King's Gate
courtesy of Col Ronnie Jenkins/Dover Museum (d24362)

'Steady the Drums and Fifes' - painted at Constable's Tower *(see page 65)*
courtesy of The Princess of Wales's Royal Regt

The Princess of Wales's Royal Regiment Drums and Silver display at Dover Castle

At this time also, Mr Biggs, the storekeeper in Dover Castle, was expected to supply ships in the Downs, 'for fitting out the cutters'. He requested a storeroom in Dover Town 'to prevent the Expense of Carriage to and from the Castle'. *[England at war with America, France and Spain - also trouble in Ireland]* *WO47/91*

Jun 1779–May 1780 *Det 4th Regt of Dragoons* *WO5/61,62*

Jul–Nov 1779 **Oxfordshire Militia** (8 coys) *WO17/2811*

Duties included escorting French prisoners from Dover to Deal.

1779 **1 coy Royal Military Artificers** (Carrying out repairs) *M–J*

Nov 1779–Jun 1780 **6th Foot** (6 coys) *WO17/103*

From Coxheath Camp. 4 coys in Town.

1779–1789 **1 Master Gunner, 16 gunners** *Macrae*

Aug 1779–Oct 1780 **North's Cinque Ports Provincial Militia** (5 coys) *Fazan, WO17/2811*

Also referred to as Cinque Ports Militia or Cinque Ports Volunteer Bn, Regt or Corps of Foot, trained for gun detachments – raised in the Castle by Lord North (as PM and LW), and commanded by his son, the Hon George Augustus North, the regular army being away at war. He had difficulty raising 'soldiers' among the seafaring men of the Cinque Ports! There were detachments also at Folkstone and Hythe. Lord North, supposing that the apprehension of invasion would soon be over and the (Oxfordshire) Militia then leave the Castle, wrote to Lord Amherst (Sec of State for War): 'when that happens I hope y[r] Lordship will order my Corps immediately into Dover Castle, when I have no doubt that they will be fit for every service on which they can be employed'. 6 May 1780 – reviewed by M/Gen Calcroft: 13 officers, chaplain, adjutant, QM, surgeon, 32 NCOs, 10 drummers and fifes, 278 privates – 'the Hattes were well cocked and the manual exercises performed with great steadiness – fit for immediate service'. *Fazan, WO34/120,195*

Dover Association Volunteers – 6 coys of 60 men each (1 Capt and 2 Lts each coy) volunteered for 'no other service than the defence of the Town' – service to be voluntary and independent. 300 men signed up (5 coys), with Capt Sampson's to be appointed later. *WO34/116*

1780–1786 **Capt Thos Burton's Independent Coy of Invalids** *Army List*

Jun 1780 *1 troop 20th Light Dragoons*

July–Nov 1780 **West Middlesex Militia** *WO17/2811*

Nov 1780–May 1781 **52nd Foot** *WO17/2811*

Mar 1781 **Lt Brown's Independent Coy** [raised in Castle] *WO5/63*

Jun–Nov 1781 **East Middlesex Militia** [& in Town] *WO17/2811*

Jul–Oct 1781 **4 Independent Coys**: Capts Skillinglaw's, Gillespies', Callender's and Pringle's

Moved to Dover Town, then Deal. *WO12/11597, WO5/63*

Oct 1781– *Det 22nd Light Dragoons* *WO5/63*

Nov 1781–Jun 1782 **59th Foot** *WO17/2811*

Winter quarters; from Coxheath Camp, and back there the following summer. *WO5/64*

Jun–Nov 1782 **North's Cinque Ports Provincial Militia** (5 Coys) *WO17/2811*

Or Cinque Ports Bn of Foot. From Faversham. *WO5/64*

Nov–Dec 1782 **45th Foot** *WO17/2811*

From Coxheath Camp, then to Chatham.

Oct 1782–Jun 1783 **85th Foot** (Westminster Volunteers) *WO17/2811*

Regt disb in the Castle, Jun 1783 – mostly lost at sea returning from Jamaica, Oct 1782.

May 1783 **Courtenay's Independent Coy of Invalids** *WO5/65*

Ordered from Archcliffe to Dover Castle, to await the arrival of the16th, then return to Archcliffe.

May–Oct 1783 **16th Foot** *WO17/2811*

Sep 1783– *Det 1st King's Regt of Dragoon Guards* *WO5/65*

Nov–Dec 1783 **24th Foot** *WO17/2811*

Quartered at Canterbury on arrival in Oct, until embarkation of 16th. Det to Archcliffe to replace the Invalid Coy there.

Dec 1783 **69th Foot** (4 coys) *WO17/2811*

The rest at Archcliffe. At the end of Dec, the 69th were ordered to move to Dover Town to give way to Hessian Troops.

Jan–May 1784 **Löwenstein's Grenadiers (Hessian troops)** *Home Stations*

Col the Prince of Löwenstein's Bn of Grenadiers, 450 strong, in the pay of Great Britain for 159 days. *WO4/126*

Jun–Aug 1784 **22nd Foot** (2 coys,)

Rest of regt in Deal, then moved to Chatham.

1785 **1st coy Royal Military Artificers** (later RE) *Akers*

Raised in DC.

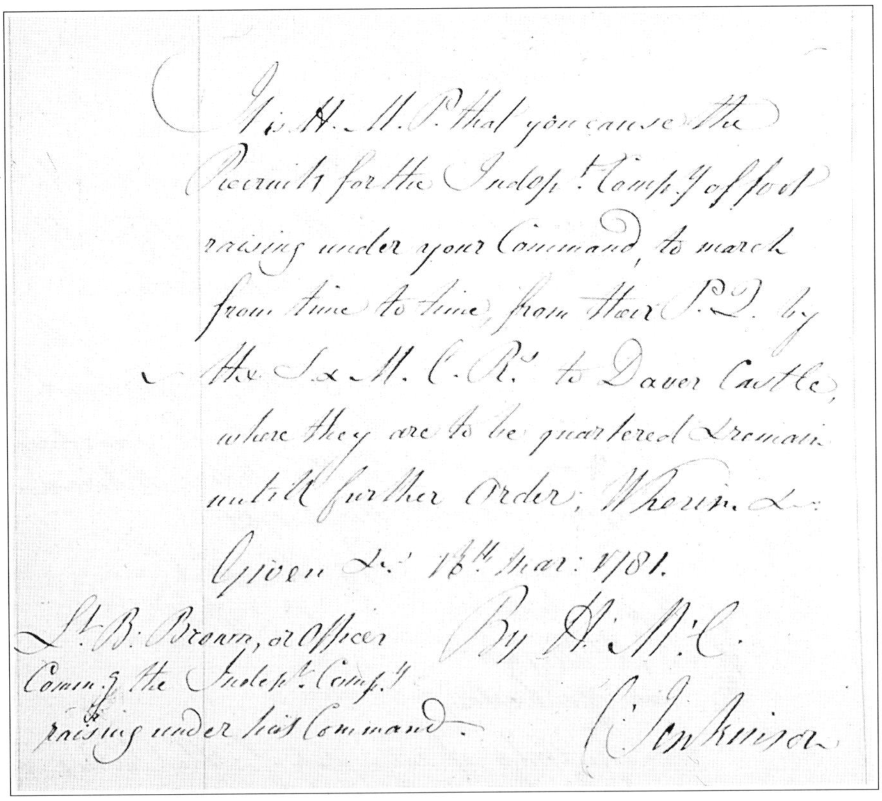

It is H. M. P. that you cause the Recruits for the Indep.t Comp.y of foot raising under your Command, to march from time to time, from their R. D. by the S. & M. C. R.ds to Dover Castle, where they are to be quartered & remain untill further Order; Wherein &c.
Given &c. 16th Mar: 1781.

By H: M.'s C.

Lt. B: Brown, or Officer Comg. the Indep.t Comp.y raising under his Command.

C. Jenkinson

'Shorthand' wording on Marching Order *(see page 37)*
courtesy of National Archives (PRO/WO5/63)

"Recruits" - Cartoon by Bunbury
courtesy of National Army Museum, 3418

Feb–Oct 1785 {**64th Foot** *WO5/66,WO17/2811*
Oct 1785–Oct 1786 " (2 coys) *WO17/2812*

8 coys in Deal, then the regt moved to Chatham. The regt complained of 'a want of all kinds of Barrack utensils and very small allowance of wood and candles, the men not having sufficient quantity to dress their Provisions. No Pump for the Tank for getting water, and ... are obliged to draw water from a well of 350 Feet deep, with a very great Labour'. After an Inspection at this time, the report reads: 'The Regiment is very weak, but for their numbers made a very good Review ... and what men they had were fine young fellows. The Recruiting service now goes on faster, they have sent out several Additional Parties, and lowered the Standard'. *WO27/54.*

Oct 1785 *Det 10th (Prince of Wales' Own) Dragoons* WO5/66

Oct 1786–Oct 1787 {**55th Foot** (2–4 coys) *WO17/2812*
Oct 1786–May 1787 2 coys; Jun–Oct, 4 coys, (and 6–4 coys in Deal).

Oct 1787–May 1788 **Capt John Watson's Independent coy of Invalids** *WO5/66,WO17/795*

Possibly until 1799. Capt Watson's Coy arrived from Sheerness Oct 1787, and moved to Archcliffe in 1788, on arrival of 5 coys of 17th. His Lieutenant was 65, with 46 years' service, the Ensign 68, with 51 years' service. The report on the state of arms: 10 sets new in 1775, 'the remainder received 50 years since and upwards', and in a bad state. *WO27/61*

Strength of Coy: 1 Captain, 1 Lieutenant, 1 Ensign, 4 Sergeants, 4 Corporals, 2 Drummers and 31 Privates (between 18–32 'effective private men'). *WO12/11601*

Capt Watson was a major in the Army, but *Captain* of the Invalid Coy (from Jun 1787). He was sick most of the time 1788–1794, and Lt Pughe was in charge, until he retired and Lt Fitzgerald was appointed.

Oct 1787–Mar 1788 **77th Foot** (10 coys) *WO27/61*

Raised in Dover Castle.

Apr–May 1788 **44th Foot** (4-5 coys) *WO17/2812*

May–Oct 1788 **17th Foot** (5 coys) *WO5/66*

WO5/66 says 5 coys Dover Castle, 5 coys in Deal; *WO17/2812* says 4 coys Dover Castle, and 6 in Deal.

Nov 1788–Nov 1789 **22nd Foot** (5 coys) *WO5/67*

10 coys from Mar-Jun 1789. 'To assist the Revenue Officers in suppressing Owlers and Smugglers'.

Nov 1789–Jun 1790 **29th Foot** (10 coys) *WO5/67*

Det remained until Feb 1791. Commanded by Lord Cathcart.

Jul–Nov 1790 **37th Foot** *WO17/2782*

Nov 1790–Feb 1791 **29th Foot** *WO5/67*

Feb–Sep 1791 Det from Chatham from **Additional Coys** of regts in India. *WO5/67*

Instruction to The Hon Col Fox at Chatham Barracks to send: 'such part of the Forces under your command as you may judge expedient to Dover Castle' – *does not specify regiments*, but 'Additional coys' are likely to have been Depôt coys, (*see* 1815 *re* Depôts). **Independent coy of Invalids** also present. *WO5/67*

Oct 1791–Apr 1792 **14th Foot** *WO5/68*

From Portsmouth; then to Chatham.

Apr 1792–Jan 1793 **54th Foot** (10 coys) *WO5/68*

Det to Chatham, Jun 1792; and to Deal, Jul 1792; 2 coys to Purfleet, Dec 1792–Feb 1793.

Feb–Mar 1793 **14th Foot** (10 coys) *WO5/68*

To embark for Flanders – also still an **Independent coy of Invalids** at DC.

[1793–1815 Napoleonic wars; 1802–3 peace]

Mar–Jun 1793 **Wiltshire Militia** *WO5/68*

Mar–Aug 1793 **Capt Hardy's Independent coy of Invalid Foot** *WO5/68*

Also drafted recruits, under orders for Holland.

Jul 1793–Apr 1794 **East Devonshire Militia** *WO17/2812*

May 1794–Apr 1795 **Somerset Militia** (8–10 coys) *WO17/2812*

Also at Archcliffe, and 4 coys in Town; Feb 1795 – 12 coys.

[1794 – *1st of the 'Three Panics* – there were three dates when there was real fear of invasion from France – 1794, 1803 & 1859, which later became known as 'The Three Panics']. *Fazan*

After the declaration of war on France, between 1793 and 1801, extensive building works, under the direction of Lt Col William Twiss, were started – a 12-year programme. 1793 – Averanches Tower was reduced in height; Horseshoe, Hudson's, East Demi and East Arrow Bastions built – all connected by passages and tunnels; new subterranean bomb–proofs opening onto the cliffs for barracks (casemates) built, and more recommended, with quarters for 56 men in the 'existing hospital'; accommodation for 724 men in the Castle barracks; up to 60 men in the ruined church; Constable's Tower was a barrack for 44 men – in all, accommodation for 1,384 men. A new well was sunk, and a new road and entrance (Canon's Gate) for access from the Town, finished in 1797. New sallyports were constructed.

Casemate Barracks, 1806, built 1793-1801
courtesy of Dover Museum, (d14117)

Casemates as they appear today

1795–7 – 'great repairs done to the outer walls'; also a new turnpike house built, on the site of an old toll house (on the Deal road). *Pattenden*

Aug 1798 – Lt Burgoyne was employed as assistant engineer on these works (later Field Marshal Sir John Burgoyne). Yet more subterranean barracks for soldiers and officers, with a well in between. *Akers*

1795– **HQ Dover Division RE** *Laws*

Plus 25 miners from Ashford to do more tunnelling. *Akers*

1795–1805 **Special Cinque Ports det Artillery Volunteers** *Laws, M-J*

1803 – The Rt Hon William Pitt was Colonel Commandant & CDC; Viscount Mahon, his nephew, was CO & LtDC.

1795–1805 **Det Marching Coy RA** *Laws*

'Additional gunners' found from the fleet, infantry garrison or county militia were no longer considered enough, and Marching Coys and detachments from other regular RA coys were sent to assist the Invalid gunners, a detachment comprising 1 officer and 22 Ors. *M-J*

There was at this time a certain amount of discussion between the RA and RE Cols as to who claimed seniority, and therefore the grazing rights within the Castle and at Archcliffe! *WO46/141*

Apr–Nov 1795 **Lancashire Militia** (10 coys) *WO17/2782*

They were required to maintain elaborate precautions for the defence of the fortifications. Guards and pickets were changed at 10am each day, and numbered 100 men, with 80 in the outer forts. On an alarm, the sentries at all gates were to be doubled. The pickets were to sleep in one room in their clothes. To keep the regiment in fighting trim there were two parades a day, and a field–day once a week, while 30 men were sent off to learn the use of the great guns in the fort. From the outer forts, sentries were posted all along the beach to prevent surprise. At night they were relieved every two hours; they had to call 'all's well' along the line every half hour, and a patrol visited them all an hour after each relief. *WO34/117*

Oct 1795–May 1797 **2nd Yorkshire, West Riding Militia** (10 coys) *WO17/999, WO17/2782*

At work on Dover Castle, together with some men of the Cornish & Montgomery Militias, who were quartered in the Town. They then exchanged quarters in Ashford with the East Suffolk Militia.

Mar 1797 – working on heightening the embrasures and merlons over the guns on turning carriages, and making trenches. *& Pattenden*

1797 was 'a dangerous year' – Spain declared war; regular regiments had to garrison the colonies, or be kept in hand for expeditions to the continent, so the preservation of law and order devolved on the Militia. *JSAHR 1972, Moyse-Bartlett*

500 Dover Volunteers 'ever keeping watch and ward' in the first line of defence. *Pattenden*

May–Nov 1797 **East Suffolk Militia** (10 coys) *Pattenden*

From Ashford. Also engaged on the building works. 5 Jun 1797 – Dover Volunteers, with the regulars and militia, were drawn up on the new road to the Castle to fire a salute on the King's birthday. *Pattenden*

Oct 1797–Sep 1798 **Sussex Militia** (12 coys) *WO17/2783-4*

Together with the **Glamorgan Militia**, who were quartered in the Town, but employed on the building works in the Castle.

Aug 1798 – soldiers quartered in the Cliff casemates, but the officers' accommodation not yet ready. *& Pattenden*

1797–1824 **Dover Artillery Volunteers** *& Pattenden*

Sep 1798–May 1799 **Denbigh Militia** (6 coys) *WO17/2784*

With the Hertford Militia, to replace the Sussex. *& Pattenden*

Sep 1798–May 1799 **Hertford Militia** (10 coys) *WO17/2784*

Nov 1798–Mar 1799 **Merioneth Militia** (3 coys) *WO17/2784*

The rest quartered in the Town.

There exists a letter written from the Debtor's prison at this time: 'Honrd Father and Mother, I takes this Houptenty *[opportunity]* to right to lett you Now that I Hame now in Condfindment at the Wight Houses, but I don't now wen that shall Be moved from this but I dearsay that et will be en Shoart time. I have Ben Brott From St Healer *[Helier?]* to Stan triell Fore the Charge consarning the *[loss?]* of Charles Twyman all thou I hope my self enset *[innocent?]*. Thank God. I remain you Doubtiful *[dutiful?]* son, David Twyman'. This was probably actually written at Portsmouth, and presumably he was transferred to Dover shortly after. *EK/U1453 0101*

16 Feb 1799 – A severe winter. Several bad cliff falls between soldiers' and officers' subterranean barracks, where there was an opening to give light to the well. One fall 'owing to frost and thaw' demolished an accommodation hut killing an artilleryman and his wife – but the baby survived! Miners had to come and remove some of the overhanging cliff. *Pattenden*

May–Jun 1799 **South Gloucester Militia** (10 coys)

Jul–Nov 1799 **South Middlesex Militia** (10 coys) *WO17/2784*

Castle & Town.

Nov 1799 **1st Bn, Northamptonshire Militia** (10 coys) *WO17/2784*

Nov 1799–May 1800 **29th Regt of Foot** *R/H*

Nov 1799–Apr 1800 **1st & 2nd Bns 17th Foot** (10 coys each) *WO17/2784-5,Pattenden*

Return of the Bombproofs provided in Dover Castle for the Lodgment of the Garrison, distinguishing what are appropriate for the men off Duty, for those on Picquet, and them on Guard. *Akers*

			Off Duty					
			Present berths contain	May be fitted to lodge during a siege	On Picquet	On guard of which one–third will be sentries	Where arty or picked men must be kept	
Out– works	East Demi Bastion	Sally Port	–	–	12	17	–	1 Officer
		Guard Room	–	–	12	17	–	1 Officer
		Suffocating Chambers	–	–	–	–	3	–
		East Arrow	–	–	–	10	–	–
		East Ravelin	–	–	–	14	–	1 Officer
	Hudson's	Communication	–	52	–	–	–	&offrs
		Guard Room	–	–	34	29	–	& offrs
		Suffocating Chambers	–	–	–	–	7	–
		Curtain	–	–	–	–	8	–
	Averanche's	Guard Room	–	–	24	17	–	& offrs
		Suffocating Chamber	–	–	–	–	16	–
	Spur Bastion old entrance	Guard Room	–	–	–	28	8	–
	Low flank	Guard Room	–	–	–	14	–	–
	curtain	Guard Room	–	–	–	14	–	–
	Flat Bastion	Guard Room	–	–	–	8	8	–
	Guilford's Battery		–	–	–	– 24	12	1 Officer
Caponnieres	East	Upper floor	–	18	–	–	–	& offrs
		Ground floor	–	50	–	–	–	–
		Entrance	–	–	–	11	4	–
	Spur	Floor	–	20	–	–	4	& officer
		Round Tower	–	16	–	–	–	–
		East Wing	–	–	–	–	12	–
		Entrance	–	–	–	15	4	& officer
		West Wing	–	–	–	–	12	–
	Old Entrance	Ground floor & entrance	–	–	–	17	–	& offrs
		1st floor	–	10	–	–	4	
		2nd floor	–	8	–	–	–	
		3rd floor	–	8	–	–	–	
	New Entrance	Sally Port	–	–	–	17	–	–
		1st floor	20	20	–	–	4	–
		2nd floor	27	27	–	–	–	–
Ramparts	Hudson's	Entrance	–	60	–	–	–	& offrs
	Averanche's	Casemated flank	–	–	–	–	–	–
		Lower flank	–	–	–	–	–	–
	Between the Spur and Averanches		–	–	–	–		May be made for 300 men This year probably 100.
	Spur	on two floors	320	400	–	–	–	No 1 for officers
	Old entrance		–	– –		– 17	–	–
	Bake House		–	– –		– 17	–	–
	Shaft		–	–	–	–	–	10 Master Artificers & Overseers
	Four cliff casemates having 2 floors each		392	592	–	–	–	& offrs
	Roman Intrenchment		72	72	–	–	–	& offrs
	Keep		100	400	–	–	–	& offrs
		Total	931	1753	82	312	122	

ⁿiform, *Cinque Ports Vol*

Officer, Cinque Ports Volunteers,
1794-1800
(Fazan)

Uniforms of Cinque Ports Volunteers, c 1803
(see page 45) *(Fazan)*

William Pitt, Lord Warden and Colonel Commandant of Cinque Ports Volunteers

courtesy of Dover Museum (d01004)

Jan–Jul 1800 **Lewis' Coy, 3rd Bn, RA** *Laws*

17 (Corunna) Fd Bty RA.

Apr–Jun 1800 **1st Bn, 27th Inniskilling Regt of Foot** *WO17/2785*

Also the **2nd Bn**, which was formed at Dover Castle on 24th May. Thos Bellingham of 27th Foot scratched his name in the Keep (on spiral stairs). Men again billeted on the Town – part of the Castle barracks burnt down 1800.

Jul 1800–Jun 1801 West Essex Militia (8 coys) *WO17/2785*

Jul 1800–Mar 1802 **Hutton's Coy, 5 Bn RA** [70 Fd Bty] *Laws*

To assist Invalid Gunners.

May–Nov 1801 **Northamptonshire Militia** (8 coys) *WO17/2785–6*

Aug–Nov 1801 **North Gloucestershire Militia** (8 coys) WO17/2786

Oct 1801 **Huntingdon Militia** (2 coys) *WO17/2786*

Oct 1801–Nov 1802 **2nd Bn, 52nd Regt of Foot** (10 coys) *WO17/2786*

From Ashford. Jun 1802 – dets at Shorncliffe and Hythe; Oct 1802, a det to Dungeness Bty. Moved to Chatham.

Feb–May 1802 **Riou's Coy, 5 Bn RA** *Laws*

Oct 1802 **70th Regt of Foot** (10 coys) *WO17/2786*

From Jersey, then on to Chatham.

Nov 1802–May 1803 **1st Bn, 4th Regt of Foot** (6 coys) *WO17/2786*

Also 4 coys in Deal. From Dec 1802 – 10 coys in the Castle, 4 in Deal, and a det at St Margaret's Bay.

May 1803–Jun 1805 **Leicester Militia** (7–10 coys) *WO17/2786–7*

1000 strong. Dec 1803 – a det at Guilford Bty; Feb 1804 – 1 coy each at St Margaret's Bay, Archcliffe & Western Heights; Jan–Jun 1805 – 7 coys Dover Castle & 1 at St Margaret's Bay.

[2nd of the 'Three Panics' 1803 - Fazan] – Invasion was again considered imminent, and large supplies of ammunition and provisions were laid in the Castle, and the guard increased. 'The degree of defence aimed at was that the enemy shall not possess this Castle in fourteen days from the day he has made his landing good'. *Akers*

Col Wm Twiss stated that 'a proportion of cavalry should be in Dover Castle, to be employed, among other duties, in catching the enemy's reconnoitring officers', but I have found no specific entries for cavalry at this time. The CRE recommended 'that a set of young soldiers who can run well should be employed to catch the enemy's engineers while reconnoitring at night'. *Akers*

May–Jul 1803 **Northamptonshire Militia** (10 coys) *WO17/2786*

Then 9 coys to Deal, 1 to St Margaret's Bay, and a det to Sandown Castle.

May 1803–Oct 1804 **Oxfordshire Militia** (8 coys) *WO17/2786–7*

Frequent swapping around of coys: Jul/Aug 1803 – 8 coys Castle, 2 W/H; Sep 1803 – 10/11 coys at Dover Castle and 1/2 at W/H; Jan 1804 – 1 coy also at St Margaret's Bay; May 1804 – 10 coys 'Castle & Town'.

Plus **Dover Volunteers** to man the Castle guns. Jul 1803 – 125 inhabitants of Dover formed a coy to learn the use of the great guns of the Castle, to act as artillerymen in case of invasion. *Pattenden*

Jul 1803–Feb 1808 **Beevor's Coy, 3 Bn RA** *Laws*

1 Aug 1803 – Pitt came with the Duke of York to inspect the fortifications and review the regiments in garrison. 'While they were firing a Royal Salute one of the guns went off and blew one of the poor artillerymen quite over the wall of the Castle, and he fell down dead to the bottom of the trench.' *Pattenden, Moyse-Bartlett*

Jan–Feb 1804 **Newhouse's Coy, 3 Bn RA** *Laws*

1803–1810 HQ (& 1st Bn) Pitt's Regt of Cinque Ports Volunteers

1803 – Pitt was then Lord Warden of the Cinque Ports and Colonel Commandant of the Volunteers. His raising of the Cinque Ports Volunteers as a local militia 'to serve during the war, but not to be sent out of the kingdom' virtually cancelled the ancient and special privileges of the men of the Cinque Ports, who claimed exemption from serving outside their own port areas – 'they were not to be marched beyond their own jurisdiction, unless it was for the assistance of eachother' *(Lyon)*. Portsmen were eager to become *volunteers* in a crisis, though there still survived a noted objection to *enforced* service of any kind, probably due to the false belief that they were exempt from the ballot in return for providing ships, even long after that obligation had ceased to exist *(Fazan)*. Pitt raised three battalions of Cinque Ports Volunteers; the HQ was in Dover, but I am not sure they were actually in the Castle. Viscount Mahon, nephew of Pitt, commanded the 1st Bn, and was LtDC at the time.

It seems the regular army did not think much of the capabilities of the volunteers. There is an anecdote about M/Gen Sir John Moore, when asked by Pitt where his corps would be placed in an invasion, being told by Moore that they would be drawn up on a hill 'where you will make a most formidable appearance to the enemy, while I with the soldiers shall be fighting on the beach' *(Fazan)*. They were 'held together by mutual consent, rather than a strict code of discipline', and it seems the feelings were mutual – the volunteers claiming: 'what the Army lost in discipline, it would gain in intelligence'. They were mostly middle class, officers and men often of the same social standing, with virtually no military experience. *Ian F W Beckett 'The Amateur Military Tradition', 1558-1945, JSAHR Vol LV*

1806 – Windham, as Secretary of State for War after Pitt's death, had no love of the Volunteers either ('painted cherries which none but the simple would take for real fruit'), and practically destroyed them by his Training Act –

compulsory training by drill sergeants, to be inflicted on an 'armed peasantry', deprived of officers and uniforms. Castlereagh restored their clothing allowance in 1807. *JSAHR 1972, Moyse-Bartlett, 'Dover at War'*

Nov 1804–Oct 1805 **Northamptonshire Militia** (6 coys) *WO17/2788*

Also 1 coy at Sandown Castle, 1 at St Margaret's Bay, 2 at Forts Nos 1 & 2 (?). Jun 1805 – 11 coys DC, 1 at Archcliffe.

1 Jul 1805 – 'Saw through my glass the rows of tents on the hills each side of Boulogne – they appear to be of a great length'. Yet another threat of invasion – frustrated by the Royal Navy, who successfully blockaded the invasion transports. Nearly 2000 men in DC at this time. *Pattenden*

Nov 1804–Jul 1809 **Cornish Miners** (Royal Miners Regt) *WO17/2788–92, WO17/892, WO13/2485*

Between 1–5 coys of Miners were present on and off as needed. Sep 1805 – 2 coys, (& 3 at Fort Pitt, Chatham); Nov 1805 – 5 coys (280 men). Quartered at W/H mostly, but working in Dover Castle much of the time – presumably tunnelling.

Jan–Dec 1805 *11th Dragoons (1 troop)*

RE at Archcliffe – 1 coy Royal Artificers

Jan 1805–Jun 1806 **Newhouse's Coy, 3 Bn RA** *Laws*

There were 98 guns in Dover Fortress at this time.

Aug 1805–May 1806 **East Kent Militia** (Det) *WO17/2798*

Jul 1805–Apr 1806 **Hereford Militia** (8 coys) *& Pattenden*

From W/H, then moved to Colchester.

Oct 1805 (2 weeks) **1st Bn, The Coldstream Regt of Footguards** (DC & W/H) *R/H*

Dec 1805–Apr 1806 **South Lincolnshire Militia** (8 coys) *WO17/2790*

May–Nov 1805 – 7 coys at W/H and 1 coy at Archcliffe.

1806 *12th Dragoons (2 troops)*

Jan–Oct 1806 **Fifeshire Militia** (8 coys) *WO17/2789–90*

Apr 1806 **Northumberland Militia** (10 coys) *WO17/2790*

May–Jun 1806 at W/H; In July on to Woodbridge.

Apr–Oct 1806 **Renfrewshire Militia** (6 coys) *WO17/2790*

Dec 1805–Apr 1806 – at W/H & 1 coy at Archcliffe. Moved to Ashford.

Royal Miners Regt (*see* Cornish Miners *above*) *Pattenden*

Apr–Oct 1806 **1st Bn, Surrey Militia** (8 coys) *WO17/2790*

From W/H, Mar–Apr 1806, and back to W/H Nov 1806–Jan 1807.

Nov–Dec 1806 **1st & 2nd Bns, 6th Foot** (10 coys each) *WO17/2790, WO17/104*

1st Bn from Canada, and then on to Colchester; 2nd Bn for November only, from Deal and on to Ospringe.

Nov 1806–Jan 1807 **13th Foot** (10 coys) *WO17/2790*

Jan–Feb 1807 **Newhouse's Coy. 3 Bn RA** *Laws*

1807–1811 **Dover Coy, RE** *Laws*

Jan–Nov 1807 **East Essex Militia** (8 coys) *WO17/2790*

Jan 1807–May 1809 **Shropshire Militia** (9-12 coys) *WO17/2790*

The burial ground at Northfall outside the Castle walls was for men of the Shropshire Light Infantry who died of smallpox, and not cholera, as is sometimes reported. *Pattenden*

Jan 1807 **Denbighshire Militia** (5 coys)

Mar–Jun 1808 **Crawford's Coy, 6 Bn RA** *Laws*

Jun 1808–Aug 1809 **2nd Bn, Yorkshire, West Riding Militia** (9-12 coys) *WO17/2791*

April/May 1808 – Regt in the Citadel. Aug 1809 – the regt moved to Chatham. A det of 62 men (13 artificers and 49 labourers) stayed on to assist RE working on accommodation *(see below at Cornish Miners).* *Nugent*

[1808–1814 Peninsular War - Wellington]

Jun 1808–Aug 1811 **Cornish Miners** (5 coys) *WO17/2791*

Working with RE under M/Gen Twiss on new accommodation at the Castle, but quartered at W/H. *Nugent*

6–13 Mar they had to move out of Dover to Canterbury during the election, as was usual.

Jul 1808–Jun 1809 **Adye's Coy, 5 Bn RA** *Laws*

Sep 1808 & Aug 1809–Jun 1810 **Perthshire Militia** (10 coys) *WO17/2791,2 & Nugent*

Oct 1808–Jul 1809 – Perthshire Militia at Redoubt and Citadel (5 coys each)

'The precaution was taken of stationing militiamen as far as possible outside their own counties, so that they would never be called upon to fight their families and relations (on anti–smuggling duties).' *(see* 1717 & 1747*)* *Western*

An order was issued in 1807 'reminding all men of the importance of the suppression of smuggling, and setting out the reward structure for officers and men who make a seizure, rewards which were considerable'.

There was also a small RA det – 1 bombardier & 8 gunners, plus 1 bombardier & 9 invalid gunners. *Nugent*

Jun/Jul 1809 20th Foot (briefly - before embarkation to Walcheren Is) *WO17/2791*

Jul 1809–Aug 1810 **Crawford's Coy, 6 Bn RA** *Laws*

Number of guns at DC: 15 mortars (13", 10" & 8"), 36 carronades (24, 18 & 12–pdrs), and 38 guns (32, 24 & 18–pdrs) *[carronade – a short cannon of large calibre, more usually used on ships].* *Nugent*

Aug–Dec 1809 **Montgomeryshire Militia** (4 coys) *Nugent*

Sep 1809 – Dover Castle still not fully fitted up as Barracks since the fire in 1800, but there were guard beds for 717 men (Cliff Casemates 250) – some will have again been billeted on the Town. A det of 220 men from the **2nd Bn 95th regt** also to assist with the building; the rest of the 95th was at Shorncliffe 'in a sickly state', from 'that ill-fated expedition' to Walcheren. 106 men died in action, 4000 from dysentery and fever (malaria). *Nugent*

Walcheren Is. captured 15 Aug 1809 – '35 naval vessels and 200 transports carrying 40,000 troops waited for the Earl of Chatham *[William Pitt]* and Sir Richard Strachan to make up their minds what they intended to do' – indecision and serious outbreaks of disease compelled the whole expedition to return with nothing accomplished. *Gordon*

Sep–Oct 1809 – Many sick and wounded from Walcheren accommodated in Dover Castle – 174 from many different regts in Castle hospital (nearly 19,000 troops in Kent). Accommodation when finished provided for 1750 men. By Oct 1809 there were (infantry): 29 officers, 1696 NCOs and privates, and 80 patients in the Castle, and (cavalry): 2 officers, 53 NCOs and privates, and 50 horses in Guilford Battery. *(Lt Gen Nugent – Commander Kent District with HQ in Canterbury).*

Nov 1809 – a det of **West Yorkshire Militia** (52 men), and Dec 1809, a det (220 men) of **6th Foot** also to assist with the building works.

Jan–Aug 1810 **1st Bn, 6th Foot** (10 coys) *WO17/2792*

From 1810, the records are not very clear about the Castle - sometimes only 'Dover' or 'Dover Barracks', since the building of the Western Heights Barracks, but there was always at least a small detachment in Dover Castle, and often Battalions were split, with several coys in each place.

July 1810 – Gen Twiss recommended one iron bedstead per man, which was 'considered quite a modern innovation'. Up to then two men per bed had been the norm. *Akers*

Sep 1810–Nov 1814 **Massey's Coy, 9 Bn** (*became* Jones' Coy 1812 – Massey died Apr 1812)

Sep 1810–Aug 1811 **West Middlesex Militia** (9 coys) *WO17/2793*

Also 1 coy at St Margaret's Bay until Jul 1811.

Dec 1810 *18th Light Dragoons (1 troop)*

A det to Walmer in Jan, on Coast duty.

9–22 Sep 1811 – An assembly of Dover Division Cinque Ports Volunteers

Nov 1811 *23rd Light Dragoons (1 troop)*

Mar 1812 **Derbyshire Militia** (some coys)

And at Redoubt, Citadel and Archcliffe – 12 coys in Dover. *WO25/3227*

George Calladine was in the Derbyshire Militia for two years, having been in Chelmsford and Hythe. On 2nd March 1812, he marched to Dover; on 4th May 1812 he and a friend decided to 'volunteer into the Line' *(as opposed to the county militia)*, and selected the 19th Foot – the regt was stationed in the East Indies and the depôt in Hull, 'and we wished to have a long march through the country'. He describes the well: 'water was drawn up by not less than 80 buckets; it took 12 men to work it, four hours a day at a spell, being a garrison fatigue'. *Calladine*

Apr–May 1812 **3rd Bn Lancashire Militia** (10 coys) *WO17/2793*

Sep 1810–Mar 1812 at 'Dover B' – this can *sometimes* refer to DC, but more often means W/H. Moved to Canterbury in May. Dec 1811 – a det to St Margaret's Bay.

3rd Coy, 2nd Bn, RE – Royal Military Artificers (Archcliffe)

May–Dec 1812 Tipperary Militia (Artillery) *WO17/2793*

Some coys DC – 10 coys in Dover. Det at St Margaret's Bay.

Jun 1812 *3rd Light Dragoons (KGL – King's German Legion)*

1812–1814 – some baptisms are recorded in Dover Castle for the following militia regts, so possibly the whole regt was there, or maybe only some coys.

Jan–May 1813 West Meath Militia (6 coys) *WO17/2793*

May–Jun 1813 Tipperary Militia (Artillery) (10coys) *WO17/2793*

Jun–Oct 1813 1st Bn, West Yorkshire Militia (10-12 coys) *WO17/2794*

Nov 1813–Jan 1814 Aberdeen Militia (10 coys) *WO17/874*

Feb–Sep 1814 Londonderry Militia (10 coys) *WO17/2794*

May–Jun 1814 Rutland Militia *WO17/2794*

Aug 1814– 2nd Bn, 86th Foot (4 coys)

Oct 1814–Mar 1815 { **95th Foot,** 1st & 2nd Bns *R/H*

Mar–May 1815 " Depôts " *StJP/R*

1802–1816 known as Rifle Brigade (*see also* Nov 1818)

Dec 1814–Apr 1815 **Morrison's Coy, 4 Bn RA** (44 Bty) *Laws*

Averanches Tower, c1820
courtesy of Dover Museum (d02009)

May 1815–Jul 1816 **Brandreth's Coy, 8 Bn RA** (disb 1819) *Laws*

1815 **Detachment of Sappers and Miners** *Laws*

Jun 1815 **3rd Bn, 14th Foot** *[briefly]* *R/H*

On arrival back from Waterloo (much Waterloo traffic passed through Dover). Many years later, Lord Albemarle thus described the landing of the 14th Foot: 'Public feeling had undergone a great revulsion in regard to us soldiers. The country was saturated with glory, and was brooding over the bill that it had to pay for the article. Waterloo and Waterloo men were at a discount. We were made painfully sensible of the change. If we had been convicts disembarking from a hulk we could not have met with less consideration. 'It's us pays they chaps' was the remark of a country bumpkin as we came ashore. It was a bitter cold day when we landed; no cheers, like those which greeted the Crimean army, welcomed us home. The only persons who took any notice of us were the custom-house officers, and they kept us under arms for hours in the cold, while they subjected us to a rigid search. Those functionaries were unusually on the alert because a day or two before a brigade of artillery, with guns loaded to the muzzles with French lace, had slipped through their fingers. Our treatment was all of a piece. Towards dark we were ordered to Dover Castle, part of which building served as a prison. Our barracks were strictly in keeping with such a locality – cold, dark, gloomy, dungeon-like. No food was to be got but our rations, no furniture but what the barrack store afforded'. *from 'Fifty Years of My Life' in R/H*

1815–1856 – 42 years of peace, and the Army, regarded as a nuisance and unnecessary expense, was reduced in strength as far as possible. After Waterloo, Volunteers were disbanded and local militia disembodied in 1816; the next great volunteer movement was not until 1859.

'God and the soldier we alike adore In time of danger, not before; The danger past and all things righted God is forgotten, the soldier slighted.' *(Thomas Jordan, 1612–1686)*	*or another version:*	'When war is proclaimed and danger's nigh, God and our soldiers is the people's cry; But when peace is proclaimed and all things righted, God is forgot and the soldier slighted.' *(Anon)*

There were 87 guns mounted at the Castle during the war, reduced to only 18 afterwards. Guns were fired to celebrate royal birthdays, and feux de joie for various victories – Nelson at Trafalgar, Wellington at Waterloo, for instance. *[Waterloo: 18th June 1815].* *Pattenden*

Dover Castle continued to house **HQ RA and one company**, with small parties scattered at outforts.

Jun–Dec 1815 **2nd Bn, 40th Foot** (disb in Castle) *R/H*

Dec 1815–Mar 1817 **40th Foot** (Depôt) *WO17/306 & 788*

Depôts – At this time each Infantry Bn in the UK, as well as those abroad (except East Indies) was to consist of 6 Service coys and 4 Depôt coys – the Depôts of such regts as were serving at home were to continue united with their respective Bns; depôts of those on foreign stations to be exercised together, but to remain independent. Depôt coys (recruits and training) moved frequently, often between the Castle and Western Heights, or had dets in both. Depôt Bns were also at Walmer, Deal and Shorncliffe. A Depôt could comprise from only 50–100 men up to 280–300 men.

Jan 1816 **4th Bn, 1st Foot** *WO17/304*

Disb in Castle, and men transferred between other 3 Bns.

2–5 Jan 1816 51st Light Infantry (3 days!) *Reg/Sec*

A Waterloo regt returning from France, en route for Portsmouth. *Letters of Private Wheeler*

Feb–May 1816 **3rd Bn, 1st Foot,** (det – 109 men) *WO17/304*

The whole Bn was in Dover in Mar 1817, more likely at W/H.

Jul 1816–Aug 1817 **5th Foot** (Depôt) *WO17/316 &788, WO17/304*

Depôt (50–60 men) at Dover Castle first, and 'later at Dover Heights' – until Sep 1818.

1817 – there is an instruction that each soldier is to have three nights rest for one night on duty. *HO50/11*

Sep 1816–Feb 1819 **Monro's Coy, 9 Bn. RA**

Disb at Dover, Feb 1819.

Sep 1817–Aug 1818 **67th Foot** (Depôt) *WO17/2794*

Jul–Sep 1818 **31st Foot** (8 coys) *WO17/327*

Sep–Oct 1818 **6th Foot** (Depôt)

Oct 1818 – 71st landed at Dover and marched straight on to Chelmsford – possibly some sick left at the Castle.

Nov 1818 **Rifle Brigade** (Depôt)

95th renamed The Rifle Brigade (4 Bns) in 1816. Bn at Shorncliffe. *WO17/2795*

Nov 1818 **7th Foot** *R/H*

From France, en route to Cork, 11 days only; embarked at Deal. *WO17/326*

Jan–Jul 1819 **47th Foot** (Depôt)

Jan 1819–Apr 1820 **17th & 24th Foot** (Depôts) [Aug 1819 in Deal]

Mar 1819–Jan 1822 **Monro's Coy, 8 Bn RA** *was:* Taylor's, 8 Bn from Woolwich.

Aug 1819 **85th Foot**

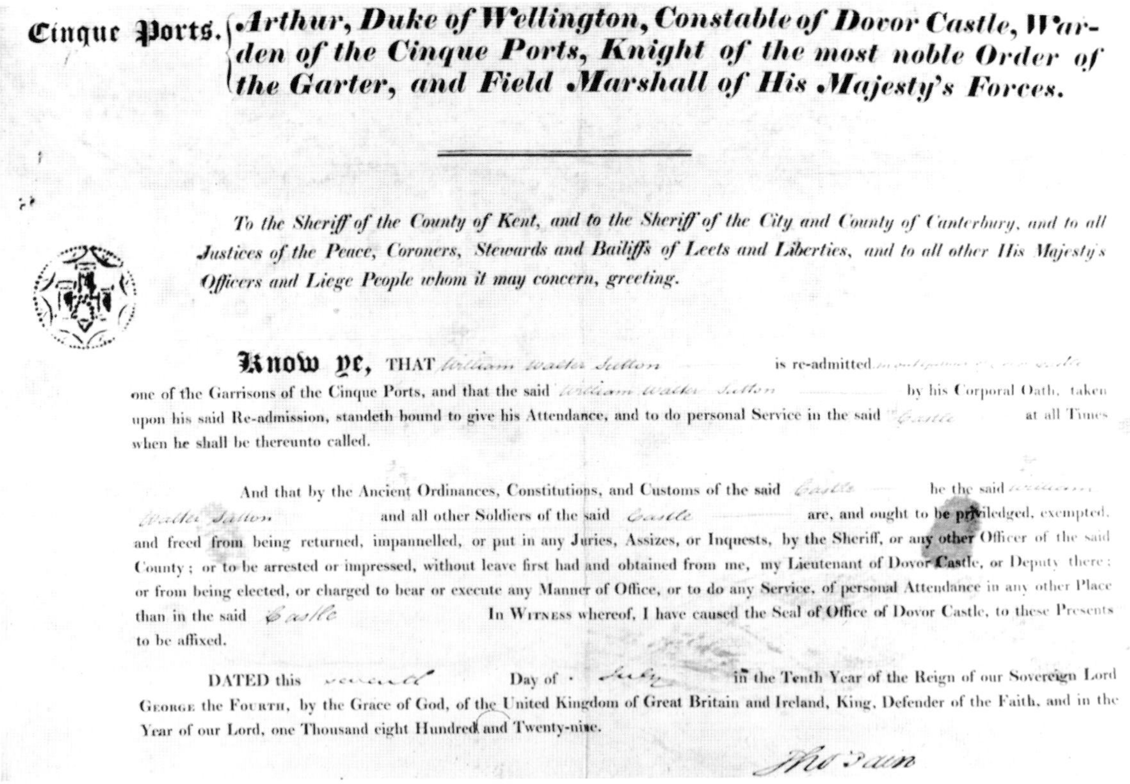

Cinque Ports. *Arthur, Duke of Wellington, Constable of Dover Castle, Warden of the Cinque Ports, Knight of the most noble Order of the Garter, and Field Marshall of His Majesty's Forces.*

To the Sheriff of the County of Kent, and to the Sheriff of the City and County of Canterbury, and to all Justices of the Peace, Coroners, Stewards and Bailiffs of Leets and Liberties, and to all other His Majesty's Officers and Liege People whom it may concern, greeting.

Know ye, THAT William Walter Sutton is re-admitted [illegible] one of the Garrisons of the Cinque Ports, and that the said William Walter Sutton by his Corporal Oath, taken upon his said Re-admission, standeth bound to give his Attendance, and to do personal Service in the said Castle at all Times when he shall be thereunto called.

And that by the Ancient Ordinances, Constitutions, and Customs of the said Castle he the said William Walter Sutton and all other Soldiers of the said Castle are, and ought to be priviledged, exempted, and freed from being returned, impannelled, or put in any Juries, Assizes, or Inquests, by the Sheriff, or any other Officer of the said County; or to be arrested or impressed, without leave first had and obtained from me, my Lieutenant of Dover Castle, or Deputy there; or from being elected, or charged to bear or execute any Manner of Office, or to do any Service, of personal Attendance in any other Place than in the said Castle In Witness whereof, I have caused the Seal of Office of Dover Castle, to these Presents to be affixed.

DATED this seventh Day of July in the Tenth Year of the Reign of our Sovereign Lord George the Fourth, by the Grace of God, of the United Kingdom of Great Britain and Ireland, King, Defender of the Faith, and in the Year of our Lord, one Thousand eight Hundred and Twenty-nine.

Appointment of an Out Gunner
courtesy of Dover Museum (d07114)

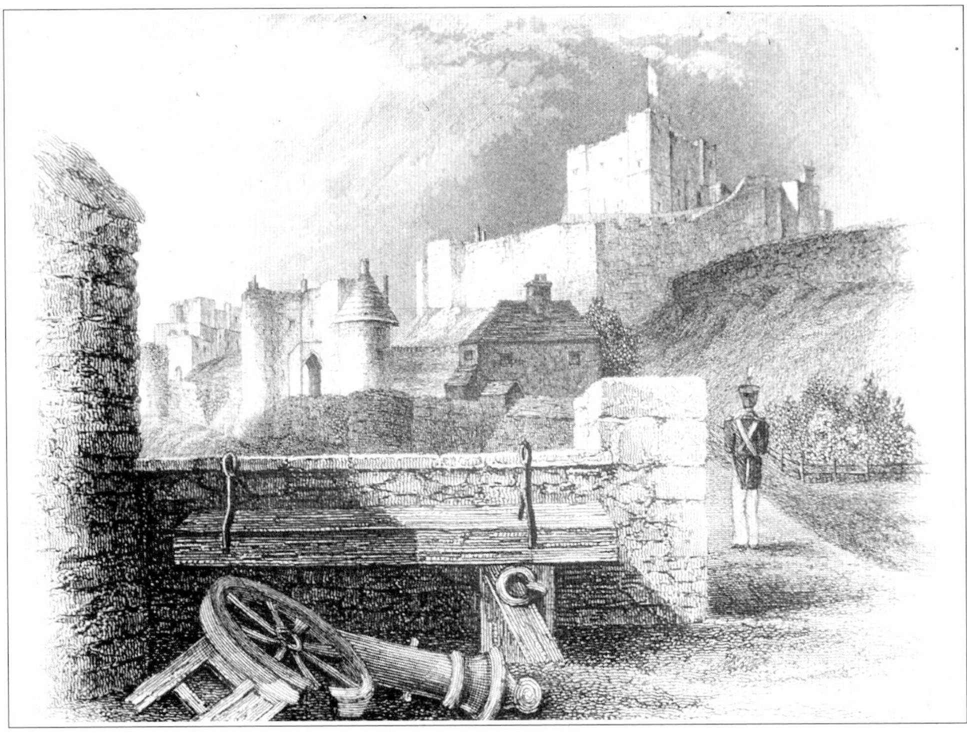

Broken gun carriage, showing dilapidated state, c 1829-1844
courtesy of Ivan Green

Nov 1819–Jun 1820 **84th Foot** (10 coys) *WO17/346*

1820–1850 1 Garrison Coy RA – mostly named below. *M/J*

Not many RA at Castle until 1860; they were mainly at Drop Redoubt until then, from where salutes were fired One Garrison coy RA 1820–1850; 2 coys 1850–1860. *M/J*

May–Nov 1820 **6th Royal Veteran Bn** (1 coy) *WO17/2794*

May 1821–Mar 1822 **71st Foot** (1 coy)

Feb–May 1822 **Sandham's Coy, 4 Bn RA** *Laws*

Mar 1822–Aug 1825 No infantry in Dover Castle – only an RA coy (c60 men). *WO17/2797*

Jun 1822–Nov 1826 **Taylor's Coy, 3 Bn RA** *became:* **3 Coy**, Jan 1825 *Laws*

–1824 **Special Cinque Ports det Artillery Volunteers**

Aug 1825–Dec 1826 **85th Foot** (Depôt) (Regt at W/H) *WO17/391 &*

Oct 1825–Oct 1826 **89th Foot** (Depôt) *Dov/Tel*

Dec 1826–Apr 1832 **Trelawney's Coy, (8 Coy, 2 Bn RA)**
became: Grantham's, May 1831 *Laws*

Dec 1826–Feb 1830 **41st Foot** (Depôt) (+ Det, Feb 1827) *WO17/2799*

Oct 1827-Mar 1828 **49th Foot** (Depôt) *WO17/2800*

Regiment in Capetown 1822–1827, then India from 1827. *St.J P/R* has entries for the regiment up to 1829, so this must have been the Depôt. This then moved to Glasgow, was back in Dover Oct-Dec 1828, then at Chatham all 1829.

Apr–May 1828 **63rd Foot** (2 coys) (8 coys at W/H) *R/H*

Jun–Nov 1828 **47th Foot** (Depôt) (then by sea to Portsmouth) *WO17/417*

1828 'Seamen and Marines' in Dover Castle *St.J P/R*

Jan 1829 – Appointment of Duke of Wellington as Lord Warden.

May 1829–1852 – The establisment of Cinque Ports posts for Dover Castle was:

Lt Gov, Deputy Lt Gov, A Master Gunner, 2 Resident Gunners, 3 Out Gunners, and a Porter *WO43/440*

These were Invalid appointments made by the Lord Warden. It was the Lord Warden's responsibility to appoint his Cinque Ports officers, i.e. Captains or Governors, gunners, etc. of the various Castles (Walmer, Deal, Sandgate, Sandown), also Archcliffe Fort and Moate's Bulwark. They were not regular army appointments, and the Duke of Wellington's principle was to confer these sinecures on men invalided in the service of the country, alternately to seamen, RA invalids and regiments of the line – preferably to natives of the Cinque Ports. R.H. Jenkinson was Lt Gov Dover Castle, and Samuel Latham, Deputy Lt Gov. Payment for the Cinque Ports Garrison seems to have been a long–standing 'thorn' to the Treasury, and there are continual pleas from the Lt Gov or his deputy justifying their existence! As most appointees were fairly aged, frequent vacancies occurred, which the Duke of Wellington invariably managed to fill again. These posts were also filled after the Duke's death, 1852–1858, under Lord Dalhousie who succeeded him as Lord Warden. *WO43/631A*

Archcliffe	Capt, Lt, Master Gunner, 2 gunners, Porter
Moate's Bulwark	Capt, Lt, Master Gunner, 3 gunners, Porter
Sandgate Castle	Capt, Lt, 7 gunners, Porter, Under Porter
Walmer Castle	Capt, Lt, 7 gunners, Resident Porter, Upper Porter
Deal Castle	Capt, Lt, 9 gunners, Resident Porter
Sandown Castle	Capt, Lt, 6 gunners, Upper & Under Porters

WO43/440

Sep 1829–Nov 1833 **2nd Bn The Rifle Bde (95th)** (Depôt & 1 coy) *WO17/2799,2800*

A det remained until Apr 1834.

May 1832–May 1836 **5 Coy, 2 Bn RA** (MacLachlan's) *Laws*

Apr–Sep 1834 **73rd Foot** (Depôt) *WO17/2801, WO17/473*

In Dover since Nov 1833, and moved to DC Apr 1834. Then to Deal early Sep.

1834 – Death of Samuel Latham, Deputy Lt Gov Dover Castle, 'at an advanced age' – Col Henry Smart (late a Lt Col RE) appointed in Latham's place.

The military presence was popular socially at this time, and relations cordial with the Town. There was comment in the local press about the inadequacy of depôts to man the Castle and other defences properly. The Duke regularly entertained officers of the garrison when he was at Walmer Castle. *Dover Telegraph*

Jan–Aug 1835 **88th Foot** (Depôt HQ & 3 coys) (Connaught Rangers) *WO17/2801*

Sep–Dec 1834 – At W/H. Then embarked at Dover for Kinsale, Ireland. Regt in Corfu. Departed to a fond farewell from Dover, having arrived from Chatham with an unfortunate reputation preceding them – when 'unfounded calumnies were disseminated to our disadvantage' (CO). *Dov/Tel*

[Aug 1835–Oct 1836 ? Det 5th Foot – Depôt at W/H] *WO17/488*

Jun 1836–Mar 1842 **2 Coy, 3 Bn RA** (Stopford's) *became:* Somerville's, Nov 1841

Troops outside the casemates, and tunnel connecting to Canon's Gate, c 1840s

Apart from railings, the gallery has changed little.

courtesy of Dover Museum (d00778)

Jun 1836–Mar 1837– **Det of 2 men only of Royal Invalid Arty** *WO10/1720*

A bombardier and a gunner. They were allowed 1d a day beer money, and about 1/9d a day subsistence.

Oct 1836–Aug 1837 **2nd Bn, The Rifle Bde** (1 coy) *Dov/Tel*

4 coys from June – Aug 1837. Depôt at W/H.

Aug 1837 **56th Foot** (Depôt) – Regt in Jamaica. *WO17/502, Dov/Tel*

Sep 1837–Jun 1838 **69th Foot** (Det)

Depôt at W/H, moved to Castle Jun–Aug 1838. Regt in Demerara. *WO17/512, Dov/Tel*

Aug 1838–Sep 1839 **27th Enniskillen** (Depôt) *WO17/510*

Jan–Feb 1839 – Also **1st Bn**. 1st Bn embarked for Cape of Good Hope, Feb 1839.

Aug 1839–Aug 1840 **90th Foot** (Det – c40 men)

Depôt at Castle Barracks. Depôts 27th and 90th provided the guard of honour for the Cinque Ports banquet for the Duke of Wellington, 30 August 1839. Depôt then moved to Kinsale, Ireland. Regt in Ceylon.

1840 – Duke of Wellington decreed 'one body of Infantry to be allotted to the defence of Dover Castle, its gates and approaches' (usually a detachment from W/H). *B-J*

There were no guns mounted in the Castle at this time; the recommendation was for 6 x 24–pdrs and 5 x carronades or howitzers.

Aug 1840–Jul 1841 **34th Foot** (Depôt) – Regt in Canada. *WO17/530, 540*

Dec 1840–Apr 1841 **54th Foot** (2 coys) *WO17/531, Dov/Tel*

Regt at W/H – after 21 yrs in India.

Jul–Nov 1841 **16th Foot** (Jul–Sep, 4 coys; Sep–Nov, 2 coys) *Dov/Tel*

Sep–Nov 1841 – 2 Coys to W/H. 17–24 Sep – rest of regt marched from Canterbury to Dover (W/H) during elections, and back to Canterbury, leaving 2 coys at Dover Castle until 15 Nov.

17–24 Sep 1841 **26th & 49th Foot** (Depôts) *WO17/541, Dov/Tel*

marched from Canterbury to Dover, and back, during the East Kent elections in Canterbury. *WO17/340*

Nov–Dec 1841 **7th Royal Fusiliers** (Depôt) [then at W/H] *WO17/538*

Apr–May 1842 (5 weeks) **6th Foot** (HQ and 2 coys – c 160 men) *Dov/Tel*

Regt arrived back from India (1000+). Jan 1842 to Canterbury; HQ moved to Dover Castle Apr, then to Deal in May to join the Depôt and rest of regt.

Apr 1842–Jul 1844 **7 Coy, 7 Bn RA** (Eyre's) *Laws*

Nov 1842–Oct 1843 **19th Foot** (Depôt) *WO17/559, Dov/Tel*

Regt in Malta and Corfu; depôt moved to Jersey.

14 Nov 1842 – Queen Victoria visited Dover Castle from Walmer, was received by the Governor, Col Jenkinson, and the 19th Foot provided a Guard of Honour.

1842 – Castle opened to public again, and a new guidebook issued.

1843 – HQ RA & RE at Archcliffe Fort.

[1843–69 New Zealand; 1845–6 1st Sikh War] Many troops returning from these campaigns quartered in and about Dover Castle.

Oct 1843–Jan 1844 **95th Foot** (Depôt) *Dov/Tel*

From Sheerness, and then moved to W/H. Regt in Corfu. *WO17/564*

Jan–Jun 1844 **77th Foot** (Depôt) *Dov/Tel*

From Sheerness, and then moved to Chatham to embark for Cork, thence to Clonmel. Regt in Jamaica.

Jun–Jul 1844 **68th Foot** (Depôt & 2 coys) *Dov/Tel*

Regt arrived back from Canada; HQ at W/H, then moved to Canterbury. *WO17/571*

Jul 1844–Jun 1845 **52nd Oxford Light Infantry** (Depôt) *WO17/579,WO17/2804*

Aug 1844–Nov 1847 **1 Coy, 7 Bn RA** (O'Brien's; *became* Stace's, Apr 1846) *Laws*

Jun–Jul 1845 **14th Foot** (Depôt) *Dov/Tel*

For 10 days from W/H, and thence embarked for Plymouth; the regt in Quebec. *WO17/577*

Jul 1845 **68th Light Infantry** (Depôt & 2 coys) *Dov/Tel*

2 weeks, then to Canterbury and Walmer. Regt in Quebec.

Jul–Nov 1845 **43rd Monmouth Light Infantry** (Depôt) *Dov/Tel*

Then moved to W/H. A det remained in DC till Jan 1847. *WO17/579.*

Nov 1845–Feb 1846 **40th Foot** (Depôt) *Dov/Tel*

Feb–May 1846 **1st Bn, The Rifle Bde** (Depôt coys) *Dov/Tel*

Jan–May 1847 **57th Foot** *Dov/Tel*

Also at W/H. Jan 1847 – Duke of Wellington stated Dover garrison should be 10,000 strong the moment war was declared, as it was more vulnerable since the arrival of steamships. For about 25 years up to this time there had been only Depôt Coys, and there was again comment in the local press on their inadequacy to man the Castle and

Officer and Private, Grendier Company,
19th Foot, circa1854

Dover Castle.

View from Gatton Tower,
Probably 89th Foot
courtesy of Dover Museum (d01470)

other defences properly. Dover was a fashionable watering place and marine resort at this time, and seems to have been very keen to have the military, not least for the social scene!

Apr 1847–Feb 1849 **3 Coy, 10 Bn RA** (Beresford's) – at Spur Barracks. *Laws*

May–Nov 1847 **89th Foot** (& at W/H) *Dov/Tel*

Nov 1847–Apr 1848 **17th Foot** (& at W/H) *R/H*

Dec 1847–Jan 1850 **4 Coy, 8 Bn RA** (Mee's) *Laws*

Apr 1848 **50th Foot** (Depôt) – to Walmer 400 strong, May-Aug. *Dov/Tel,R/H*

May–Aug 1848 **46th Foot** (Depôt) *Dov/Tel*

From Guernsey. Regt at W/H. Recipes found for 46th: 'Salt meat for 50 men. Put the meat in the boiler and fill it with water the night previous. The next morning wash the meat well and remove it from the boiler. When breakfast has been cooked, put the meat back again, fill up with water and boil gently for three hours. Skim off the fat and serve. The fat when cold is an excellent substitute for butter'. 'Soldiers' soup for 50 men: Put 60 pints of water (or 5 camp kettles full) in the boiler, 50 pounds of meat, Beef or Mutton, the rations of preserved or fresh vegetables, ten small tablespoonfuls of salt. Simmer for three hours and serve. Rice when issued to be put in when boiling, two pounds is sufficient.' *EK/U888 019 EK*

Aug 1848–Apr 1850 **50th Foot** (Depôt) [Regt at W/H] *Dov/Tel*

Mar 1850 – The Duke of Wellington (LW & CDC) twice declined requests to take County Court prisoners in the Castle prison. 'Dover Castle is used as a place of confinement for Debtors within the district of the Cinque Ports', and 'there is no accommodation for females'.

Mar 1849–Jan 1852 **3 Coy, 11 Bn RA** (Tulloh's) *Laws*

Feb–Dec 1852 – Drop Redoubt.

Jan 1850–Nov 1853 **4 Coy, 12 Bn RA** (Townsend's) *Laws*

Plus a 'detachment' of 2 Independent Invalid Arty: 1 corporal and 1 gunner. The Duke of Wellington's appointees – since 1836 (and possibly 1828). *WO10/2143*

?from 1850s–1899+? **HQ Dover Fortress**

Apr 1850–Jan 1851 **91st (Argyllshire) Foot** (1 coy) [rest at W/H] *Dov/Tel*

Jan 1851–Jan 1852 **1st Bn, The Rifle Bde** (5 coys) *WO17/2806*

HQ & 5 coys at W/H.

1851 – Castle reported to be in an intolerable state of disrepair, and unarmed. *WO55/785*

Jan 1852–May 1853 **30th Foot** (Depôt) *Dov/Tel*

14th Sepember,1852 – Death of the Duke of Wellington at Walmer Castle. He had been LW and CDC since 1829. The Earl of Dalhousie was appointed LW after the death of the Duke; he was abroad for 1853, and the LW's salary ceased. The Duke had paid from his own salary for the Admiralty Judge, the Chaplain and the Bodar (keeper of the Debtors' Prison) – all Cinque Ports officers, but civilians. The Lt DC (R H Jenkinson) and his deputy (Henry Smart) had great trouble extracting money from the Treasury for these men – the jobs were regarded as sinecures 'and do not form part of the effective garrison of a place of strength required to be maintained for purposes of national defence'. Dalhousie never received any pay himself, but after much pleading extracted about £100 pa for a paid assistant in 1858, as paymaster for the Cinque Ports Garrison, *(described at* 1828*)*, and reduced after the Duke's death to 2 resident and 2 out gunners. The Treasury view was that the salaries would cease as vacancies occurred and would not be replaced. The Debtors' Prison closed 1855. *WO43/440*

Jan 1852–Sep 1853 **7 Coy, 6 Bn RA** (Riddell's) *Laws*

Jan 1853–Jan 1854 **3 Coy, 11 Bn RA** (Swinton's, was Tulloh's) *Laws*

May 1853–1854 **1st Bn,The Rifle Bde** (Depôt) – from Walmer *Dov/Tel*

Jan–Apr 1854 **The Rifle Bde** (1 coy) [1st Bn to W/H] *Dov/Tel*

Oct 1853–May 1854 **5 Coy, 6 Bn RA** (Mundy's; *became:* Brandling's, Feb, & Thompson's, Apr 1854) *Laws*

Dec 1853–Nov 1854 **4 Coy, 1 Bn RA** (Price's; *became* Lawson's, Jun 1854) *Laws*

Feb 1854–Jun 1855 **1 Coy, 7 Bn RA** (Fisher's) *Laws*

Apr–May 1854 **Kent Artillery Militia** (3 coys) – for 28 days *WO68/340*

May 1854–Mar 1855 **1st Bn, The King' Own Staffordshire Militia** (1 coy - 81 men) *WO17/2806*

Regt at W/H. *Dov/Tel*

Sep 1854 **44th Foot** (Depôt) *Dov/Tel*

Sep–Oct 1854 **19th Foot** (Det) *Dov/Tel*

From & back to depôt at Walmer. *[1854–1856 – Crimean War]*

Oct 1854 **38th Foot** (Det) *Dov/Tel*

Regt in Crimea, depôt at Walmer.

Terracing for the new barracks and officers' mess, possibly 93rd Foot.
The earth was carted away through a tunnel which had been cut beneath the ancient outer walls of the castle, when it was shot onto the cliffs

courtesy of Dover Museum (d00285)

New Officers' Mess, early 1860s

courtesy of Ivan Green

Jan–Jul 1855 **Kent Artillery Militia** (230 men) *WO68/340, WO17/929*

1855–1863 – Kent Artillery Militia came for annual training in Dover Castle (21-28 days gunnery practice); 1864–1869 at Western Heights; 1869–1876 again at the Castle, thereafter at Fort Burgoyne. In 1883 became 2 Bde Cinque Ports Div RA, and recruits were still drilled at Dover Castle up to 1900.

Jul 1855–Sep 1856 **1 Coy, 14 Bn RA** (Chancellor's) *Laws*

Jul 1855–Jul 1856 **British Swiss Legion** *WO3/190, WO33/2*

Also at W/H. 1856 – Again many troops encamped in and around Dover Castle. The camp became a tourist attraction – to see the Crimea heroes! The British Swiss Legion, one of the auxiliary contingents raised during the Crimea, were among those encamped; they were in dispute over their bounty prior to disbandment and repatriation, which was £6 per man, but with a £3 drawback in case of barrack damages – a system they did not understand!

Jul–Sep 1856 **79th Foot** *WO17/680*

1856–60 – Much new building of earthworks and quarters, including Salvin's Officers' Mess (1856); and the restoration of St Mary's-en-Castro church was begun; Shoulder of Mutton Battery (in cliffs below Castle) built c1862. In 1855, Gen Sir John Burgoyne had considered DC so outdated and weak as to be beyond improvement, and recommended a detached fort to command the high ground to the north – Fort Burgoyne (or Castle Hill Fort) was started six years later. *Akers*

One of the ramparts 'looking towards St Margaret's, Deal' (probably East Arrow Bastion) was a very lonely sentry post, and was known as 'Mount Misery' to the garrison. *'A Day's Ramble about Dover Castle'*

Oct 1856–Oct 1857 **2 Coy, 1 Bn RA** (Newton's) *Laws*

Oct 1856–May 1857 **93rd Sutherland Highlanders** (12 coys) *WO17/2807*

From camp at W/H and Shaft Barracks. The 42nd (at W/H), 79th and 93rd had all arrived home from Crimea in July 1856, and left for India, May 1857, having been employed on the building works much of the time.

Jul–Oct 1857 **25th Foot** *R/H,D/Ex*

Back from the Crimea. Then toW/H till Jan 1858. There was the usual farewell eulogy from the Mayor of Dover on their leaving Dover for Gibraltar – 'heartfelt satisfaction at the universal kind manner and deportment of the officers, the quiet and exemplary behaviour of the NCOs and men composing your regiment during your stay in Dover'. *[1857–1859 – Indian Mutiny]*

Aug 1857–Jan 1860 **3 Coy, 1 Bn RA** (Clifford's) *became:* **7 Bty, 2Bde**, Jul 1859 *Laws*

Nov 1857–May 1858 Queen's Royal Rifles (Antrim Militia Corps) – & at W/H *Dov/Tel*

Sep–Oct 1858 **Kent Artillery Militia**

c280 men – also W/H (South Lines & Citadel). 21 days annual training. *WO68/340*

Jun 1858–Jun 1859 **Bedfordshire Light Infantry Militia** *Dov/Exp*

The regt was the first to occupy the new officers' mess. 'The visitors and inhabitants continue to be indebted to the courtesy of the officers of the regts stationed in this garrison for the performance of the bands of the respective corps upon the marine promenade. These concerts are most fashionably attended, and are evidently among the most attractive of our manifold sources of out-door recreation and enjoyment'. *Dov/Exp*

Oct 1858–Jun 1859 **Royal Lancashire Artillery Militia**

In Spur Bks. Dover Castle contained 23 officers, 580 men – 'a fine, hearty set of fellows', plus Invalid Arty of 1 Master Gunner, 2 Sergeants, 1 gunner. *Dov/Exp*

Jun 1858– **Bde HQ RA**

Jun–Aug 1859 **6 Coy, 1 Bn RA** (Lennox's) *became:* **6 Bty, 2 Bde**, Jul 1859 *Laws*

Re-organization of RA into brigades.

1859 – Invasion scare from Napoleon III *[3rd of the 'Three Panics' – Fazan]*.

A report in the Dover Express of 30 July 1859 reads: 'the other day two of our windows were blown out by the sharp reverberation of the cannon which were being used for ball practice at the new battery immediately over our office. On mentioning the subject to a colonel of artillery, who luckily happened to be passing at the moment, we were informed, as we quite anticipated, that no redress was to be obtained for the damage our glass had undergone – in short, that individual grievances could not be weighed against the national advantage to be derived from practising at this particular battery. The public service, said the gallant colonel, could *not* be impeded. He also, with professional severity of manner, put it to us whether we would rather have our windows blown out by the practice of English cannon, or be blown altogether into space by the rifled cannon of French invaders. Of course, there was but one view to be taken of this alarming hypothesis ... however, we do not share the invasion panic'. Warnings were later issued by the Mayor on days when practice firing was to take place, urging people to take due precautions for the preservation of windows, etc. The Castle was temporarily closed to visitors except with written passes during the panic.

Jun 1859–Feb 1861 **3 Coy, 5 Bn RA** (Woolsey's) *became* **2 Bty, 2 Bde**, Jul 1859 *Laws*

Jul 1859–Apr 1864 **3 Coy, 4 Bn RA** (Bolton's) *became* **8 Bty, 2 Bde**. Jul 1859 *Laws*

Jul 1859 **Kent Artillery Militia** [Castle & Citadel] *WO68/340*

Aug 1859–Apr 1862 **5 Bty, 2 Bde RA** (Mitchell's, *became* Smith's, Feb 1862) *Laws*

Ruined church and Pharos, c 1800-1820
courtesy of Dover Museum (d05932)

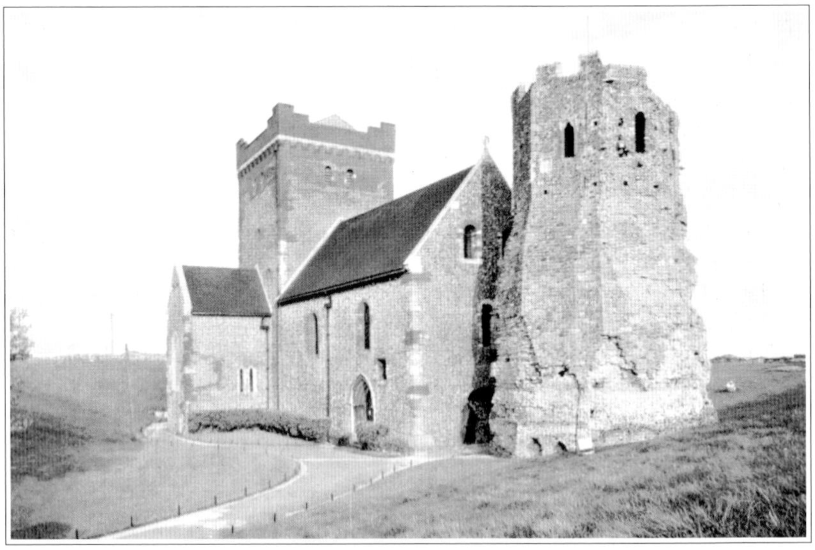

Restored church and Pharos

The Cinque Ports Volunteer Artillery, 1860, Archcliffe Fort
courtesy of Dover Museum (d00848)
(see page 63)

Sep 1859–May 1860 **Wiltshire Militia** – c 500 strong. Depôt at Walmer *Dov/Tel*

Sep 1859–Feb 1861 & Jun 1862–Sep 1864 **1 Bty, 2 Bde RA** (McCrea's, *became* Field's, Jan 1860, *and* Kelly's, Jun 1864) *Laws*

Sep 1859–May 1862 & May 1863–Sep 1864 **3 Bty, 2 Bde RA** (Hay's) *became* Johnston's, May 1861 *Laws* *and* Talbot's, Sep 1863 [Alderney, Jun 1862-Feb 1863] *Laws*

HQ Dover Garrison – Guilford Battery

HQ SE Coast Defences

HQ Dover Division RE – 3rd Coy RE at Castle Hill Fort (Burgoyne).

Feb 1860–May 1862 & Mar 1863–Sep 1864 **6 Bty, 2 Bde RA** (Taswell's, *was* Lennox's, *see* 1859) (at Shoeburyness, Sep 1859-Jan 1860).

After 1860, Dover Castle was kept for RA only, with a detachment of Infantry (from now on, the main body of which was normally at Western Heights, or 'Castle Hill Fort' (Fort Burgoyne)) to 'guard the gates and approaches'. HQ RA. Of 8 Btys in the Bde. only 4–6 Btys were in the Castle at one time, and the rest at outforts and the Western Heights. (c.1820–1850 – 1 Garrison Coy RA; 1850–1860 – 2 Garrison Coys in the Castle).

Gun salutes were fired from the Castle at 6am, noon ('Time Gun'), and 8.30pm.

From 1860, Dover became one of the chief coastal defence fortresses in England, along with Portsmouth and Plymouth.

The system of District Establishments in coast forts (comprising a Master Gunner and a squad of district gunners) continued as for ages (since H VIII) until final disbandment in 1956. They were responsible for maintaining, caring and accounting for guns, ammunition and stores. Frequent re-organizations of RA 1859–1890, including the introduction of the Brigade system in 1859. *M-J*

Apr/May 1860 **Kent Artillery Militia** – 28 days annual training. *WO68/340*

Apr 1860–Apr 1861 **47th Foot** (Det) – & at W/H.

Nov 1860–Apr 1862 **21st Foot** (Det) *Dov/Ex*

HQ, 2nd Bn at Shorncliffe; 1st Bn West Indies. *WO379/9*

Apr 1861 **Kent Artillery Militia** *WO68/340*

Apr 1861 **1st Bn, 3rd Foot** (Buffs) *WO68/340*

The Buffs moved into Dover Castle on arrival from active service in China, but only for about 10 days, before moving to Western Heights, 20th April. Kent Artillery Militia moved out to billets after only 5 of their usual 27 days annual training, 'the Barracks being required for 3rd Buffs arrived from China', under command of Col Ambrose. *WO68/340*

<u>The Arrival of the Buffs</u> (To the tune of 'The British Grenadiers')

'Twas on an April morning
  The news to Dover came
The gallant Buffs were coming home -
  A regiment of great fame
And all the dear young ladies,
  In hoops, and hats and muffs,
Came down a husband to select
  From out the gallant Buffs.

From both the Crescent and Parade
  The girls they came in swarms,
To see what damage they could do
  By virtue of their charms.
And one young damsel I heard say
  'Dear me, they look like 'roughs'
But still, I think I'd like a beau
  From out the gallant Buffs'.

'And don't you think I'll have a chance,
  When the Rifles give their Ball?
I'll get some fellow out to dance
  In the Apollonian Hall!';
''Tis not the slightest use', said I,
  'Don't think these men are muffs;
Your arms will have but small effect,
  On the gallant, gallant Buffs'.

May 1861–Sep 1864 **4 Bty, 2 Bde** (Rotton's) *Laws*

May 1862 **Kent Artillery Militia** – annual training *WO68/340*

1862 – The Bishop of Sierra Leone formally inaugurated the resumption of Divine Service in the Church of St Mary–en–Castro, after major restoration by Sir Gilbert Scott, 1860–1862. It appears that, despite being a ruin for so many years, it did not need re–*consecrating*. In the intervening years since its abandonment in 1690, it had been variously used as: a barrack room, prison, stables, store, granary, coal store, chicken coop and rubbish heap. Meanwhile the garrison had used the church of St James at the foot of the hill.

Jun 1862–Aug 1864 **7 Bty, 2 Bde** (Gordon's)

Jun 1862–Sep 1864 **2 Bty, 2 Bde** (Taswell's, *became:* Woolsey's, Mar 1863)

March 1863 – 6 Bty, 2Bde, Taswell and Woolsey exchanged Btys twice. Woolsey to Jersey, Jun 1862–Feb 1863.

Mar 1863–Sep 1864 **5 Bty, 2 Bde** (Smith's, *became:* Gordon's, Apr 1864)

Apr 1863 **Kent Artillery Militia** *WO68/340*

1864–1869 – annual training took place at W/H.

Sep 1864–Nov 1866 & Sep 1867–May 1868 **1 & 2 Btys, 13 Bde** (Johnston's & Davis') [Dec 1866–Aug 1867 in Cork]. *Laws*

Sep 1864–May 1868 **7 Bty, 13 Bde** (Crauford's, *becam:* Turner's, Nov 1865)

Oct 1864–Dec 1867 **3 & 4 Btys, 13 Bde** (Govan's & Cockburn's)

Oct 1864–Apr 1868 **5 Bty, 13 Bde** (Singleton's)

Oct 1864–Apr 1868 **6 Bty. 13 Bde** (Hay's, *became:* Godby's, Feb 1865)

8 guns at Saluting battery - the Time Gun is in the foreground. Possibly known as Seven-Gun Battery in the 18th century, it is near the site of the present-day beacon
courtesy of Dover Museum (d02012)

The Time Gun
courtesy of Dover Museum (d06244)

Armstrong Gun, 1856 *(see page 63)*

Officers of 2 Bde RA, 1862
courtesy of Ivan Green

Men of 2 Bde, RA in the Keep yard; door No 4 can still be seen…it is now the entrance to the 'Ladies'!
courtesy of Dover Museum (d13294)

Volunteer Review, 1869 -
Assault on the castle
courtesy of Dover Museum (d08896)

Volunteer Review, 1869
Traction engines & artillery train
courtesy of Dover Museum (d08892)

Volunteer Review, 1869 -
Divine Service
courtesy of Dover Museum (d08901)

Oct 1864–May 1868 **8 Bty, 13 Bde** (Curtis')

Oct 1864 – 5 btys of 13 Bde arrived Dover Castle.

Jul 1866 – a report on SE Division from Shorncliffe: 'a new canteen at Dover Castle is very much wanted. *EK/U888 018*

April 1867 (Easter week-end) – About 25,000 troops (24,000 of them Volunteers) from all over the country came for a mass review by HRH the Duke of Cambridge (C-in-C), and a mock battle on the plateau behind the Castle – the first time the Volunteer review had been held in Dover, and also with regular troops. The 1st Sussex and the Cinque Ports Volunteer Artillery worked the guns defending the Castle – 70 guns were brought in, among them 4 x 42–pdrs on Bell Battery and 2 x 68–pdrs on top of the keep; Armstrong guns *(see page 60)* were also used, as also by the Royal Navy who took part in the assault. It was deemed a success, and another was held two years later, in 1869. This time only about 15,000 took part, and it was nearly cancelled due to a storm with icy wind and rain in the morning, when the troops assembled on the Esplanade were drenched with huge waves. They were told to disperse and find shelter, but the Duke of Cambridge ordered them back (a few by then the worse for drink), and they marched up to Castle Hill Fort a few hours later to be reviewed, then continued with the mock battle, attacking the Castle. The heavy guns of the Cinque Ports Volunteer Artillery were drawn by enormous carthorses 'directed by drivers in smock frocks and leather leggings'. The opinion was expressed of the great value of exercising the Volunteers with regular troops, and that the same should apply to the Militia, but that to be more realistic they should camp the nights before and after and be fed in the field, to test the commissariat and their ability to pitch and strike camps, and transport them. *Dov/Tel*

May–Sep 1868 & Mar 1869–Apr 1870 & May 1871–Mar 1872 **4 Bty. 17 Bde** (Couchman's) [Oct 1868-Feb 1869, Shoeburyness] [Apr 1872–May 1873, W/H] *Laws*

Jun 1868–Mar 1869 & May 1870–Apr 1872 **1 Bty 17 Bde** (Lumsden's) – Entertainments of readings and singing were given by 17 Bde in the Recreation Room at Dover Castle.

Jun 1868–Feb 1871 **2 Bty, 17 Bde** (Wilson's, *became:* McCausland's, Jan 1870)

Jun 1868–Mar 1869 & Apr 1869–Apr 1870 & Apr 1872–May 1873 **3 Bty, 17 Bde** (Trevor's, *became:* Cairnes', Nov 1871) [Greencastle; May 1870-Mar 1872, then W/H] [moved from W/H back to Dover Castle]

Jun 1868–Apr 1870 & May 1871–Mar 1873 **5 Bty, 17 Bde** (Magrath's *became:* Hoyes'. Aug 1870) [Greencastle; May 1870-Apr 1871; W/H, Apr-May 1873]

Jun-Sep 1868 & Mar 1869–Mar 1871 **6 Bty, 17 Bde** (Blair's, *became:* Hadow's, Apr 1870) [Sep 1868-Mar 1869, Shoeburyness; to W/H April-Oct 1870 and back to DC].

Jun 1868–Oct 1870 **7 Bty, 17 Bde** (Baker's)

Moved to W/H, Oct 1870–Mar 1871.

Jun 1868–Jan 1871 **8 Bty, 17 Bde** (Forster's) [disb, 1 Feb 1871]

April 1869 **3rd Kent Artillery Volunteers** *WO68/340*

Cliff Casemates for annual training.

Aug 1873 **10th Coy RE**

Apr 1873–1876 **Kent Artillery Volunteers** *WO68/340*

Back at the Castle for annual training, Apr or May, for approx 27/28 days.

Sep–Nov 1873 **28th Coy RE**

Jun 1873–May 1876 **2 Bty, 3 Bde** (Hardy's, *became:* Cane's, Apr 1875) *Laws*

Jun 1873–Jul 1874 **6 Bty, 3 Bde** (Lluellyn's)

Jun 1873–Jul 1874 **7 Bty, 3 Bde** (de Moleyne's, *became:* Purcell's, May 1874)

Jun 1873–Jul 1875 **8 Bty, 3 Bde** (Anderson's)

Aug 1874–May 1876 **3 Bty, 3 Bde** (de Moleyne's, from May 1874, *became:* Still's, Mar 1875)

Aug 1874–May 1876 **4 Bty, 3 Bde** (de Cetto's)

Sep 1875–May 1876 **5 Bty, 3 Bde** (Cardew's)

Feb 1875 **2 Coast Division** (McCallum's)

Mar–May 1875 **7 Coast Division** (Anderson's)

Mid–1870s – About 1000 men in Dover Castle.

1875 – 'a voluntary offer was made by a large number of men to garrison Dover Castle. Happily, their services were never required, but no less that 450 officers and men of the East Kent Volunteers gave in their names to the Colonel as willing volunteers for garrison duty.' *Igglesden*

May 1876–Jul 1877 **1 Bty, 10 Bde** (Vachell's) *became:* **3 Bty, 9 Bde,** July 1877 *Laws*

Jun 1876–Jun 1877 **5 Bty, 10 Bde** (Lyle's) *became:* **7 Bty 9 Bde** "

Jun 1876–Nov 1878 **6 Bty, 10 Bde** (Sandham's) *became:* **8 Bty, 9 Bde** (Brackenbury's)

Lady Butler in her studio, Constable's Tower
(The Art Annual)

Jun 1876–Apr 1880 **7 Bty, 10 Bde** (Farrell's) *became:* **9 Bty, 9 Bde**

May–Jul 1877 **4 Bty, 1 Div, RA Depôt** *became* **Depôt Bty, 9 Bde**; (*see *Apr 1882*)

Jun 1877–Apr 1880 **4 Bty, 10 Bde** (Newman's) *became*: **6 Bty, 9 Bde GA**

Jul 1877–Mar 1882 **HQ 9 Bde, RGA** (Royal Garrison Artillery)

1877 **Army Service Corps (Det)** *Dov/Lib*

1882 Re-organization of RA and re-designations took place in Dover Castle. (Cardwell reforms, 1881)

Apr 1880–Mar 1883 **12 Bty, 11 Bde GA** *became:* **2 Bty, 4 Cinque Ports Division** , Apr 1882

Apr 1880–Apr 1883 **13 Bty, 11 Bde GA** *became:* **1 Bty, 4 Cinque Ports Division** "

Feb 1881–May 1884 **10 Bty, 8 Bde GA** *became:* **3 Bty, 4 Cinque Ports Division** "

May 1881–Sep 1883 **14 Bty, 8 Bde GA** *became:* **2 Bty, Eastern Division** "

Nov 1881–Jun 1884 **18 Bty, 7 Bde GA** *became:* **4 Bty, 4 Cinque Ports Division** "

Mar 1882 **18 Bty, 8 Bde GA** *reduced* Apr 1882

1883/4 – Constable's Tower was greatly enlarged to provide suitable accommodation for the General Officer commanding S E District, using some of the stone from the ruined Sandown Castle. *B–J*

Apr 1882–Jul 1899 ***Depôt, 4 Cinque Ports Division** [1882–1908]

Depôt remained but changed designation – (* *see also at* 1889, 1895, 1902)

Apr 1883–Feb 1885 **2 Bty, 1 Northern Division GA**

Nov 1883–Dec 1886 **7 Bty, 8 Scottish Division GA**

May 1884–Oct 1886 **4 Bty, 7 Western Division GA**

Apr 1883–Jan 1886 **3 Bty, 1 Northern Division GA**

May 1884–-Sep 1886 **3 Bty, 6 Southern Division GA**

Sep 1885–Oct 1887 **9 Bty, 9 Welsh Division GA**

Nov 1886–Nov 1893 **8 Bty, 2 Lancashire Division,** *became:* **17 Bty Eastern Division GA,** Jul 1899

Jul 1889–1895 ***Depôt, Eastern Division GA** (*see* Apr 1882)

Nov 1886–May 1891 **4 Bty, 5 London Division,** *became*: **20 Bty Eastern Division GA,** Jul 1889

Nov 1886–Apr 1889 **5 Bty, 5 London Division GA**

Sep 1887–Sep 1891 **10 Bty, 8 Scottish Division GA,** *became*: **29 Eastern Division GA,** Jul 1899

Apr 1890–Jan 1895 **2 Coy, Eastern Division GA**

Apr 1890–-May 1894 **11 Coy, Eastern Division GA**

Jul 1890–Oct 1895 **25 Coy, Eastern Division GA**

Jul 1894–Sep 1899 **7 Coy, Eastern Division GA**

1895 – 1902 ***No 1 Depôt, Eastern Division GA** (*see* Apr 1882) [recruits at DC]

Jan 1895–Sep 1898 **10 Coy, Eastern Division GA**

Oct 1895–Dec 1897 **20 Coy, Eastern Division GA**

Apr 1897 – Surrey Bde of Volunteers (c 3000) came for military training during Easter – billeted in schools, the convict prison and Shaft Barracks.

Dec 1897–Jun 1900 **15 Coy, Eastern Division GA**

1896–8 – Gen Sir William Butler at Constable's Tower, as Deputy Constable, and Commander S E District; Lady Butler did her famous painting 'Steady, the Drums and Fifes!' here (57th Regt). Writing in her autobiography, she said: 'The Castle was the very ideal, to me, of a residence. Here was History, picturesqueness, a wide view of the silver sea, and the line of the French coast to free the mind of insularity. It was a pleasure to give dances at the Constable's Tower, and the dinners were like feasts in the feudal times under that vaulted ceiling of the Banqueting Hall. Our boys' bedroom in the older part… had witnessed the death of King Stephen *(? – a popular legend, but he died at St Martin's Priory, Dover!)*, and the winding staircase conducted the unappreciative London servants by a rope to their remote domiciles. My studio had a balcony which overhung the moat and drawbridge. What could I have better than that? No wonder I accomplished a creditable picture there, for I had many advantages. I place *'Steady, the Drums and Fifes*!' amongst those of my works with which I am the least dissatisfied'. She used her own sons, and the 'well–drilled lads' from the Gordon Boys' Home as some of her models.

Sep 1898–Mar 1900 **6 Coy, Eastern Division GA**

1899 – 'Dover Fortress', i.e. the whole garrison, not just the Castle, comprised 4,700 men (850 regulars, 1230 artillery militia, 568 volunteers RA, 500 volunteers RE, 1500 infantry militia).

Nov 1899–Apr 1900 **12 Coy, Eastern Division GA**

Feb 1900–Aug 1903 **30 Coy, Eastern Division GA,** *became*: **24 Coy, RGA,** Dec 1901

Oct 1900–Feb 1904 **12 Coy, Eastern Division GA,** *became*: **23 Coy, RGA,** Dec 1901

Dec 1900–Nov 1903 **3 Coy Southern Division,** *became*: **7 Coy, RGA,** Dec 1901

The Port War Signal Station (PWSS)

1902–Sep 1908 ***No 1 Depôt RGA, Eastern Command** (*see* Apr 1882)

Apr 1903–Sep 1908 **107 Siege Train Coy RGA**

Feb 1904–Sep 1905 **35 (Heavy) Coy RGA**

Nov 1903–1914 **40 Coy, RGA**

Then moved to Langdon Battery.

Mar 1903–1914 **41 Coy, RGA**

? Plymouth 1904; 1 Coy Kent RGA(TF*) (M/J);* 1908 – Formation of the TA, or Territorial Force (TF).

Feb 1905--1914 **46 Coy, RGA**

Became Dover Fire Command. The Fire Command Post was built in 1905 on the site of a former muzzle–loader emplacement from the Napoleonic wars. *Peck*

1905–1915/1918–1922 **RGA Records & District Staff**

RGA Records in Dover Castle at start of war, moved to Victoria Park 1915, then to western block of Waterloo Crescent (1922–1926 at Western Heights).

Jun 1906–May 1918 **3rd Dover Fortress Coy RE** *WO73/97*

?since 1858– **HQ SE Coast Defences**

1900–Aug 1914 **HQ 12 Inf Bde** *WO33/602*

Dover Castle was HQ for 12 Inf Bde only during peacetime. *[War declared 4 Aug 1914]*

–1912–1925 **HQ Dover Garrison** (or Dover Fortress) (?since 1899)

Aug 1914– **HQ Kent Inf Bde & HQ for 2 coys RGA, CRA**

Jul–Oct 1914 **5th Bn. (Cinque Ports) Royal Sussex Regt (TA).** (4 coys)

Dec 1914- – **A Special Service Section of cyclists** from the above (3 officers and 42 ORs) *Fortress Orders, DYRMS*

1914–1918 At the outbreak of war (4th August), reservists replaced regulars almost immediately, and numbered 16,000 in the garrison. 5th Bn Royal Sussex Regt were the successors to Pitt's Cinque Ports Volunteers - one of their first tasks was digging and constructing more earthworks along the perimeter of the Castle. They arrived at their next post (The Tower of London) 'so bronzed after two months' digging in the sun at Dover as to be taken for a regular Bn back from India' *(Fazan).* There was also a Dover Fortress Civil Labour Corps employed on these defence works.

Aug 1914 **4th Bn, Royal Sussex Regt**.(a few weeks before going to France) *D92 44949*

Aug 1914–Mar 1915 **3rd Reserve Bn, The Royal Sussex Regt**

'From its long association with the Cinque Ports, no station could have been more appropriate for the Bn than Dover Castle – the regular garrison, then on their way with the BEF to France, was replaced by Special Reserve units fully occupied in training drafts for overseas. (*see also* 1916). Hence there fell to the Bn not only the normal garrison duties of Dover Fortress, but much heavy work besides. The Dover defences were so vulnerable to attack from inland that three large working parties, each of two coys under a captain, were required daily to dig and construct earthworks along the perimeter, and also an outpost coy with piquets (pickets) on the main roads to search all motor cars. Spy scares were the cause of much activity, including the arrest of a former German officer, whose new Ford motor became a useful car for Bn HQ *(Fazan).* As numbers were depleted from these Reserve Bns by constant drafts to the Front, they were replaced by 'Kitcheners' – hastily recruited from the famous poster: Lord Kitchener saying 'Your Country Needs You' (Lord Kitchner was Secretary of State for War). In Dec 1914, 4 Bns of Kitcheners were formed at Dover, and were billeted mainly among civilians in the Town or in temporary camps. (*Dover & the European War, 1914-1918', Dover Express).* By 16th, Aug 1914, DC was so overcrowded, 4 coys and the Corps of Drums of Royal Sussex had to move out to South Front Barracks. *Fazan*

Aug 1914–1919 **Dover & Folkestone Coys (Kent & Sussex) RGA**

Aug 1914–1918+ **11 (Kent & Sussex) Fire Command** (from 40 & 46 Coys, RGA) *became*:

Oct 1918–1921 **HQ Dover Fire Command East** (at Hospital Bty)

Oct 1914 Guard duty – 'It having been brought to notice that in a great many cases commanders of guards and sentries have only very vague ideas of what their duties and orders are, officers commanding units will arrange for all NCOs and men to be instructed in this most important duty'. *Fortress Orders, DYRMS*

Nov 1914 – Attached to the HQ in DC were several details: 9 naval ratings manning the searchlight; a school (Adult Education) for map reading, simple French, geography of the seat of war; 13 Army Pay Corps; 1 NCO and 8 men of 15th Bn Royal Fusiliers (Bn at DYRMS) on police duty, who relieved a similar party of 3rd Bn Royal Sussex.

Dec 1914 – 'complaints having been made of men throwing missiles over the cliffs, all ranks are warned that this practice is extremely dangerous and is strictly prohibited. Serious notice is to be taken of any breach of this order'. *Fortress Orders, DYRMS*

Dover was made one of the chief ports for the reception of wounded, after the retreat from Belgium.

1914–1918 **Port War Signal Station** (PWSS)

PWSS was erected 1914, directly over the Fire Command Post. Dover Fire Command (commanding Citadel, Pier Turret and Langdon Fort) was manned throughout World War I, for 10 days during the Munich crisis in 1938, then Aug 1939-July 1945.

Searchlight on roof of Keep, WWI
courtesy of Dover Museum (d16105)

The Seaforth Highlanders on parade, 1933
courtesy of The Times/Dover Museum (d01345)

1914–1918 – The Keep was used as an armoury, with vast stocks of rifles and machine guns (up to 20,000), and to store ammunition. Constable's Tower was used as a Hospital, Court Martial Room, Signals Office; it became the residence of the commander 12 Inf Bde again in March 1920.
Dover Castle was kept relatively empty during the war, as an ultimate retreat for outlying troops – reserve rations for 5500 men for 7 days were held.

1914 – **Volunteer Hampshire Fortress Coy, RE** (S/L) *RE records*
'To man defence electric lights'. Then to Connaught Bks.

Nov 1914–Aug 1916 **1 Coy local Anti-Aircraft Corps RNVR** *EK/D92 44949*
2 crews of 1 Sub Lt, 3 Petty Offrs, 18 S/L workers (ABs) working alternate nights of three watches, in the Keep. The Control house was at Dover Castle with telephone communication with the other two stations, FC Post and all AA guns.

Aug 1916–1939 **Dover Searchlight Corps RE(T)** (1st Kent Bty RFA)[The Keep]]
Aug 1916 – The military authorities did not like admiralty control of AA guns and S/L units, so AA Corps RNVR was demobbed, and RE Chatham took over command; the AA HQ was then at Maison Dieu, with 3 out-stations: at the Keep, Drop Redoubt and Langdon Battery. The S/L Corps Control House was at Dover Castle. Black balls hoisted at the Castle gave warning of daylight raids as well as sirens. In peacetime black balls were used as warning of firing practice by RA.

Aug 1914–1918 **Det of 468 Coy RE (TF)** *Mr Godfrey, ex RE*

Jul 1915–Sep 1916 **HQ 6th Wing, Royal Flying Corps**

1916– **RE Signal Centre** (Constable's Tower)

1916– **HQ 7th Reserve Inf Bde**

1916–Jan 1919 **2nd Dover Special Reserve Inf Bde** (HQ Constable's Tower)
Aug 1916 – Formation of Training Reserve as regimental reserve units were unable to cope with the number of recruits. Reserve Infantry Bns became Training Reserve Bns, and Bdes as Reserve Bdes.

Feb 1917– **386 Siege Bty, RA** – formed at DC. *JBM Frederick*

Feb/Mar 1917– **396 Siege Bty, RA** – formed at DC.
Spring 1918 – 'The whole army passed through Dover, plus many American troops'. *(EK)D92 44949*
At the end of the war, there were many returning prisoners, and Dover was one of the chief de-mob centres.
May 1918 – Battalions reduced to Training Cadres, and a major re-organization took place. 'The Regular Army, in keeping with historical precedent, reverted to its former estate – short of men and short of money'. *Ascoli*
Dec 1918 – 'The sight of the cliffs of Dover, and the great Castle crowning them, with our Empire's flag – the worldwide emblem of freedom for which we have fought – floating over all this is a most inspiring spectacle, and itself repays us for all that we have been privileged to do in the discharge of our duty to our King and Country'. *(Field Marshal Lord Haig, Dec 1918, speaking at Dover on return from the Front).*

Jun 1919 **1st Bn, Connaught Rangers** (very briefly)
Regiment disbanded in Connaught Barracks, Dover, 1922.

Apr 1921–Apr 1924 **'K' & 'L' Btys, Coast Defence** (were 46 & 40 Btys, RGA)

Apr 1921–Aug 1924 **HQ & District Establishments**

1925 – Dover Castle again became an Infantry station, and the RA moved out.

Jun 1925–Oct 1927 **1st Bn, The King' Own Yorkshire Light Infantry** *R/Sec*
1925 – the battalion was under canvas at Swingate aerodrome until the new barracks were completed. One of their duties was guarding Dover Harbour installations during the General Strike of 1926. In 1979, a retired railwayman from Yorkshire spent his 70th birthday revisiting Dover Castle, and recounted having spent many hours, as one of his duties, polishing Queen Elizabeth's Pocket Pistol when stationed there as a drummer with KOYLI in 1925 – it is no longer kept polished!
The steep bank outside the Officers' Mess building has evidently proved a problem to drivers on occasion. Brig A R Forbes (retd) tells of an officer trying to drive someone else's car in front of the Mess who went down the bank, and ended up perched perilously on the edge of one of the enormous airshafts.

1925–Sep 1939 **HQ 12 Infantry Bde** *(?from 1920)*

1925–Nov 1940 **HQ Dover Garrison** *WO166/1343*

Nov 1927–Aug 1929 **1st Bn, The Lincolnshire Regt** *HB(A), R/H*
& Sep 1929–Feb 1930 – temporary move to London for one month, Aug–Sep 1929. *WO380/112*

Feb 1930–Dec 1933 **1st Bn, The Seaforth Highlanders** *R/Sec*
Moved from Citadel. Nov 1933 – The Prince of Wales (Edward VIII), as Colonel–in–Chief, inspected the regt's farewell parade, prior to their departure for Palestine. Home Details remained in occupation until the arrival of the 2nd Bn, which they joined, in April 1934, as about 100 were considered too young to go abroad.

2nd Bn The Seaforth Highlanders.
The Prince of Wales presenting new Colours

courtesy of The Regimental Museum, The Highlanders

The Officers' Mess, taken c 1870, but showing cannon balls

courtesy of Dover Museum (d06212)

Lord Ballantrae (Bernard Fergusson) told of another motoring incident at the Officers' Mess, when dining with the Seaforth Highlanders in 1932: 'My fellow guest, John Montagu-Douglas-Scott, in the 9th Lancers, drove his car half over the edge of the steep bank while turning it round after dinner to go home. It seesawed precariously as he clambered out and he was lucky not to break his neck. We anchored it for the night with ropes, and hauled it back up the slope the next day.'

Winter 1930 – the War Office handed over the Keep to the Office of Works; some of the last stores to be removed were 10,300 Blankets and 4000 Rugs, Horse – considered a fire risk. *WORK 14/289*

1932–Dec 1940 { **HQ Fixed Defences, RA** *became:*
HQ 12 Corps CA *WO192/45*

1932–Dec 1940 **Fortress Coy Signals, Bde Signals** *WO192/45*

HQ AA, RA

Field Security Police

Jul 1932–Jun 1940 **HQ Kent & Sussex Heavy Regt, RA** (TA), *split into:* *Laws*

Jun 1940–Nov 1945 { 519 & 520 (Kent & Sussex) Coast Regt, RA(TA), & *became:*

Nov 1945–Jan 1946 Holding Bn, RA [disbanded 1946])

Manned the Fire Command Post until formation of Coast Artillery (12 Corps) in 1940. HQ 519 was at Dover Castle, 520 Fire Command Post was at the Citadel.

Apr 1934–Sep 1937 **2nd Bn, The Seaforth Highlanders** *R/Sec*

Dets arrived Dec 1933, and left Mar 1938, for handover periods between the 1st & 2nd Bns, and the Black Watch.

27th Feb 1935: 1st Bn East Lancs stayed one night on return from Saarbrucken. 2nd Seaforths escorted them with pipes and drums from the docks to the Castle in pouring rain – 'a night I shall never forget'. *Major A J Wallace, R/Sec*

July 1935 – The Prince of Wales presented new Colours to the 2nd Bn.

1934–Jun 1940 **HQ Cinque Ports Fortress Coy, RE** *WO166/1343*

Mar 1938–Sep 1939 **1st Bn, The Black Watch** *R/Sec, WO73/141*

Dets arrived Jan 1938, and left Oct 1939. Cannon–balls were once piled at the top of the steps to the Officers' Mess. There are tales of after–dinner races, rolling them down the steps (thereby damaging the steps as can still be seen), and on down the hill!

Aug 1938–Sep 1940 **PF** [?Permanent Force] **Hospital 3**. [In casemates] *WO192/45*

Aug 1938–Sep 1940 **Fire Command Post** (FCPF)

Situated on top of the cliffs in front of Cliff Block, and directly beneath the naval PWSS, the FC Post was equipped with a DPF (Depression Position Finder) – standard equipment before the advent of RADAR. FC Posts were tactically controlled by the Coast Artillery Ops Rooms in Dover Castle. The job of the Fire Commander was the operational control of all the harbour batteries and searchlights, including Western Heights and Langdon, with a staff of 18 telephonists, plotters and rangetakers, and another 12 on the Ashford Flank Radar Station set just above the FC post; they supplied all shipping details and movements to the FC. All were members of 519 (K & S) Coast Regt RA. *Arnold*

Sep 1938 **Port War Signal Station** (PWSS) *[Munich]*

HQ Vice Admiral, Dover *Arnold*

Aug 1939–Jul 1945 **Port War Signal Station** (RN) *WO192/192*

Dover Mil. Telephone Exchange East

Sep 1940–1948 ?+ **Main Dressing Station/Mil. Hospital** *WO166/6044*

–July 1942 **129 Field Ambulance RAMC**

Aug 1942– **182 " " "**

Aug 1939–Nov 1945 **HQ Vice Admiral, Dover**

Aug 1939–Apr 1942 – Admiral Sir Bertram Ramsay, who had served in the Dover Patrol 1915–1918, was Vice Admiral Dover; he was charged with bringing the soldiers back from Dunkirk in 1940 – Operation 'Dynamo' – so named, according to one commonly repeated story, because the Ops Room used by Ramsay had been originally intended to house a dynamo *(Barker, p 85)*. Another theory claims the room had housed auxiliary electrical equipment (a dynamo) in World War I, and was therefore known as the Dynamo Room, but the truth appears to be that the name was merely next on the list issued for code–names of Operations! Initially Ramsay had a naval staff of only 18 men. It was said that the tunnels were infested with rats and bats on first occupation.

There were up to 100 RN Officers and 1000 WRNS working in Dover Castle, mainly in the Underground HQ. An ex-Wren *(Mrs Anne Sandys)* says: 'for a time before the invasion, we found ourselves working alongside sailors and soldiers – coding, plotting, signals, met. office, etc. This, we understood, was in case of counter invasion – the women would be removed inland, and so we helped train up some men in case of emergency, to leave behind in the casemates'.

Once again, 'the plan was drawn up so that in the event of Dover being cut off on the landwards side, and the withdrawal of the Infantry to within the Castle, the whole unit would become completely self-contained, able to

Admiral Ramsay
courtesy of The Imperial War Museum (HU90020)

Admiral Ramsay in his room in the casemates
courtesy of The Imperial War Museum (HU90019)

Naval Plotting, Admiralty Casemate
courtesy of The Imperial War Museum (A28263)

S O I Office, Admiralty Casemate, 1941
courtesy of The Imperial War Museum (A9916)

Cartoon, Knotting Class *(It is has not been possible to trace the sailors in PWSS who produced this cartoon; copied from Arnold, p110)*

Emblem of 12th Corps *(Arnold)*

HM the King inspecting RA, 1940
courtesy of The Kent Messenger Group

operate seawards, and remain a strong point behind the enemy's lines of communications' – a plan also applying to the Citadel and Fort Burgogne. *Arnold, Maj W H Fox*

In July 1945, command reverted to C-in-C Nore, but the VA remained in station until Nov 1945. Apr 1942-1945 the VA was Admiral Pridham Whipple (variously spelt Wippel, Whippel). Ramsay went on to command the Navy at D-Day, and tragically was killed in an air crash in 1945.

468 S/L Bty, TA RE (att RA) *Mr May*

RA took over responsibility fo S/L units July/Aug 1940, previously manned by TA(RE).

In September 1939, the order came for Territorials to remove the 'T' from the shoulders of their uniform, denoting their volunteer status – a move resented by the men, and known as 'Striptease'. *Arnold*

1939– **42 Kent Coy, ATS** *WO166/71*

1939– **Movement Control, SE Ports** *WO73/142*

Sep 1939–Oct 1940 **4th Signal Training Regt, RA** (C Bty) *WO166/1343*

Oct 1939–1945 **310 AA Ops Room & Gun Control Room** *WO166/14355*

Feb 1940– **Coast Artillery Ops Room, Combined Plotting Room**

Apr 1940 – King George VI visited Dover and inspected the RA in DC; he lunched afterwards in Constable's Tower – the menu for this occasion is still there.

Jul 1940–Oct 1944 **HQ 'B' Flt, 961 Sqn RAF, 5 Balloon dets** *WO166/6649*

Jul 1940–Dec 1944 **HQ 519 (Kent & Sussex) Coast Regt, RA**

Housed in Cliff Block (behind PWSS) from where all the administration of the garrison regiments was carried out – postings, pay, promotions, sustenance, etc. Btys were at: Langdon, Eastern Arm, South Breakwater (2), Pier Extension, Pier Turret, Western Heights, and Citadel.

Col Arnold organised a knot instruction class for Fire Command personnel and telephonists in Dover Castle in 1941. *(The cartoon was produced by sailors in PWSS above the Fire Command Post, p110 - Arnold).* *Arnold*

Jul 1940–Feb 1941 **HQ 520 Coast Regt RA**

July 1940 – formation of 520 (Kent & Sussex) Coast Regt, RA, and Dover Citadel Fire Command Post. The RHQ was established in the Castle with, at that time, no operational role. Feb 1941, RHQ moved from Dover Castle to South Front Bks (W/H). *WO166/1723*

Autumn 1940-Spring 1941: *Defence of Dover Castle.* 'France fell. "We will never surrender", Churchill told Hitler, "We will fight on the beaches...". The grapevine had it that when (not if) the Germans landed, the first line of defence would be at the River Stour (Canterbury), and the second major line of defence would be the River Medway. The civilian population of Kent would be overrun by the Blitzkrieg and would surrender but, although the Castle might be besieged by the Germans (as it had been by the French long ago) it would never surrender; the heroic garrison would rather die. I, a young airman from RAF Hawkinge, arrived at Dover Castle in the autumn of 1940, as did a whole motley of volunteers from the tattered remnants of the BEF and other units. We mounted a 24-hour watch along the battlements. We had no weapons. Between times we attended lectures on military tactics and on stripping and cleaning arms (working from diagrams) and on the use of grenades (working with one dummy grenade) remembering always to remove the pin with one's teeth whilst keeping the grip most firmly depressed. We were promised real grenades and real rifles at any moment - they never arrived. The 24-hour watches continued, and when the winter snows fell we were instructed to make snowballs and to practise lobbing them over the ramparts as if they were grenades. For arms we could go to the Keep and remove from the walls the weapons of olden times - battleaxes, lances, swords and shields. Thus was Dover Castle defended by intrepid volunteers with snowballs and ancient arms against Stuka bombers and the threatened Blitzkrieg until Spring 1941, when it became clear that the German invasion was but a myth, and we could return to our units'. *F/Lt A R Goodburn*

There was a restaurant near the seafront in Dover, called The Crypt – very popular with all ranks. It was said at one time that if anyone forgot the password to re-enter Dover Castle, it could always be obtained from the barmaid at the Crypt! *Arnold*

Nov 1940–Apr 1941 **HQ 130 Inf Bde** [absorbed HQ Dover Garrison] *WO166/1343*

4th Bn, The Dorsetshire Regt (TA) (HQ,A,B,& C Coys) *WO166/4208*

Mar–Oct 1941 **HQ 540 Coast Regt RA** *WO166/1072*

Then moved to South Foreland. Regt was at Wanstone, South Foreland and Fan Bay. *WO166/348 &1740*

Nov 1940–May 1941 **540 Coast Regt RA** *WO166/140*

In the Castle only whilst guns were being installed – 3 x 6" at Fan Bay; 4 x 9.2" at South Foreland; 2 x 15" ('Clem' and 'Jane') at Wanstone. The great railway–mounted cross–Channel 14" guns 'Winnie' and 'Pooh' were near St Margaret's.

Nov 1940–1944 **HQ 12th Corps, Coast Artillery** *WO166/72*

12th Corps – the Corps Commander was General Montgomery. The Corps emblem now worn as a sleeve badge by the Coast Artillery regt was the three trees: the oak, the ash and the thorn, selected to link the name of the first

Napoleonic tunnel
courtesy of Ivan Green

Tunnellers
courtesy of Dover Museum (d02551)

Tunnel down to DUMPY level
courtesy of Ivan Green

corps commander, Sir A F Thorne, with the three trees mentioned in Sir Rudyard Kipling's book 'Puck of Pook's Hill. It was the coastline covered by 12th Corps which was Pook's Hill country. *Arnold*

'Of all the trees that grow so fair, Old England to adorn
Greater are none beneath the sun than the Oak, the Ash and Thorn.' *A Tree song, c AD1200*

(The Bulldog badge worn later was for South Eastern Comd and then, postwar, Eastern Comd).

Nov 1940–1944 **Coast Artillery (CCA) & Ops Room**

1941–1943 **Ashford Det, 20 Bomb Disposal Coy, RE** *Mr Shatwell, ex RE*

Jan–Feb 1941 **11 Coast Artillery Group** *WO166/348*

Feb 1941–Nov 1942 **HQ 219 Indep Inf Bde** [in casemates] *WO166/1072*

Feb 1941–Aug 1942 **15th Bn, Queen's Royal Surrey Regt** (Bn HQ & HQ Coy) *WO166/1072*

Rest of the Bn was at W/H employed defending the beaches at Dover.

Constables Tower was used as an Officers' Mess – for 20 officers ('A' Mess). Fred Potticary, an officer's batman, recalls a 'smelly oil bomb' striking the doorway of the Tower. He lived in the batman's quarters next to Constables Tower. *WO199/454*

2nd Bn East Surrey Regt was lost in Malaya, but resuscitated May 1942 – the formation parade took place in Dover Castle, July 1942, and the Bn was stationed at the Citadel. *Col Les Wilson*

Feb 1941–Nov 1946 **HQ Dover Garrison** [reinstated] *WO166/1343, 6649*

In the Casemates. They moved to the Keep, Oct 1942–Jul 1943, during tunnelling.

Mar 1941– **Eastern Counter Bombardment Fire Comd** *WO166/348*

681 & 702 General Construction Coy, RE *WO166/140*

Based at Northfall Meadow. Constructing the hospital under Dover Castle, and Pioneer Corps later took over. During slack periods the Coy alternated between Capel and the Castle. The HQ was in Tunbridge Wells. (10 Pioneers per Sapper). There was also a Gas Decontamination chamber and Telephone Exchange.

A valuable 3" astronomical telescope, sent by a Canadian, Mr B H Witts, on loan for the duration, was installed on the Keep roof for watching the Channel.

Mar 1941 et al 1945 **5,7,8,16 & 20 Coast Observer Dets** *WO33/1836*

Mar 1941–1945 **HQ AA Combined Ops Room, Gun Ops Room** (GOR)

Mar 1941–1944 **290 Coast Bty** (519 Coast Regt) *WO33/1835*

May–Jun 1941 **11th Bn, The Buffs** (D Coy) *V Pieri*

The Bn was at Grand Shaft, and one of their duties was combing the beach for mines.

1941–1942 **Fixed Defences, E & W Reserve Coys** *WO166/1072*

The RA officers lived in the Corps Commander Coast Artillery (CCCA) Mess, known as RA Fixed Defences – end block of the old Officers' Mess ('B' Mess) with accommodation for 50 officers.

1941–1944 **Dets 171 & 172 Tunnelling Coys, RE** *WO199/462*

A tunnelling coy consisted of: a major, a captain, 4 subs and 208 men.

1941 – constructing a Dressing Station at a level above the Napoleonic casemates, which later became a hospital (Annexe).

1941–3 – Much tunnelling, not without mishap from subsidence and rock falls at Casemate level, led to the construction of Battle HQ (Combined HQ) at yet a lower level in solid chalk, 40' below the naval accommodation, which became known as 'DUMPY' (translated by some as: Deep Underground Military Position Yellow, but a dumpy level is also a surveyor's spirit level). They were using a new system of horizontal boring and steel arch linings, and were known as the Moles. Civilian electricians (DCRE, the civilian branch of RE) also worked on the construction of Comb HQ (Battle HQ) in the Cliff Casemates. Their official address was c/o GPO Dover – the actual address a secret due to the sensitive nature of their work. *WO166/348*

1943 – In the interest of better co-operation between RA and RN Ops Rooms, some 'amateur and unauthorised' excavation was undertaken by Coast Defence RA, with materials from RN sources, causing cracks in VA Dover's accommodation – they had removed the support of arch rings in the two casemates they tried to connect. 'To be discontinued forthwith'! RE stationed at Connaught Barracks, but working in Dover Castle. *WO199/454*

Jul–Aug 1942 **HQ 129 Inf Bde** *WO166/6594*

Jun–Jul 1942 **4th Bn, Wiltshire Regt** *WO166/6044*

Sep–Nov 1942 **8th Bn, The Buffs** (Bn HQ, HQ + 1 Coys) *WO166/6649*

at Oct 1942+ **9 Defence Troop RA, Bofors Det** *WO166/6649*

Det 8 S/L Bty, Sec 553 Field Coy

Det SE Comd Signals, Garrison Engineer *WO166/6649*

Elec Pl, RAPC, RAMC, APTC, RMP *WO166/6649*

GPO Pl

24 civilian GPO engineers maintained the equipment throughout the war.

Senior Chaplain, NAAFI *WO166/6649*

Brigadier Rawlings in the Coast Artillery Plotting Room

courtesy of the Kent Messenger Group

WRAC, Coast Artillery Plotting Room

courtesy of The Imperial War Museum (H24862)

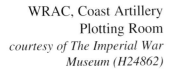

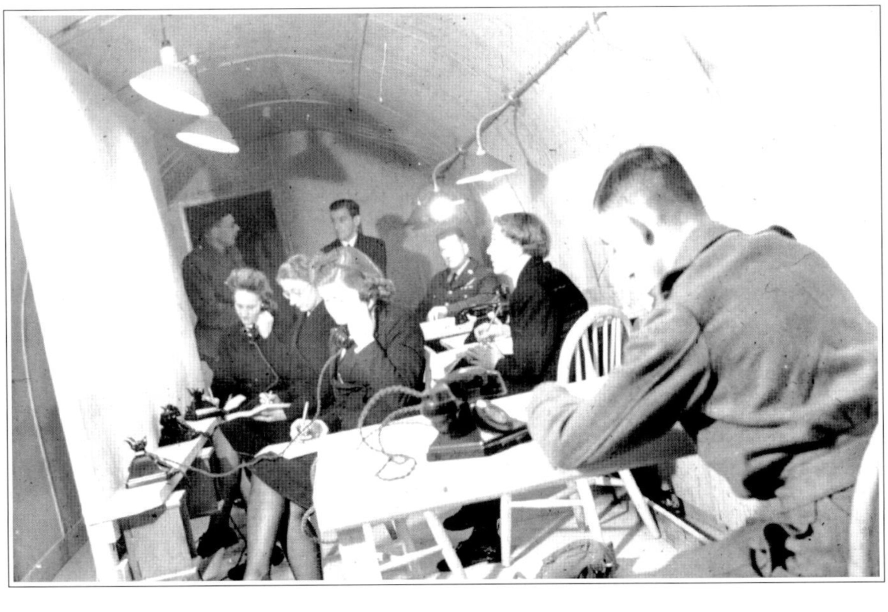

Combined Operations Room

courtesy of Dover Museum (d02548)

Dets ATS & WRNS, Air Sea Rescue *WO166/6649*

1943/4 – ATS were attached to 71 AA Bde, with HQ at Saltwood. They worked in the Gun Ops Room in 3 teams of 8 covering 24 hours: 0600–1400; 1400–2200; 2200–0600, rotating watches. Quartered at River. *WO166/14678*

Dec 1942–May 1943 **HQ 206 Independent Inf Bde** *WO166/6641*

Dec 1942–Mar 1943 **9th Bn, The King' Regt** (Bn HQ & HQ Coy) *WO166/10808*

Mar–May 1943 **9th Bn, The Buffs** ('B' Coy) [Bn at Grand Shaft] *WO166/10808*

1943 **Dets 1 & 2 Canadian Tunnelling Coys CRE** *WO179/2072*

1943–5 **Brigade Signals** *WO166/10352*

2nd War Office Signals *WO166/14678*

Attached 71 AA Bde. Known as the 'Dover Soles'. *Ken Flint*

May 1943–Oct 1944 **Combined HQ Ops Room** (CA & RN)(ATS & WRNS)

The Combined Ops Room (CHQ, or Battle HQ) was nicknamed 'The Hole', (as was also the underground HQ at Uxbridge, the Battle of Britain HQ Ops Room). Included an RAF section, special radar men and women, 18 wireless mechanics, 20 WAAF telephone and teleprinter operators.

Combined Plotting Room +(RAF & WAAF)

May–Oct 1943 **HQ 115 Inf Bde & LAD** [Aug-Sep: Victoria Park, Dover] *WO166/10808*

8th Bn, The Royal Welch Fusiliers (1 coy) *WO/10771*

May 1943 (2 weeks) **2nd Army HQ** (Formation Exercise) *WO199/1066*

Oct 1943–Sep 1944 **HQ 182 Inf Bde** *WO166/10800*

Mar–Jun 1944 – moved to Victoria Park, Dover to make room for Canadian HQ, (*see below)*

Apr–Jul 1944 – Bde HQ ceased to command its units, and became HQ Residue Concentration Area, re: Invasion of Europe. It reverted to normal rôle 18 Jul 1944. Royal Corps of Signals and WRNS worked with II Canadian Corps of Signals in the tunnels under DC. Sep 1944 – Bde HQ moved to Burgoyne Bks, Shorncliffe.

Oct 1943 – 182 & 192 Field Ambulance, 32 FDS (Field Dressing Station).

Oct 1943–Oct 1944 **2/7th Bn, The Warwickshire Regt** (1 coy) *WO166/10800*

Feb–Apr 1944 **9th Bn, Royal Worcestershire Regt** (1 coy) *WO166/14408*

Feb 1944 – there was a US unit (120 AAA Bn, with c100 men) in Dover at this time, with HQ at the Citadel, connected to GOR (Gun Ops Room in Dover Castle), and under command AADC, Dover (OC 173 HAA Regt). *(Operation 'Crossbow'?)*

Mar–Jun 1944 **HQ II Canadian Corps** *WO166/14408*

Based at Old Park Barracks, but moved to the Castle as part of *'Overlord'* Cover Plan *WO166/14408*

Apr 1944 **3 Canadian SW Sec** (I Canadian Army) *WO166/14408*

Sep–Oct 1944 **HQ 183 Inf Bde** [from Old Park Bks] *WO166/14356*

Oct 1944 **Advance Party RE; Met Office** [The Keep] *WO166/14408*

Oct 1944 – Intensive troop movements, and major re-organization of Home Forces. Dover was a busy port of embarkation for reinforcements of men, munitions and machinery.

Constable's Tower was used as an Officers' Mess in World War II. Became the residence of GOC Home Counties in 1946.

Nov 1944–Mar 1945 **832 Pioneer Coy** *WO166/14192*

Jan–Dec 1945 **HQ Garrison Engineer RE** (Dover East) *WO166/16366*

Also at W/H and Kearsney. Moved to Archcliffe, under DCRE

Mar 1945– **234 Pioneer Coy, det RMP** *WO166/16366,17583*

Mar 1945 **HQ 540 Coast Regt, RA** *WO166/16366*

Mar 1945–Jun 1946 **HQ E Kent Sub-District** (Keep) *WO166/16559*

Apr–Nov 1945 **Kent Comd Coast Artillery, and CA Plotting Room** *WO166/16366*

Jun 1945–Oct 1951 {**4th Coast Trg. Regt** *absorbed* 540 Coast Regt RA, & *became:*
47 Coast Regt RA, Apr 1947} *WO166/16366WO166/305/54*

at Nov 1945 **HQ Dover Harbour 'District', CA** *WO166/16366*

HQ & District Establishments SE Ports, CA *WO166/16366*

135 Heavy AA Regt, RA (466, 467 & 478 Btys) *WO166/16366*

110 (Indep) Laundry Unit (Northfall Meadows) *WO166/16366*

Jun 1948–1956 **HQ & District Establishments RA, Defended Ports** *WO166/16366*

HQ SE Comd

–Jun 1946 **E Kent Group, ATS** (att 71 AA Bde) *WO166/16366*

Winston Churchill inspecting guard of honour, 1946.
It will be noticed that an epaulette is missing - this was later refitted!
courtesy of Daily Graphic (The Times)/Dover Museum (d00680)

Gun salute for the accession of HM Queen Elizabeth II, 1952
courtesy of the Kent Messenger Group

det RMP, RAMC

1945 – there was a detachment of RMP as Dover Castle had detention facilities for prisoners from other regiments in the area. The underground hospital (Annexe) was still used for families for some years after the war - ante-natal clinics, innoculations, etc.

Nov 1945–Jan 1946 **Holding Unit RA** [was 519 Coast Regt, RA]

Feb–Jun 1946 **6th Bn, The Royal Berkshire Regt** [& 1st Bn, May 1946]

6th Bn (TA) arrived in Dover, to await arrival of the remnants of the 1st Bn from Burma, their numbers reduced by war casualties, demob, etc to 2 officers and 18 ORs, after four years in the Far East, and then quarantined on board by smallpox – known as 'The little Bn'. Bns amalgamated in the Castle, and went out as 1st Bn to BAOR in June.

Spring 1946 **HQ Kent Sub-division of SE District** *Dover Exp*

Aug 1946 The Installation of Sir Winston Churchill as Lord Warden and Constable of Dover Castle. He had been appointed in Sep 1941, but was not installed until after the war. A guard of honour was provided by 4th Coast Training Regt, RA.

May 1948–1956 **223 Indep Maintenance Bty** (East Cliff)

End May 1948–1955/?1958 – Ordnance Survey Triangulation Station established on the roof of the Keep. Royal Observer Corps did four exercises a year there.

Jan–Jun 1951 **1st Bn, The Royal Norfolk Regt** *(left for Korea)* *Dover Exp,Gen Mans*

1951 - Although the Bn was technically stationed in the Castle, most of the troops were away training for Korea at the Stamford Training Area, and large numbers of Z reservists were called up for re-training.

Jun–Oct 1951 **1st Bn, The Border Regt** *(left for Suez)* *Reg/Sec*

Oct 1951–Oct 1952 *[Castle empty of troops - Korea]* *Dover Express*

On 7th Feb, 1952 – Salute was fired from Dover Castle by 72 LAA Regt, RA (the town's only garrison regt at the time), on the occasion of the death of King George VI – 56 minute–guns, equivalent to the age of the King. Also for the accession of HM Queen Elizabeth II, a 41–gun salute on 15th Feb. *Dover Express*

Oct 1952–Sep 1953 **1st Bn, The Royal Inniskilling Fusiliers** *Dover Express*

On leave until Jan 1953; on flood relief in Norfolk, Feb 1953. Left for Kenya, Sep.

Mar 1953–1955 **HQ 29 Bde** – moved to Old Park Bks. *Gen Mans*

Sep 1953–Jul 1955 *[Castle empty of troops - Kenya/Mau Mau]*

Jul 1955–Aug 1957 **1st Bn, The York & Lancaster Regt**

The advance party arrived July, the main body in August, 1955. Aug-Dec 1956 – Bn in Suez.

Nov-Dec 1956 – Hungarian Refugees were housed in the Castle at this time.

June 1957 – new Colours were presented at Crabble Cricket Ground, and the old Colours laid up the following day in St Mary-in-the-Castle, the Garrison church – the chaplain saying: '...greatly honoured by this solemn trust, and the Colours will repose in this Ancient Church as long as the Regiment so desires' *(Reg/Mag)*. The Bn was popular in Dover – 'one of the friendliest, best–behaved battalions ever to have served in our garrison.' *(The Mayor)* *Dover Express*

1956 – Coast Artillery disbanded.

Sep/Oct 1957–Feb 1958 **1st Bn, The Buffs** *Reg/Sec*

Advance party of 110 arrived in September, and a somewhat depleted Bn in October, after two years in Germany. They experienced a very severe cold winter. There was no central heating – large log fires were kept permanently burning in the Mess ante–rooms, but everywhere else was freezing. The Bn's previous recent stays in Dover had been in Old Park Barracks – the Castle was regarded as 'more august' surroundings, but rather less comfortable! New drafts arrived from the regimental Depôt, as well as from the Royal Fusiliers, the East Surreys and the Royal Sussex Depôts, to rebuild the Bn. Intensive training and being issued with tropical equipment for Aden seemed incongruous in the snow in January! Great emphasis was placed on physical fitness, and every Friday afternoon a 5–mile Bn cross–country run along the cliff tops was organised, with the carrot of a 48–hour weekend pass for those who came in before the very fit CO! 'A' Coy, No 3 Platoon's quarters were underground in the old Field Dressing Station under the Officers' Mess – 'although their quarters resemble a cross between a submarine and the late Goodge Street Deep Shelter of happy or unhappy memories, they surface frequently for fresh air and exercise, and are fit in spite of a troglodyte existence'. On leaving: 'Our stay in the Castle has been a happy one and we shall be sorry to leave. Once one had unravelled the labyrinth of passages and tunnels, and leg muscles had developed sufficiently to deal with the hills, life became pleasant, and of course to be in Kent with the opportunity for many of getting home, offset any other disadvantages. All too soon will we sweat up rocky mountain sides in a temperature well in the hundreds with a 30lb tripod on our backs. Under these circumstances we shall be longing to be back in the inclemencies of an English winter'. *'The Dragon' (Regt Mag)*

Apr–Oct 1958 **1st Bn, The Queen's Own Cameron Highlanders**

Advance party arrived March, and the Bn was then away on leave, followed by training at Stanford in Norfolk until mid–July. Described as 'our romantic but exceedingly weather-beaten Castle'. On returning from the heat of Aden: 'very little in the way of weather escapes it *(the Castle)*; hail descended on Muster Parade, biting winds whipped round us as we climbed up to meals, and icy draughts followed us down the strange tunnels and passages we were discovering as short cuts'. The QM's staff complained – 'Dover Castle is not the barracks one would choose; the

Queen's Own Cameron Highlanders - guard of honour
courtesy of Queen's Own Cameron Highlanders, 79th News

Queen's Own Cameron Highlanders - dancing display
courtesy of Queen's Own Cameron Highlanders, 79th News

QM stores are dank, dismal dungeons, suitable for growing mushrooms. The traditional light-springing footsteps are inclined to lag somewhat on the last stages of the one-in-four ascent to the QM Office'. On 26th July, the regt held their Lucknow Centenary Reunion parade in the Castle. *79th Regt News*

Oct 1958 – Bn moved to Connaught Barracks. Maj Gen Willow Turner, the General resident in Constable's Tower, was the local territorial district commander (GOC Home Counties District). The Bn resident in the Castle was not in his command except for 'housekeeping' (part of 3 Div, with HQ in Colchester). He deemed the huts outside the Castle unfit for occupation, so they were demolished, and the Castle Barracks were then too small for an Infantry Battalion.

The Royal Navy also moved out of the Casemates in 1958. Dumpy level was taken over by the Home Office and modernised as an alternative Regional (South Eastern) Seat of Government in the event of nuclear war. In 1988, it was abandoned, though not declassified until 1992.

1959–1961 **REME Workshop and RAOC, and Garrison Works Engineer** *Gen Turner*

No troops were quartered in the Castle after 1958, but, 'as a result of local pressure and for the good of community relationships, a small quarter-guard or piquet (picket) continued at Canon's Gate, found from the battalion at Connaught Barracks, until c1961. This was quite a strain on manpower, not popular with the Jocks, and was not continued by the relieving Bn in Connaught Barracks.' *(Gen Sir Peter Hunt, then commanding the Cameron Highlanders).*

The Castle was finally handed over to the civilian authorities, at that time the Ministry of Works (Ancient Monuments Branch), in Feb 1963. It is now in the care of English Heritage.

Appendix A

STATUTES OF DOVER CASTLE

Promulgated in the reign of Henry III, and in due course declared by Sir Stephen de Pencestre, appointed Constable of the Castle at Dover in the year 1267.

I. At sunset the bridge shall be drawn, and the gates shut; afterwards the guard shall be mounted by twenty warders on the Castle walls.

II. Any warder found outside the walls, or otherwise off his guard, shall be put in the Donjon prison, and punished besides in body and goods at the Constable's discretion, since for that watch the Castle was trusted to him, not to be surprised through his default.

III. After the last mount, two sergeants shall turn out of their houses to serve as chief guards. They shall make continual rounds within the Castle to visit the warders on the walls and see that they right loyally keep their watch without going to sleep, by reason that they have the Constable's leave to sleep as much as they like in the daytime.

IV. It is established by ancient rule that if a chief guard discover a warder asleep, he shall take something from him as he lies, or carry away his staff, or cut a piece out of part of his clothes, to witness against him in case the warder should deny having been asleep, and he shall lose his day's wage, viz: jjd. *[2d]*

V. And if it happen that the sergeant will not make such arrest, for pity's sake, or even for life's sake, then he shall be brought before the Constable, and be sentenced to prison *dur et fort*, after which he shall be led to the great gate, in presence of the garrison, and there be expelled the Castle. He shall, besides, lose his wage, and forfeit all his chattels found within the Castle walls.

VI. Either sergeant or warder using vile language shall be brought before the Constable, who shall have the matter considered, and the offence fairly enquired into. He who was in the wrong shall lose his day's pay - if the Constable so wills.

VII. If a sergeant or a warder strike another with the flat hand, he shall be liable to an *amende* as high as vs. *[5/-]*, and shall for the rest be held at the mercy of the court. If he hit with his fist he shall be liable to and *amende* as high as xs. *[10/-]*, and be at the mercy of the court. If a sergeant or warder wound another the fine shall be as high as xvs. *[15/-]*, and the offender shall forfeit his station in the Castle, if the Constable so adjudge.

VIII. Because the Castle is out of common jurisdiction, it is ordained that at every quarter of the year shall the whole garrison be mustered in the presence of the Constable, and any shall then before him be addressed and reprehended who may be accused of any notable crime, which ought of right by Holy Church to be dealt. And if the Constable find himself in any perplexity thereupon, he may take counsel of some Parson of Holy Church who shall advise him what to do in any such case.

IX. There shall be one sergeant and one guard, elected in full garrison assembled, who shall be sworn to leal keeping of that light in Holy Church which is not burning inside the chancel.

X. And because the priests are sworn on their consciences to keep leal *(sic)* watch over the chancel lights, if any one of them knows of the others doing other than they ought, he shall report and accuse them before the Constable; unless indeed they be willing to inflict penance on themselves, and then he may excuse them.

XI. Reliques are appointed to be shown, and, especially such as are of the true Cross, shall be brought out every Friday and placed on the High Altar from the ringing of prime to the end of high mass.

XII. Meantime the reliques shall be open to all who wish to visit them, for the honour of God, and the benefit of the Chapel. One of the Chaplains or a Clerk, vested in a surplice, shall remain by the reliques and may shew and explain them, and pronounce absolution to a person in a dying state who may desire it.

XIII. At all great feasts of the year, that is *(scilicet=to wit)* at the Feasts of our Lord, and our Lady, of S. John, of SS. Peter and Paul, and of All Saints, and such as are double and solemn, shall mass*[1] be sung. And on the vigils shall be grand *seynsey**[2]; and afterwards at the procession and sequence at matins and vespers shall be a Te Deum, Laus Deo, and Gloria in Excelsis.

XIV. At Christmas, Easter, Ascension, Pentecost and Feasts of our Lady, as well as at all chief Festivals, shall all the peals, great and small, be rung; and once all together for the sake of the greater solemnity.

XV. Item, after the same manner it is ordered, that if a knight, a lady, or a chaplain in the said Castle die, the commendation shall be made by all the priests who shall be vested in *'chapes de goer'*.*[3]

XVI. And at the burial, in like manner, of a deacon or sub-deacon shall all the priests attend, similarly vested.

XVII. At the funeral of a sergeant the first Chaplain is to attend in his hood; and the other two in surplices. At the funeral of a watchman the Chaplain is to wear his gown. At the burial of a soldier, his surplice.

XVIII. Every Sunday after high mass, holy bread shall be given in the chancel to all who have attended the festivals, marriages, or sermons during the preceding week.

XIX. The priests are to pray for the recovery of the Holy Land, the success of Christianity, and King and Royal Family, the Barons of the Realm, the Constable and all the Garrison.

XX. The Rector, or one of the Chaplains at this request, after Gospel for the day is to deliver a discourse to all the garrison, or to as many as attend high mass.

XXI. The font, Eucharist, the oil and ointments are to be well guarded, and kept under key by the Rector, who is also to provide a clerk qualified to read and chant daily at matins, mass and vespers.

XXII. When one of the garrison dies his *'obiit'* is to be placed in the Calendar, and high mass said for him on the first anniversary.

Some Statutes from the same period:

After the mass matinal for the watchmen, the Chaplains shall say one for the soldiers, and the clerk is to ring out the bell, so that it may be heard on the high road by any person walking from the town towards the Castle.

During the summer, the first mass matinal is to begin at sun rising, from Easter to the festival of S. Michael. Every evening, during the summer, the bell is to be tolled after the ringing of the curfew bell; and in the winter, between the reveille and the relieving guard, at the break of day.

The Lieutenant-Governor, the Clerk of the Exchequer, the Marshal, the Carpenter, and other artificers, are, at the times appointed, to survey the walls of the Castle, both within and without, and shall order the requisite repairs of all houses and buildings.

The porters at the gate shall not suffer any persons to enter, until they have taken particular notice of them, and if they be strangers they shall not step within the sill of the wicket, but one of the porters is to call the Constable, and in his absence, his Lieutenant; but every person asking admittance is to receive civil treatment. The porters are to attend to these orders under penalty of heavy forfeitures. The gates are never to be left during the day to the care of any persons but the porters, and they are always to have the wicket secured with bolts. After the bridge is drawn up and the great gates shut, they are not to be opened until the rising of the sun.

If the King arrives unexpectedly in the night, the great gates shall not be opened to him, but he shall go to the postern called the King's Gate, towards the north, and there the Constable and those who accompany him, may admit the King and a certain number of his suite. When the King is admitted he has the command, and in the morning, when it is full day, he may admit the remainder of his company.

Translated from the document, in old Norman French, originally in the Surrenden collection of manuscripts.

Notes

*[1] XIII - *Puckle* has ....'shall ('nonné'?) be sung'. I believe this could mean 'none', the 6th canonical hour, meaning the 9th hour of the day, which was c3pm. [i.e. Matins, Lauds, Prime, Terce, Sext, **None**, Vespers, Compline].

*[2] XIII - *Puckle* ....'shall be grand celebration (?)' *(grand seynsy/seynsey)*, I think probably means celebration of holy communion - if 'tous les seyns' is All Saints, 'seynsy' could possibly be French 'sainte' = holy, and can, I believe, refer to holy communion or mass, but this is only a guess.

*[3] XV - ....shall be vested in 'Chapes de goer'. One explanation from Brother Mark, a Capuchin monk in Canterbury, is: 'Chapes de goer' - a war cape. Goer = guerre - war (Latin - guerra); chape = mantle/cape/cloak/cope (Latin - capa/cappa). Hence: 'chapel' = a place for precious relics, originally the sanctuary of St Martin's cloak; and 'chaplain' = protector/custodian of the cloak. So, he suggests, a protective cape to shield the sacrament carried to troops during battle, and could then have come to be a form of ceremonial dress for priests.

Brother Mark compiled the tree of Mediaeval Constables and their Kin, now hanging in the Keep, and is the son of the Rev Stanley Elvins, Rector of St Mary-en-Castro 1949-53.

Appendix B

HENRY REX - Le Roy - Le Veult *CPW/RO1*

Whereas the Castle of Dover whereof the King's Maj^tie^ is very owner in the Right of the Imperiall Crowne of this his Realme is not only a very Honble strong and Defensive Fortresse sett and standing next unto the Sea on the East Parts and Frontiers of this his Realme But alsoe is soe necessary a thing for the Defence and Safeguard of the same that itt may not in any wise bee Lacked or Forborne Wherefore the King Our Sovereigne Lord hath hitherto to his great Costs and Charges Repaired and Sustayned the same And alsoe continually keepeth and maintayneth therein a great number of all soldiers there always keeping watch and ward Furnished sufficiently with Harnesse Artillerie and other Municons of Warr for the Safeguard of this Realm toward and for the continuall sustentacon of which said Castle and Furnitures of the same Our said Sovereigne Lord and his most Noble Progenitors Kings of this Realme have had from tyme out of minde many sundry Revenewes and namely Rents com'only called Castle Wardys due and to be paid by reason of the same Castle of and for divers other Castles Mannores Lordshippes Lands Tenem^ts^ and Hereditaments holden of the King and his said Progenitors (that is to say) some of them holden of the Constablerie of the same Castle and there holden severally of the Honors of Crevecure *(Crêvecoeur)* Hagenett *(?Magminot)* Ffobert *(Fulbert)* and other Hon^bles^ being members of the said Castle of Dover which said Rents called Castle Wardys ben att this present tyme much decayed and deminished by reason and causes under written (that is to say) because that divers of the Mannores Lands and Tenements which were holden of the said Castle been come to the possession of Our said Sovereign Lord in Estates of Inheritance and others have bee given by his Grace or his said Progenitors to divers their Subjects to bee holden by other Services And divers other bee and ---? hereafter shall be in the possession of the King's Maj^tie^ by reason of Wardshipp 'primer seysin' purchase exchaundge or otherwise by guift or any estate of Inheritance whereby some of the said Rents called Castle Wardes by the Laudes of this Realme be and shall be utterly extincted for ever and many other of the same Rents by Longtimes shall be suspended and not due to be paid By occasion whereof the said Castle and the Officers and Soldiers thereof cannot be nor shall be susteyned as heretofore honorably have been - unless that convenient remedy therefore be provided In consideration whereof Our said Sovereign Lord the King is contented and pleased that itt be ordayned and enacted by Authority of this present Parliament that where the Tenants and Owners of the Castle, Mannor^s^ Lands and Tenements which been holden of the said Castle of Dover and lye in many Shoires of this Realme farr distant from the same Castle been bounden by their tenures thereof to pay and yield at the same Castle of Dover the said Rents called Castle Wardes and divers and sundry daies of the yeare to their great costs and charges and upon great penaltyes and forfeitures comonly called in the said Castle of Dover Sursyses. And all and singular those Tenants which now hould or hereafter shall hould any Lands Tenements and Hereditaments by the said Service to pay the said Rents called Castle Wardes shall yield and pay the same Rents from and after the ffeast of St Michael the Archangel next coming to the King our Sovereigne Lord his heirs and successors att the King's Court of Excheq^r^ yearly in the ffeasts of St Symon and Jude - or without ffifteen days next after that ffeast and not att the said Castle of Dover nor to the Constable or other Officer or Minister of the same Castle And bee itt enacted that if any Tenant make default of Payment of such Rent contrary to the forme of this Act then every Tenant so making default of payment shall yield and pay to Our said Sovereigne Lord the King his heirs and successors for every such default the double of his Rent that is to say Twice his Rent then being due to be paid without any other Sursise Penalty or Forfeiture for Non payment thereof And that every of the said Tenants which hold any of their Lands Tenements and Hereditaments by the Service to make repairs or build any house or houses within the said Castle shall doe and performe the same according to theire said Dutys and Tenures Provided allway and bee itt enacted by the Authority aforesaid that dureing all such time as any Lands Tenements and Hereditaments houlden of the said Castle of Dover by Rent of Castle Warde shall bee in the hands or Custody of Our said Sovereigne Lord the King or of his heirs and successors Kings of this Realme by reason of Wardshipps 'primer seyson' or otherwise that by and for all such tyme the same Lands Tenements and Hereditaments and every Tenant and Owner thereof and the Heirs and Successors and Assignes of every of them shall be discharged of the said Rent called Castle Warde against the King and his said Heirs and Successors for ever without any payment thereof for any such tyme to be made or yeilden att any time after that the same Lands Tenements and Hereditaments shall be devested sued or had out or from the King's hands or possession And because that the more ready and undelayed payments hereafter shall be had and made to all Officers Ministers and Soldiers of the said Castle of Dover for the tyme being without any Defalcacon *(?)* abbridgement or restraynt of any of their ffees Stipends Salaries or Wages in any wise to bee made bee itt ordayned and enacted by Authority of this prent Parliament and the Constable of the said Castle of Dover and every of his Successos being Constable of the same Castle shall have as annexed united and appropriated to the same Office from henceforth for ever an Annuall or yearly Rent of One hundred and Threescore Pounds of Lawfull Money to be paid yearly to the same Constable or his Lawfull Deputy or Assignes in the Citty of Canterbury att the Dore of the Co55mon Hall called the Court Hall of the Kings Revenues of the Augmentacons of his Crowne yearly growing and comeing within the County of Kent by the head of the Kings General Receiver for the tyme being of the said Revenues of that County in the ffeasts of St Michael the Archangel the Nativity of Our Lord God the Annunciatõn of Our Lady St Mary and the Nativity of St John Baptist or within three days next ensuing every of the same ffeasts by even porcon yearly to be paid And bee itt further enacted that if the Kings said General Receiver for the tyme being doe not fully pay to the said Constable or his Lawfull Deputy or Assigne the said Annual Rent for One Hundred and Threescore Pounds according to the tenor of this Act before written

Except thereof and to be retayned by the said Receiver onely Eightpence for the making of the Acquittance of every of his payments Then the same Receiver shall forfeit and loose to the said Constable for the tyme being for every such default of Payment thereof soe to be made att any tyme or place of Payment thereof before Lymitted ffive Pounds of Lawfull money ffor which penaltie and all arrerages *(?arrears)* of the said Annual Rent the said Constable shall have his remedy Accon *(?action)* of Debte Scirefacon *(?satisfaction)* to be grounded upon this Act or any other Lawfull Remedy to be pursued against the said Receiver for the tyme being in any Competent Court of the Kings Lawds In which Suite none Esson/Essai? Proteccon or Wager of Lawd shall Lye or be allowed And where our Our said Sovereigne Lord the King by his exceeding great Costs and Charges hath lately Builded and made nye unto the Seas divers Castles Blockhouses Bullworks and other houses and places of great defence with the Lymits of the ffive Portes and their members or betweene the same in the Shires of Kent and Sussex for the Safeguard and Surety of this his Realme and subjects of the same Our said Sovereigne Lord the King willing the same newmade Castles Blockhouses Bullworks and other defensive houses and places to bee well surely and safely kept and fullfilled with such and as many Officers Ministers Soldiers Gunners and other Persons as his Maj[tie] hath ordayned and established and hereafter shall Ordayne and Establish to bee and remaine att and in every or any of them And that every of the same persons shall daily and nightly and from tyme to tyme continually doe his Office and Duty in and att the same without any Extorcon Oppression or other injurie offence or misbehaviour by them or any of them to be done or committed by Sea or by Land to or upon any whatsoever person or persons or to or upon any theire Shipps Boates Goods or Cattles hath Ordayned and enacted by Authority of this present Parliam[t] that the Warden of the said ffive Portes and Constable of the said Castle of Dover which now is and commonly heretofore hath been one person and every of his successors being Warden of the said Portes and his Ltfor the tyme being or either of them shall have full power and authority by virtue of this Act to survey viewe and controll as often as by his discretion he shall think necessary or expedient all and singular Captaines and Keepers and other Head Officers of every of the said new Castles Blockhouses Bullworks and other defensive houses and places and all Soldiers Gunners and other Ministers and Persons of any of them and all the Artilleries Stores and Municons of Warre many of them being and by his Discretion as well shall Examine every of the said Captaines Keepers Officers Soldiers Gunners Ministers and Persons by their Oathes upon a Booke or otherwise as well of such Offences Crymes Misorders Ommissions and Defaults as shall be thought by them necessary to be inserched *(?)* tryed or knowne As alsoe of all excesses wastes imbosilings *(embezzling?)* miskeepings and misusing of the said Artilleries Stores and Municons and shall comand and enjoyne them and every of them by his discretion to make reformacon and redresse therein as by his discretion shall be considered to stand with reason and equity And if the importance or urgency of the Cause or Matter shall soe require the said Constable shall make Relacon and Notification thereof to the Kings Maj[tie] or to his Hon[ble] Counsell And alsoe bee itt enacted that if any of the said Captaines Keepers Officers Soldiers Gunners Ministers or other Persons of any of the said new Castles Blockhouse Bullworks or other Defensive Houses or Places in anywise Resist Contempne Disobey of otherwise Offend against the said Warden of the said ffive Portes for the tyme being in any of the premises Then it shall bee lawfull to the said Warden to comitt every such Offender to Warde into the said Castle of Dover or elsewhere in the said Portos or their members to remaine by the Discretion of the said Warden And of any such person soe once punished shall oftsomes offend in any of the premises against the said Warden then every such Offender shall theretofore forfeite and Loose att the Kings pleasure his said Office Rooms and Service And shall further bee punished att the pleasure of Our said Sovereigne Lord the King Provided allway and bee it enacted that the said General Receiver may keepe and retayne in his hands soe much of the Kings Revenues as shall amount for satisfaccon of the said yearely Rent to bee paid as is aforesaid And shall alsoe as well bee discharged and allowed for the payment thereof as of and for such costs and expenses as he shall sustayne by Occasion of the same as by the Discretion of the Chancellor and Ministers of the said Court of Augmentacon shall bee thought reasonable upon the Accompt of the said General Receiver

32 HVIII - 1540/41

Appendix C

Ordenances made by King Henry VIII, c.1541 - (Extracts) *EK/CPW/RO1*

Ordenances and Statutes Devised by the King's most Excellent Majestie for the Government and Surety of his Highness Castles Bullworks and other ffortresses appointed to the Survey of the Lord Warden of the Cinque Ports.

1. First itt is Ordered that the Captaine be resident continually upon his Office and never to Lye out of the hould above Eight Nights in any one month without the Special Lycense of the Kings Maj[tie] upon paine to forfeit for the First tyme a Months wages, for the Second tyme three Months wages, for the third tyme to Loose his Office, and further to be punished att the Kings Highness pleasure. — Captains to be resident

2. Item that the Deputy never Lye out of the Houlde above fower nights in any one month and that to be att the discretion and by the Lycense of the Captaine, and also when the same Captaine shall be present himselfe in the house, soe as the Captain and the Deputy be never out of the houlde att one tyme upon paine for the first time...*(see above* 1. *for first and second times)* ... for the third time to Loose his Rooms with imprisonment at the Kings Highness pleasure. — Lieutenants to be resident

3. Item that none of the Porters lye out of their hould three nights in any one month...*(to alternate if there are two porters, or find a replacement within the garrison if one - punishments as at 2).* — Porters to be resident

4. Item that everyday Captain of the Gunners and Soldiers doe warde besides the Porters as the numbers will beare the certainty to be determined by the Lord Warden of the Cinque Ports, and if any shall have reasonable cause of excuse, by sickness absence or otherwise, then he to find another to warde for him, upon paine for every such default to forfeit double wages to him which by the commendment of the Captaine shall supply his place. — Warding daily

5. Item that every night two of the Gunners and Soldiers where the number will beare itt doe watch as their courses shall happen, the same watch to be nightly sett at one houre convenient by the Captaine or the Deputy, and if any of the Watch shall att any tyme be found sleeping, or shall goe from his place and circuit appointed shall for every such default of sleeping forfeit for the first tyme 2 days' wages, for the second a fortnight's wages, for the third to Loose his Rooms, and for the Departure he shall loose his Rooms with further imprisonment att the King's Highnes pleasure. — Watch by night

6. ....(Gate shutt and opene)

7. ....(Strangers borne forbidden to enter)

8. ....(Bribery and exaccon *(?exaction)* of Shippes passing by etc. forbidden)

9. ....that neither the Captaine Deputy Porter nor any of the Soldiers or Gunners shall hunt course or otherwise take or kill (except hee or they have sufficient warrant for the same) any manner of Deere, Hares or Coneys within any fforest Chases, Parkes Warrens or other Grounds where any Deeres, Hares or Coneys bee kept and nourished, nor shall in noe place Hawke or otherwise destroy or take with any kind of Cynne *(?Gin trap)* Snare or other Trinkett nor Shoote with Crossbow or Gunne at any Hawkes ffesants Partriches or Shoveleres *(?duck)* upon paine to forfeit his or theire Office for any such Offences, and to suffer imprisonment at the King's Will — Hunting forbidden

10. Item that every of the said Garrison furnish himselfe with convenient Weapons, as a Dagger and a Sworde with an Halbert or a Bill, and also Harnis and every Gunner alsoe to have a Handgunne or a Hagbush *(an early gun - Harquebus?)* at his owne Charge between this and Midsomer...*(if not to forfeit three days' pay for every day without!)* — Weapons for Garrison

11. ....(Shooting of Ordnance or Palsing *(?)* of Shipps)

12. ....(Suites against any of the Garrison to the Lord Warden)

13. ....(Payment by the Guarrison for Victualls before they receive wages)

14. ....(Lycence of Soldiers to be absent - not more than two at once and for no more than 3 days in a month)

15. ....(Allowances of Powder - for exercising and halseing *(?)* of Shipps, Trying of Peeres at the discretion of the Lord Warden

16. ....(Every of the Captaines, Deputies, Porters and Gunners to have their Bills signed by the King's Majestie)

17. ....(Musters of the Guarrison quarterly)

18. ....(Inventories of Municion)

19. ....(Departure etc., putting away of Soldiers)

20. ....(Certificate of death of any of the Guarrison to the Lord Warden)

21. ....(Affray by any of the Guarrison - to lose his Rooms, with imprisonment at Will)

22. ....(How the Guarrison Soldiers are punished for violacion of their Oathes or other Crimes)

Appendix D

Infantry regiments – with amalgamations and disbandments, from 1881

Number until 1881	*Named as at 1947*	*Later designations * = a 'large' regt, also **Bold = present designation*
1st	**The Royal Scots (The Royal Regt)**	
2nd	The Queen's Royal Regt (Royal West Surrey Regt,1881) – *with* 31st/70th (East Surrey) = Queen's Royal Surrey Regt, 1959 – *with* Queen's Own Buffs, Royal Sussex & Middlessex = 1st Bn,*The Queen'.Regt, 1966 (4th Bn disb, 1970) – *with* Royal Hampshire = ****The Princess of Wales's Royal Regt, 1992**	
3rd	The Buffs (Royal East Kent Regt, 1935) – with 50th/97th (Royal West Kent) = The Queen's Own Buffs, 1961 – *with* Queen's Royal Surrey, Royal Sussex & Middlessex = 2nd Bn,The Queen's Regt, 1966 (4th Bn disb, 1970) – *with* Royal Hampshire =****The Princess of Wales's Royal Regt, 1992**	
4th	The King's Own Royal Regt (Lancaster) – *with* 34th/55th (Border) = **The King's Own Royal Border Regt. 1959**	
5th	The Northumberland Fusiliers (Royal, 1935) – *with* 6th, 7th & 20th = ***The Royal Regt of Fusiliers, 1968** (reduced to 3 Bns, 1969)	
6th	The Royal Warwickshire Regt (Fusiliers, 1963) – *with* 5th, 7th & 20th = ***The Royal Regt of Fusiliers, 1968** (reduced to 3 Bns, 1969)	
7th	The Royal Fusiliers (City of London Regt) – *with* 5th, 6th & 20th = ***The Royal Regt of Fusiliers, 1968** (reduced to 3 Bns, 1969)	
8th	The King's Regt (Liverpool) – *with* 63rd/96th (Manchester) = King's (Manchester & Liverpool), 1958; **The King's Regt, 1968**	
9th	The Royal Norfolk Regt – *with* 12th (The Suffolk Regt) = 1st East Anglian (Royal Norfolk & Suffolk), 1959 – *with* 2nd East Anglian (10th & 48th/58th), 3rd East Anglian (16th & 44th/56th) & 17th (Royal Leicestershire) = ***The Royal Anglian Regt, 1964** (reduced to3 Bns, 1970)	
10th	The Royal Lincolnshire Regt – *with* 48th/58th (Northamptonshire) = 2nd East Anglian (Duchess of Gloucester's Own), 1960 – *with* 1st & 3rd East Anglian &17th (Royal Leicestershire) = ***The Royal Anglian Regt, 1964** (4th Bn disb, 1970)	
11th	The Devonshire Regt – *with* 39th/54th (Dorset) = **The Devonshire and Dorset Regt, 1958**	
12th	The Suffolk Regt – *with* 9th (The Royal Norfolk) = 1st East Anglian (Royal Norfolk & Suffolk), 1959 – *with* 2nd & 3rd East Anglian & 17th (Royal Leicestershire) = ***The Royal Anglian Regt, 1964** (reduced to 3 Bns 1970)	
13th	The Somerset Light Infantry (Prince Albert's) – *with* 32nd/46th (Duke of Cornwall's LI) = Somerset & Cornwall LI, 1959 – *with* King's Own Yorkshire LI, King's Shropshire LI & Durham LI = ***The Light Infantry, 1968** (4th Bn disb, 1968)	
14th	The West Yorkshire Regt (The Prince of Wales's Own) } *with*	
15th	The East Yorkshire Regt (The Duke of York's Own) } = **The Prince of Wales's Own Regt of Yorkshire, 1958**	
16th	The Bedfordshire (& Hertfordshire Regt, 1919) – *with* 44th/56th (Essex) = 3rd East Anglian(16th/44th), 1958 – *with* 1st & 2nd East Anglian & Royal Leicestershire = ***The Royal Anglian Regt, 1964** (4th Bn disb, 1970)	
17th	The Royal Leicestershire Regt – *with* 1st, 2nd & 3rd East Anglian = ***The Royal Anglian Regt, 1964** (4th Bn disb, 1970)	
18th	The Royal Irish Regt (disbanded 1922)	
19th	**The Green Howards (Alexandra, Princess of Wales's Own Yorkshire Regt)**	

20th The Lancashire Fusiliers – *with* 5th, 6th & 7th = ***The Royal Regt of Fusiliers, 1968** (reduced to3 Bns, 1969)

21st The Royal Scots Fusiliers – *with* 71st/74th (Highland Light Infantry) = **The Royal Highland Fusiliers, 1959**

22nd **The Cheshire Regt**

23rd **The Royal Welch Fusiliers**

24th The South Wales Borderers – *with* 41st/69th (Welch, 1881) = **The Royal Regt of Wales (24th/41st Foot), 1969**

25th **The King's Own Scottish Borderers**

[1st – 25th had two battalions each until 1948]

26th/90th (1st & 2nd Bns), The Cameronians (Scottish Rifles), 1881 (disbanded 1968)

27th/108th (1st & 2nd Bns) The Royal Inniskilling Fusiliers, 1881 – *with* (83rd and 87th), =*The Royal Irish Rangers, 1968 (3rd Bn disb, 1970) – *with* The Ulster Defence Regt =****The Royal Irish Regiment (27th (Inniskilling), 83rd & 87th, & the Ulster Defence Regt), 1992**

28th/61st (1st (North) & 2nd (South) Bns), The Gloucestershire Regt, 1881 – *with* (49th/66th & 62nd/99th) = ***The Royal Gloucestershire, Berkshire & Wiltshire Regt, 1994**

29th/36th (1st & 2nd Bns), The Worcestershire Regt, 1881 – *with* 45th/95th (Sherwood Foresters = **The Worcestershire & Sherwood Foresters Regt (29th/45th Foot), 1970**

30th/59th (1st & 2nd Bns), The East Lancashire Regt, 1881 – *with* 40th/82nd (South Lancashire) = The Lancashire Regt (Prince of Wales's Volunteers), 1958 – *with* 47th/81st (Loyals) = **The Queen's Lancashire Regt, 1970**

31st/70th (1st & 2nd Bns), The East Surrey Regt, 1881 – *with* 2nd, (Queen's Royal (West Surrey)) = Queen's Royal Surrey Regt,1959 – *with* Queen's Own Buffs, Royal Sussex & Middlesex = *The Queen's Regt, 1966 (4th Bn disb, 1970) – *with* Royal Hampshire = **The **Princess of Wales's Royal Regt, 1992**

32nd/46th (1st & 2nd Bns), The Duke of Cornwall's Light Infantry (LI), 1881 – *with* 13th (Somerset LI) = Somerset & Cornwall LI, 1959 = ***The Light Infantry, 1968** (4th Bn disb, 1968)

33rd/76th (1st & 2nd Bns), The Duke of Wellington's (West Riding Regt), 1881 = **The Duke of Wellington's Regt (West Riding), 1920**

34th/55th (1st & 2nd Bns), The Border Regt, 1881 – *with* 4th (King's Own) = **The King's Own Royal Border Regt, 1959**

35th/107th (1st & 2nd Bns), The Royal Sussex Regt, 1881 – *with* Queen's Royal Surrey, Queen's Own Buffs & Middlesex = *The Queen's Regt, 1966, (4th Bn disb, 1970) – *with* Royal Hampshire = ****The Princess of Wales's Royal Regt, 1992**

36th *2nd Bn, The Worcestershire Regt (see* 29th*)*

37th/67th (1st & 2nd Bns), The Hampshire Regt, 1881,(Royal, 1946) – *with* *The Queen's Regt = ****The Princess of Wales's Royal Regt, 1992**

38th/80th (1st & 2nd Bns), The South Staffordshire Regt, 1881 – *with* 64th/98th (North Staffordshire) = **The Staffordshire Regt (Prince of Wales's), 1959**

39th/54th (1st & 2nd Bns), The Dorset Regt, 1881 – *with* 11th (Devonshire) = **The Devonshire & Dorset Regt, 1958**

40th/82nd (1st & 2nd Bns), The South Lancashire Regt (The Prince of Wales's Volunteers), 1881 – *with* 30th/59th = The Lancashire Regt, 1958 – *with* 47th/81st (Loyal North Lancashire = **The Queen's Lancashire Regt. 1970**

41st/69th (1st & 2nd Bns), The Welch Regt, 1881 – *with* 24th (South Wales Borderers) = **The Royal Regt of Wales (24th/41st), 1969**

42nd/73rd (1st & 2nd Bns), The Black Watch (Royal Highlanders), 1881;
The Black Watch (Royal Highland Regt), 1934

43rd (Monmouthshire LI) – *with* 52nd (Oxfordshire LI) = The Oxfordshire LI, 1881; The Oxfordshire & Buckinghamshire Light Infantry, 1908 – 1st Green Jackets (43rd & 52nd),1958 – *with* 2nd Green Jackets (King's Royal Rifle Corps) & 3rd Green Jackets (The Rifle Brigade)
= ***The Royal Green Jackets, 1966**

44th/56th (1st & 2nd Bns), The Essex Regt, 1881 – *with* 16th (The Bedfordshire & Hertfordshire Regt) = 3rd East Anglian (16th/44th) 1958 – *with* 1st & 2nd East Anglian & Royal Leicestershire
= ***The Royal Anglian Regt, 1964** (4th Bn disb, 1970)

45th/95th (1st & 2nd Bns), The Sherwood Foresters, 1881 – *with* 29th/36th (Worcestershire)
= **The Worcestershire & Sherwood Foresters Regt (29th/45th), 1970**

46th *2nd Bn, The Duke of Cornwall's Light Infantry,* (*see* 32nd)

47th/81st (1st & 2nd Bns), The Loyal (North Lancashire) Regt, 1881 – *with* 30th/59th & 40th/82nd (Lancashire) = **The Queen's Lancashire Regt, 1970**

48th/58th (1st & 2nd Bns), The Northamptonshire Regt, 1881 – *with* 10th (Royal Lincolnshire) = 2nd East Anglian (Duchess of Gloucester's Own), 1960 – *with* 1st & 3rd East Anglian& Royal Leicestershire
= ***The Royal Anglian Regt, 1964**

49th/66th (1st & 2nd Bns), The Royal Berkshire Regt (Princess Charlotte of Wales's), 1881 – *with* 62nd/99th (Wiltshire) = The Duke of Edinburgh's Royal Regt, 1959 – *with* The Gloucestershire Regt (28th/71st)
= ***The Royal Gloucestershire, Berkshire & Wiltshire Regt, 1994**

50th/97th (1st & 2nd Bns), The Queen's Own Royal West Kent Regt, 1881 – *with* 3rd (Buffs) = The Queen's Own Buffs, 1961 – *with* Queen's Royal Surrey, Royal Sussex & Middlesex = *The Queen's Regt. 1966 – *with* Royal Hampshire
= ****The Princess of Wales's Royal Regt, 1992**

51st/105th (1st & 2nd Bns), The King's Own Yorkshire LI, 1881 – *with* Somerset & Cornwall LI (13th & 32nd/54th), King's Shropshire LI (53rd/85th) & Durham LI (68th/106th)
= ***The Light Infantry, 1968** (4th Bn disb, 1968)

52nd *2nd Bn, The Oxfordshire & Buckinghamshire Light Infantry* (*see* 43rd)

53rd/85th (1st & 2nd Bns), The King's Shropshire LI, 1881 –*with* 13th, 32nd/46th & 51st/105th LI
= ***The Light Infantry, 1968** (4th Bn disb, 1968)

54th *2nd Bn, The Dorset Regt* (*see* 39th)

55th *2nd Bn, The Border Regt* (*see* 34th)

56th *2nd Bn, The Essex Regt* (*see* 44th)

57th/77th (1st & 2nd Bns), The Middlesex Regt (Duke of Cambridge's Own), 1881 – *with* Queen's Royal Surrey, Queen's Own Buffs & Royal Sussex = *The Queen's Regt, 1966 –*with* Royal Hampshire
= ****The Princess of Wales's Royal Regt, 1992**

58th *2nd Bn, The Northamptonshire Regt* (*see* 48th)

59th *2nd Bn, The East Lancashire Regt* (*see* 30th)

60th The King's Royal Rifle Corps – 2nd Green Jackets (The King's Royal Rifle Corps), 1958 – *with* 1st & 3rd Green Jackets
= ***The Royal Green Jackets, 1968**

61st *2nd Bn, The Gloucestershire Regt* (*see* 28th)

62nd/99th (1st & 2nd Bns) The Wiltshire Regt, 1881 – *with* 49th/66th (Royal Berkshire) = The Duke of Edinburgh's Royal Regt, 1959 – *with* The Gloucestershire Regt
= ***The Royal Gloucestershire, Berkshire & Wiltshire Regt, 1994**

63rd/96th (1st & 2nd Bns), The Manchester Regt, 1881 – *with* 8th (King's Liverpool) = The King's Regt (Manchester & Liverpool), 1958; **= The King's Regiment, 1968**

64th/98th (1st & 2nd Bns), The North Staffordshire Regt (The Prince of Wales's), 1881 – *with* 38th/80th = **The Staffordshire Regt, (The Prince of Wales's), 1959**

65th/84th (1st & 2nd Bns) The York & Lancaster Regt, 1881 (disbanded 1968)

66th *2nd Bn, The Royal Berkshire Regt (Princess Charlotte of Wales's)* (*see* 49th)

67th *2nd Bn, The Royal Hampshire Regt* (*see* 37th)

68th/106th (1st & 2nd Bns) The Durham Light Infantry, 1881; ***The Light Infantry, 1968** (disbanded as 4th Bn)

69th *2nd Bn, The Welch Regt* (*see* 41st)

70th *2nd Bn, The East Surrey Regt* (*see* 31st)

71st/74th (1st & 2nd Bns), The Highland LI (City of Glasgow Regt), 1881 – *with* 21st (Royal Scots Fusiliers) = **The Royal Highland Fusiliers, 1959**

72nd/78th (1st & 2nd Bns), The Seaforth Highlanders, 1881 – *with* 79th (Queen's Own Cameron Highlanders) = The Queen's Own Highlanders, 1961 – *with* The Gordon Highlanders (75th/92nd) = ***The Highlanders (Seaforth, Gordon & Cameron), 1994**

73rd *2nd Bn, The Black Watch* (*see* 42nd)

74th *2nd Bn, The Highland Light Infantry* (*see* 71st)

75th/92nd (1st & 2nd Bns), The Gordon Highlanders, 1881 – *with* The Queen's Own Highlanders (72nd/78th & 79th) = ***The Highlanders (Seaforth, Gordon & Cameron), 1994**

76th *2nd Bn, The Duke of Wellington's Regt (West Riding)* (*see* 33rd)

77th *2nd Bn, The Middlesex Regt* (*see* 57th)

78th 2nd Bn, The Seaforth Highlanders (*see* 72nd)

79th The Queen's Own Cameron Highlanders *(two Bns, 1897)* – *with* 72nd/78th (The Seaforth Highlanders) = The Queen's Own Highlanders, 1961 – *with* The Gordon Highlanders **= *The Highlanders (Seaforth, Gordon & Cameron), 1994**

80th *2nd Bn, The South Staffordshire Regt* (*see* 38th)

81st *2nd Bn, The Loyal Regt (North Lancashire)* (*see* 47th)

82nd *2nd Bn, The South Lancashire Regt (The Prince of Wales's Volunteers)* (*see* 40th)

83rd/86th (1st & 2nd Bns), The Royal Irish Rifles, 1881 (The Royal Ulster Rifles, 1921) – *with* 27th/108th (Royal Inniskilling Fusiliers)& 87th/89th (Royal Irish Fusiliers) = *The Royal Irish Rangers (27th (Inniskilling), 83rd & 87th), 1968 (3rd Bn disb. 1970) – *with* The UlsterDefence Regt **= **The Royal Irish Regt (27th (Inniskilling), 83rd & 87th, & The Ulster Defence Regt), 1992**

84th *2nd Bn, The York & Lancaster Regt* (*see* 65th)

85th *2nd Bn, The King's Shropshire Light Infantry* (*see* 53rd)

86th *2nd Bn, The Royal Ulster Rifles* (*see* 83rd)

87th/89th (1st & 2nd Bns), The Royal Irish Fusiliers (Princess Victoria's), 1881 – *with* 27th/108th (Royal Inniskilling Fusiliers) & 83rd/86th (Royal Ulster Rifles) (disb. as 3rd Bn, 1970) = *The Royal Irish Rangers (27th (Inniskilling), 83rd & 87th), 1968– *with* The Ulster Defence Regt = ****The Royal Irish Regt (27th (Inniskilling), 83rd & 87th, &The Ulster Defence Regt), 1992**

88th/94th (1st & 2nd Bns) The Connaught Rangers, 1881 *(disbanded 1922)*

89th *2nd Bn, The Royal Irish Fusiliers (Princess Victoria's)* (*see* 87th)

90th *2nd Bn, The Cameronians (Scottish Rifles)* (*see* 26th)

91st/93rd (1st & 2nd Bns), Princess Louise's The Argyll & Sutherland Highlanders, 1881, **= The Argyll & Sutherland Highlanders (Princess Louise's), 1920**

92nd *2nd Bn, The Gordon Highlanders (see* 75th*)*
93rd *2nd Bn, The Argyll & Sutherland Highlanders (Princess Louise's) (see* 91st*)*
94th *2nd Bn, The Connaught Rangers (see* 88th*)*
95th *2nd Bn, The Sherwood Foresters (see* 45th*)*
96th *2nd Bn, The Manchester Regt (see* 63rd*)*
97th *2nd Bn, The Queen's Own Royal West Kent Regt (see* 50th*)*
98th *2nd Bn, The North Staffordshire Regt (see* 64th*)*
99th *2nd Bn, The Wiltshire Regt (Duke of Edinburgh's) (see* 62nd*)*
100th/109th (1st & 2nd Bns), The Prince of Wales's Leinster Regt (Royal Canadians), 1881 (disbanded 1922)
101st/104th (1st & 2nd Bns), The Royal Munster Fusiliers, 1881 (disbanded 1922*)*
102nd/103rd (1st & 2nd Bns), The Royal Dublin Fusiliers, 1881 (disbanded 1922)
103rd *2nd Bn, The Royal Dublin Fusiliers (see* 102nd*)*
104th *2nd Bn, The Royal Munster Fusiliers (see*101st*)*
105th *2nd Bn, The King's Own Yorkshire Light Infantry (see* 51st*)*
106th *2nd Bn, The Durham Light Infantry (see* 68th*)*
107th *2nd Bn, The Royal Sussex Regt (see* 35th*)*
108th *2nd Bn, The Royal Iniskilling Fusiliers (see* 27th*)*
109th *2nd Bn, The Prince of Wales's Leinster Regt (Royal Canadians) (see* 100th*)*
previously 95th – 1816, taken out of the line and renamed The Rifle Brigade (Prince Consort's Own)(4 Bns – 3rd Green Jackets (The Rifle Brigade), 1958 – *with* 1st & 2nd Green Jackets
= *The Royal Green Jackets, 1966

Composition of Large Regiments (by original numbers)

The Princess of Wales's Royal Regt (1992)
2nd/31st/70th (Queen's Royal Surrey)
3rd/50th/97th (Queen's Own Buffs)
35th/107th (Royal Sussex)
57th/77th (Middlesex)
37th/67th (Hampshire)

The Royal Regt of Fusiliers (1968)
5th (Royal Northumberland Fusiliers)
6th (Royal Warwickshire Fusiliers),
7th (Royal Fusiliers)
20th (Lancashire Fusiliers)

The Royal Anglian Regt (1964)
9th (Royal Norfolk)
12th (Suffolk)
10th (Royal Lincolnshire)
48th/58th (Northamptonshire)
16th (Bedfordshire & Hertfordshire)
44th/56th (Essex)
17th (Royal Leicestershire)

The Light Infantry (1968)
13th/32nd/46th (Somerset & Cornwall LI)
51st/105th (King's Own Yorkshire LI)
53rd/85th (Shropshire LI)
68th/106th (Durham LI)

The Royal Irish Regiment (1992)
27th/108th (Royal Inniskilling Fusiliers)
83rd/86th (Royal Ulster Rifles)
87th/89th (Royal Irish Fusiliers)
The Ulster Defence Regt

The Royal Gloucestershire Berkshire & Wiltshire Regt (1994)
28th/61st (Gloucestershire)
49th/66th (Royal Berkshire)
62nd/99th (Wiltshire)(The Duke of Edinburgh's Royal Regt)

The Highlanders (Seaforth, Gordon & Cameron) (1994)
72nd/78th (The Seaforth Highlanders)
75th/92n (The Gordon Highlanders),
79th (The Queen's Own Cameron Highlanders)

The Royal Green Jackets (1966)
43rd/52nd (Oxfordshire LI (& Bucks, 1908))
60th (King's Royal Rifle Corps),
The Rifle Brigade

BIBLIOGRAPHY and REFERENCES

Some references used *(abbreviations used in text are in small italics)*:

Akers – Akers, Maj Gen C S, *The Fortifications of Dover*, RE Papers (1886)

Arch Cant – Archaeologia Cantiana

Arnold – Arnold, Col B E, TD, *Conflict across the Strait*, Crabwell, Dover (1982) [and personal memories]

Ascoli – Ascoli, David, *A Companion to the British Army*, 1660-1983, Harrap, London (1983)

Barker – Barker, A J, *Dunkirk, The Great Escape*, Dent (1977)

B-J – Bavington-Jones, John, *Annals of Dover*, Dover (1916)

Blaxland – Blaxland, Gregory, *South-East Britain, Eternal Battleground*, Meresborough Books, Chatham (1981)

Boynton – Boynton, Lindsay, *The Elizabethan Militia, 1558-1638*, Routledge & Kegan (1967)

Burrows – Burrows, Montagu, *Cinque Ports*, Longmans, Green & Co, London (1892)

CSP(D) – *Calendar of State Papers Domestic*, National Archives (PRO)

Calladine – *The Diary of Colour Sergeant George Calladine, 19th Foot, 1793–1837,* Eden Fisher (1922)

Camden – *Camden's Britannia (Kent)*, ed. G J Copley, London (1977)

Correlli Barnett – Barnett, Correlli, Britain and Her Army, 1509-1970, Penguin Press, London (1970)

DNB – *Dictionary of National Biography*

Douch – Douch, John,*Rough, Rude Men*, Crabwell & Buckland Publications, Dover (1985)

Dov/Tel, Dov/Exp – Local Newspapers *(Dover Library)*

Everitt – Everitt, A M, *The Community of Kent and the Great Rebellion, 1640-60*, University Press, Leicester (1966)

Fazan – Fazan, Col E A C, MC, TD, DL, *Cinque Ports Battalion* , Adams Bros, Dover (1971)

F & D – Sir Charles Firth & Godfrey Davis, *Regimental History of Cromwell's Army*, Clarendon Press, Oxford (1940)

Frederick – Frederick, J B M, *Lineage Book of British Land Forces, 1660-1978* (1984)

Gordon – Gordon, Major Lawrence L, *Military Origins*, Kaye & Ward, London, (1971)

Hardman – Hardman, F W, *Castleguard Service of Dover Castle* Arch.Cant. XLIX (1937)

Harris – Harris, John, DD, FRS, *The History of Kent*, London (1719)

Haydon – Haydon, Brigid, *Algernon Sidney, 1623-1683*, Arch Cant LXXVI (1961)

Hist of K/W – Colvin, H M (Ed), The History of the King's Works, vols I & II, London (1963)

Hist Parl – *History of Parliament, 1660–*

Hollister – C Warren Hollister, *Military Organization of Norman England*, Clarendon Press, Oxford (1965)

Home Stations – Ministry of Defence Library, Whitehall

Igglesden – Igglesden, Charles, *History of the East Kent Volunteers*, Kentish Express, Ashford (1899)

JSAHR – Journal of Society of Army Historical Research – (including *Moyse-Bartlett*)

Kentish Sources II – *Kent & the Civil War*, Kent County Council, Maidstone (1960)

Lambarde – Lambarde, William, *A Perambulation of Kent*, Baldwin, Cradock & Joy, London (1826)

Laws – Laws, Lt Col M E S, *Battery Records of the Royal Artillery, 1716-1859*, London (1952)

L & P – *Letters & Papers of HVIII*

Lyon – Lyon, Rev John, *The History of the Town & Port of Dover, & of Dover Castle*, Dover & London (1813)

M-J – Maurice Jones, Col K W, *History of the Coast Artillery in the British Army*, London (1959)

Meddicott – Meddicott, J R, *Simon de Montfort*, Cambridge University Press (1994)

Murray – Murray, K M E, *The Constitutional History of the Cinque Ports*, Manchester University Press (1935)

Nugent – Nugent, Lt Gen Sir George, *Correspondence & Returns Relating to the Kent District* (1809)

Pattenden – Pattenden, Thos, *Diaries of* .. (1797-1808)(Dover Library)

Peck – Peck, Major, *The Coast Artillery*

P/R – Parish registers of St James', Dover *(Cathedral Archives)* & of St Mary–en–Castro, Dover Castle

R/H – Regimental Histories

Reg/Mag – Regimental Magazines

R/Sec – Information from Regimental Secretaries

Statham – Statham, Rev S P H, *History of Town, Castle & Port of Dover*, London (1899)

Wolfe – *General Wolfe's Instructrions to Young Officers*, London (1790)

Other sources consulted

Coad, Jonathan – *Dover Castle,* Batsford/English Heritage (1995)
Coad, J G & Lewis, P N – *The later fortifications of Dover*, Post Medieval Archaeology, vol 16 (1982)
Dalton, Charles, FRGS – *Army Lists*, Vol I, 1661–1714, Francis Edwards Ltd, London (1960)
Dover & the European War 1914–1918, Dover Express
Elvin, Rev Chas R S, *Records of Walmer* (1890)
Firth, J B, *Dover and the Great War*, Dover (1920)
Labarge, Margaret Wade – *A Baronial Household of the Thirteenth Century*, Eyre & Spottiswoode Ltd, London (1965)
Leslie, N B, *The Succession of Colonels of the British Army from 1660 to the Present Day* (1974)
Royal Kalendars
Swinson, Ed. Arthur, *A Register of the Regiments and Corps of the British Army*, Archive Press (1972)
Walton, Col Clifford, CB, *History of the British Standing Army, AD 1660–1700*, Harrison & Sons, London (1894)
Ward, S G P, *Faithful, The Story of the DLI*, Nelson (1962)
Western, J, *English Militia in the 18th century*, Routledge & Kegan (1965)
Willson, Beckles, *The Life and Letters of James Wolfe*, Heinemann, London, (1909)

Personal names – verbal recollections of those who served in the Castle

Many classes at the Public Records Office (PRO)*(now National Archives)* have been consulted, including:
PRO/WO3,5,17,24,26,27,33,47,55,68,73,166,192,179,199,305,379,380; HO50; SP14,34; E101,315, WORK14

East Kent Archives: EK/CPW/RO1-4 (D92/44949), EK/U1475, U888, U2246